Law Made Simple

Living Wills
Simplified

Law Made Simple

Living Wills
Simplified

by **Daniel Sitarz**
Attorney-at-Law

Nova Publishing Company
Small Business and Consumer Legal Books and Software
Carbondale, Illinois

© 2002 Daniel Sitarz

Editorial assistance by Janet Harris Sitarz, Linda Jorgensen-Buhman, Melanie Bray, and Carol Kelly. Interior design by Linda Jorgensen-Buhman. Manufactured in the United States.

ISBN 0-935755-52-7   Book only   ($22.95)
ISBN 0-935755-50-0   Book w/CD   ($28.95)

Cataloging-in-Publication Data
        Sitarz, Dan, 1948-
            Living Wills Simplified / by Daniel Sitarz. -- 1st ed.
            p. cm. -- (Law Made Simple series). Includes index.
            1. Right to Die—Law and Legislation—United States—Popular Works. 2. Right to Die—
            Law and Legislation—United States—States—Forms. I. Sitarz, Daniel. II. Title. III. Series.
            ISBN 0-935755-52-7, Book only ($22.95); ISBN 0-935755-50-0, Book/CD Set ($28.95).

Nova Publishing Company is dedicated to providing up-to-date and accurate legal information to the public. All Nova publications are periodically revised to contain the latest available legal information.

1st Edition; 1st Printing   June, 2002

This publication is designed to provide accurate and authoritative information in regard to the subject matter covered. It is sold with the understanding that the publisher and author are not engaged in rendering legal, accounting, or other professional services. If legal advice or other expert assistance is required, the services of a competent professional person should be sought.
        —*From a Declaration of Principles jointly adopted by a Committee of*
        the American Bar Association and a Committee of Publishers

DISCLAIMER

Because of possible unanticipated changes in governing statutes and case law relating to the application of any information contained in this book, the author, publisher, and any and all persons or entities involved in any way in the preparation, publication, sale, or distribution of this book disclaim all responsibility for the legal effects or consequences of any document prepared or action taken in reliance upon information contained in this book. No representations, either express or implied, are made or given regarding the legal consequences of the use of any information contained in this book. Purchasers and persons intending to use this book for the preparation of any legal documents are advised to check specifically on the current applicable laws in any jurisdiction in which they intend the documents to be effective.

Nova Publishing Company
Small Business and Consumer Legal Books and Software
1103 West College Street
Carbondale, IL 62901
Editorial: (800) 748-1175

Distributed by:
National Book Network
4720 Boston Way
Lanham, MD 20706
Orders: (800) 462-6420

Table of Contents

Planning Your
Health Care Options

What is an Advance Health Care Directive?

An Advance Health Care Directive is a legal document that you may complete in any state that allows you to provide written directions relating to your future health care and financial affairs should you become incapacitated and unable to speak for yourself. Advance Health Care Directives give you a direct voice in medical decisions in situations when you cannot make those decisions yourself. Your Advance Health Care Directive will not be used as long as you are able to express your own decisions. You can always accept or refuse medical treatment and you always have the legal right to revoke your Advance Health Care Directive at any time. Instructions regarding revocations are discussed later in these instructions.

Advance Health Care Directives are not only for senior citizens. Serious life-threatening accidents or disease can strike anyone and leave them unable to communicate their desires. In fact, the rise of the use of Advance Health Care Directives can be attributed in part, to legal cases involving medical care to young people, particularly Karen Ann Quinlan and Nancy Cruzan. Anyone over the age of 18 who is mentally competent should complete an Advance Health Care Directive. Be aware, however, that Advance Health Care Directives are intended for non-emergency medical treatment. Most often, there is no time for health care providers to consult and analyze the provisions of an Advance Health Care Directive in an emergency situation.

The Advance Health Care Directives that are contained in this book contain five separate sections, each dealing with different aspects of potential situations that may arise during a possible period of incapacitation. Each section is explained in detail later in this chapter. Below is a brief explanation of each component of an Advance Health Care Directive:

The first section is a *Living Will* which is intended to allow you to declare your wishes and desires regarding the delivery of medical treatment if you are terminally ill or permanently unconscious. It allows you to decide in advance how you wish such situations to be handled. Many states use different terms to describe a Living Will, such as a 'Directive to Physicians' or a 'Medical Directive,' but they all refer to a document that allows you to make known your desires for end-of-life medical treatment. The most important items that are covered by most living wills are as follows:

- Whether medical treatment should be withheld or withdrawn, and that you be permitted to die naturally with only the administration of medication or the performance of any medical treatment deemed necessary to alleviate pain
- Whether you desire the withholding or withdrawal of artificially-provided food, water, or other artificially-provided nourishment or fluids

The second section of each Advance Health Care Directive allows for the selection of a *Health Care Agent*. This selection may be termed a Durable Power of Attorney for Health Care or numerous other designations in various states. Regardless of the title of these forms, this section of the Advance Health Care Directive provides for the selection of person of your choosing to make medical decisions on your behalf should you become incapacitated to the extent of being unable to make them yourself. Your designated Health Care Agent is bound to follow any instructions that you may include as well as any directions provided by your Living Will.

The next section provides for the selection of a person to handle your financial affairs in the event that you are unable to do so. This is referred to as a *Durable Power of Attorney for Financial Affairs*. If completed, it will allow your designated agent to handle all of your financial affairs during your infirmity.

The fourth section, *Designation of Primary Physician*, allows you to make known in advance your choice for a personal physician should you be unable to communicate your desires to health care providers.

The fifth and final section, *Organ Donation*, provides a method for you to indicate your decisions regarding the donation of any organs for research, transplant, therapy, or educational science.

The combination of these five sections provides a comprehensive method by which you may provide, in advance, for a situation in which you may be unable to communicate your desires to your family, your friends, and your health care providers. It is an opportunity to carefully plan how you would like various medical situations to be handled should they arise.

What is a Living Will?

A Living Will is a relatively new legal document that has been made necessary due to recent technological advances in the field of medicine. These advances can allow for the continued existence of a person on advanced life support systems long after any normal semblance of "life," as many people consider it, has ceased. The inherent problem that is raised by this type of extraordinary medical "life support" is that the person whose life is being artificially-continued by such means may not wish to be kept alive beyond what he or she may consider to be the proper time for their life to end. However, since a person in such condition has no method of communicating his or her wishes to the medical or legal authorities in charge, a Living Will was developed to allow him or her to make these important decisions in advance of such a situation.

As more and more advances are made in the medical field in terms of the ability to prevent "clinical" death, the difficult situations envisioned by a Living Will are destined to occur more often. The legal acceptance of a Living Will is currently at the forefront of new laws being added in all states. Although a Living Will does not address all possible contingencies regarding terminally-ill patients, it does provide a written declaration for the individual to make known his or her decisions on life-prolonging procedures. A Living Will declares your wishes to not be kept alive by artificial or mechanical means if you are suffering from a terminal condition and your death would be imminent without the use of such artificial means. It may also apply if you are considered to be in a state of "permanent unconsciousness," commonly referred to as being "brain-dead." It provides a legally-binding written set of instructions regarding your wishes about these important matters.

Even if you appoint a *Health Care Agent*, discussed below, to make medical decisions on your behalf, it is important to also prepare a Living Will. Your Living Will can provide your chosen agent with a clear picture of your desires regarding end-of-life decisions. It will also provide evidence your agent is acting in good faith, should his or her decisions regarding your medical care ever be challenged by medical or legal authorities. Plus, the provision of a Living Will can act to reassure your chosen Health Care Agent that he or she is indeed following your wishes. This can ease the burden for your agent when he or she is asked to make the very difficult decisions that may arise.

In most states, in order to qualify for the use of a Living Will, you must meet the following criteria:

• You must be at least 18 years of age
• You must be of "sound mind"
• You must be able to comprehend the nature of your action in signing such a document

The forms contained in this book are taken directly from the most recent legislation regarding Living Wills in each state. A few states (Massachusetts, Michigan, and New York) do not currently have specific legislation providing express statutory recognition of Living Wills. For those states, a Living Will has been prepared by legal professionals to comply with the basic requirements that courts in that state or other states have found important. In such states, be assured that courts, health care professionals, and physicians will be guided by this expression of your desires concerning life support as expressed in the Living Will prepared using this book. Please select the appropriate form for use in your own state.

Typical Living Will Provisions

Nearly all states have passed legislation setting up a statutorily-accepted Living Will form. Those states that have not expressed a preference for a specific type of Living Will have, nevertheless, accepted Living Wills that adhere to general legal requirements. There are many different types of Living Wills. They may range from very brief statements to lengthy and elaborate multi-page forms with detailed and very specific instructions. The following statement from the state of Illinois is an example of a short statement comprising a Living Will:

If at any time I should have an incurable and irreversible injury, disease, or illness judged to be a terminal condition by my attending physician who has personally examined me and has determined that my death is imminent except for death-delaying procedures, I direct that such procedures which would only prolong the dying process be withheld or withdrawn, and that I be permitted to die naturally with only the administration of medication, sustenance, or the performance of any medical procedure deemed necessary by my attending physician to provide me with comfort care.

The following Living Will statement from the state of Ohio is an example of a longer type of form:

I, _____ , being of sound mind and not subject to duress, fraud, or undue influence, intending to create a Living Will Declaration under Chapter 2133 of the Ohio Revised Code, do voluntarily make known my desire that my dying shall not be artificially-prolonged. If I am unable to give directions regarding the use of life-sustaining treatment when I am in a terminal condition or a permanently-unconscious state, it is my intention that this Living Will Declaration shall be honored by my family and physicians as the final expression of my legal right to refuse medical or surgical treatment. I am a competent adult who understands and accepts the consequences of such refusal and the purpose and effect of this document (*initial all the following that you choose*):

In the event I am in a terminal condition, I declare and direct that my attending physician shall (*initial all that you choose*):
[   ]   Administer NO life-sustaining treatment, including cardiopulmonary resuscitation;
[   ]   Withdraw life-sustaining treatment, including cardiopulmonary resuscitation, if such treatment has commenced, and in the case of cardiopulmonary resuscitation, issue a do-not-resuscitate order;
[   ]   Permit me to die naturally and provide me with only the care necessary to make me comfortable and to relieve my pain but not to postpone my death.

In the event I am in a permanently-unconscious state, I declare and direct that my attending physician shall (*initial all that you choose*):
[   ]   Administer NO life-sustaining treatment, including cardiopulmonary resuscitation, except for the provision of artificially- or technologically-supplied nutrition or hydration unless, in the following paragraph, I have authorized its withholding or withdrawal;
[   ]   Withdraw such treatment, including cardiopulmonary resuscitation, if such treatment has commenced; and, in the case of cardiopulmonary resuscitation issue a do-not-resuscitate order;
[   ]   Permit me to die naturally and provide me with only that care necessary to make me comfortable and to relieve my pain but not to postpone my death.

[   ]   In addition, if I have *initialed* the foregoing box, I authorize my attending physician to withhold, or in the event that treatment has already commenced, to withdraw the provision of artificially- or technologically-supplied nutrition and hydration. If I am in a permanently-unconscious state and if my attending physician and at least one (1) other physician who has examined me determine, to a reasonable degree of medical certainty and in accordance with reasonable medical standards, that such nutrition or hydration will not or will no longer serve to provide comfort to me or alleviate my pain.

All of the various state forms try to ensure that a person's own wishes are followed regarding health care decisions. Many states have drafted their legislation with the intention that you prepare both a Living Will and a Durable Power of Attorney for Health Care (or similar form) which appoints a person of your choosing to act on your behalf in making health care decisions when you are unable to make such decisions for yourself. It is advisable to prepare both of these forms in order to cover most, if not all, eventualities that may arise regarding your health care in difficult situations. In general, the purpose of your Living Will is to convey your wishes regarding life-prolonging treatment and artificially-provided nutrition and hydration if you no longer have the capacity to make your own decisions, have a terminal condition, or become permanently unconscious.

Living Wills generally provide, in the absence of your own ability to give directions regarding the use of life-prolonging treatment and artificially-provided nutrition and hydration, that it is your intention that your Living Will be honored by your attending physician, family, and anyone else as the final expression of your legal right to refuse medical or surgical treatment. Most forms also state that by signing the form you fully accept the consequences of the refusal of medical care in the circumstances that you have chosen. In addition, in many states, if you have been diagnosed as pregnant and that diagnosis is known to your attending physician, your Living Will will have no force or effect during the course of your pregnancy.

Official Notices

Many states have provided official notices on their Living Will or similar forms. The purpose of these notices is to be certain that the person signing the forms is fully aware of his or her legal rights and of the legal consequences of signing such forms. Following is a typical notice. Even if your state does not require such notices, it would be prudent to read through this statement to help you comprehend the ramifications of the decisions that you are about to make. For the purposes of this book, the entire set of advance health care decisions that you will make are called an "Advance Health Care Directive" for your particular state.

Witness Requirements

All states which have enacted legislation regarding Living Wills or their counterparts have provided protections to ensure the validity of the Advance Health Care Directive. They have also provided legal protections against persons using undue influence to force or coerce someone into signing an Advance Health Care Directive. There are various requirements regarding who may be a witness to your signing of your Advance Health Care Directive. In general, these protections are for the purpose of ensuring that the witnesses have no actual or indirect stake in your death. These witnesses should have no connection with you from a health care or beneficiary standpoint. In most states, the witnesses must:

- Not be under 18 years of age
- Not be related to you in any manner either by blood, marriage, or adoption
- Not be your attending physician
- Not be a patient or employee of your attending physician
- Not be a patient, physician, or employee of the health care facility in which you may be a patient
- Not be entitled to any portion of your estate upon your death under any laws of intestate succession, nor under your will or any codicil

Sample Official Notice for Advance Health Care Directive

You have the right to give instructions about your own health care. You also have the right to name someone else to make health care decisions for you. This form lets you do either or both of these things. With this form, you may also select a person to act on your behalf in your financial affairs should you be unable to do so yourself. It also lets you express your wishes regarding donation of organs and the designation of your primary physician. If you use this form, you may complete or modify all or any part of it. You are free to use a different form.

Part 1 of this form lets you give specific instructions about any aspect of your health care, whether or not you appoint an agent to make your health care decisions. Choices are provided for you to express your wishes regarding the provision, withholding, or withdrawal of treatment to keep you alive, as well as the provision of pain relief. Space is provided for you to add to the choices you have made or for you to write out any additional wishes. If you are satisfied to allow your agent to determine what is best for you in making end-of-life decisions, you need not fill out this part of the form.

Part 2 of this form is a power of attorney for health care. This part lets you name another individual as agent to make health care decisions for you if you become incapable of making your own decisions or if you want someone else to make those decisions for you now, even though you are still capable. Your agent may not be an operator or employee of a community care facility or a residential care facility where you are receiving care, or your supervising health care provider or employee of the health care institution where you are receiving care, unless your agent is related to you or is a co-worker. Unless the form you sign limits the authority of your agent, your agent may make all health care decisions for you. This form has a place for you to limit the authority of your agent. You need not limit the authority of your agent if you wish to rely on your agent for all health care decisions that may have to be made.

If you choose not to limit the authority of your agent, your agent will have the right to:
(1) Consent or refuse consent to any care, treatment, service, or procedure to maintain, diagnose, or otherwise affect a physical or mental condition;
(2) Select or discharge health care providers and institutions;
(3) Approve or disapprove diagnostic tests, surgical procedures, and programs of medication;
(4) Direct the provision, withholding, or withdrawal of artificial nutrition and hydration and all other forms of health care, including cardiopulmonary resuscitation; and
(5) Make anatomical gifts, authorize an autopsy, and direct the disposition of your remains.

Part 3 of this form allows you to select a person who will have authority to handle your financial affairs while you are unable to do so yourself.

Part 4 of this form lets you designate a physician to have primary responsibility for your health care.

Part 5 of this form lets you express an intention to donate your bodily organs and tissues following your death.

After completing this form, sign and date the form at the end. The form must be signed by two (2) qualified witnesses or acknowledged before a notary public. If you complete the section for a Durable Power of Attorney for Financial Affairs, you must have the form both witnessed and notarized. Give a copy of the signed and completed form to your physician, any other health care providers you may have, any health care institution at which you are receiving care, and any health care or financial affairs agents you have named. You should talk to the person you have named as agent to make sure that he or she understands your wishes and is willing to take the responsibility.

You have the right to revoke this advance health care directive or replace this form at any time.

- Not have a claim against any portion of your estate upon your death
- Not be directly financially responsible for your medical care
- Not have signed the Advance Health Care Directive for you, even at your direction
- Not be paid a fee for acting as a witness

In addition, please note that several states and the District of Columbia (Washington D.C.) have laws in effect regarding witnesses when the *declarant* (the person signing the Advance Health Care Directive) is a patient in a nursing home, boarding facility, hospital, or skilled or intermediate health care facility. In those situations, it is advisable to have a patient ombudsman, patient advocate, or the director of the health care facility act as the third witness to the signing of an Advance Health Care Directive.

These restrictions on who may be a witness to your signing of an Advance Health Care Directive require, in most cases, that the witnesses either be friends who will receive nothing from you under your will or strangers. Please review the requirements for your own state in the Appendix of this book and in the witness statements on your particular state's form.

There may be situations in which the use of a Living Will is not appropriate. For example, the official Living Will forms in some states may actually forbid a doctor from withdrawing all life support in terminal situations. These forms may forbid the withdrawal of "nutrition and hydration," essentially tube-type feeding for terminally-ill patients. You will need to review the precise terms of the Living Will form for your state to be certain that it is what you want. You may desire to complete and sign a Durable Power of Attorney for Health Care (or the equivalent form in your own state) for your health care options. This section of your Advance Health Care Directive is explained below.

Other Health Care Planning Tools

Selection of a Health Care Agent
(Durable Power of Attorney for Health Care)

These are also referred to as a Health Care Power of Attorney, or Appointment of a Health Care Proxy, or some similar title. They are useful documents that go beyond the provisions of a Living Will, provide for health care options that Living Wills do not cover, and are important additions to the use of a Living Will. Basically, a Durable Power of Attorney for Health Care allows you to appoint someone to act for you in making health care decisions when you are unable to make them for yourself. A Living Will does not provide for this. Also, a Durable Power of Attorney for Health Care generally applies to all medical decisions (unless you specifically limit the power). Most Living Wills only apply to certain decisions regarding life support at the end of your life and are most useful in "terminal illness" or "permanent unconsciousness" situations.

Additionally, Durable Powers of Attorney for Health Care can provide your chosen agent with a valuable flexibility in making decisions regarding medical choices that may arise. Often, during the course of medical treatment, unforeseen situations may occur that require immediate decision-making. If you are unable to communicate your desires regarding such choices, the appointment of a Health Care Agent for you (appointed with a Durable Power of Attorney for Health Care) will allow such decisions to be made on your behalf by a trusted person.

Finally, a Durable Power of Attorney for Health Care can provide specific detailed instructions regarding what you would like done by your attending physician in specific circumstances. Generally, Living Wills are limited to the provision or withholding of life support options. A Durable Power of Attorney for Health Care form (or its equivalent in your state) is provided for each state in this book. All states have enacted legislation regarding this type of form and recognize the validity of this type of legal document. Information regarding each state's provisions are included in the Appendix. In order to be certain that you have made provisions for most potential health care situations, it is recommended you prepare both a Living Will and a Durable Power of Attorney for Health Care. Not everyone, however, has a trusted person available to serve as their Health Care Agent. In these situations, the use of a Living Will alone will be necessary. It is, of course, possible to add additional instructions to any Living Will to clearly and specifically indicate your desires.

Your Health Care Agent can be a relative or close friend. It should be someone who knows you very well and whom you trust completely. Your agent should be someone who is not afraid to ask questions of health care providers and is able to make difficult decisions. Your agent may need to be assertive on your behalf. You should discuss your choice with your agent and make certain that he or she understands the responsibilities involved.

Many states provide for notices or warnings that explain the gravity of the decision to appoint a Health Care Agent. Such notices are provided in the forms in this book for the states that require their use. Following is a sample of such a notice, which should be read by all readers to help explain the consequences and gravity of the decision to appoint a Health Care Agent:

Sample Official Notice for Selection of a Health Care Agent
(Power of Attorney for Health Care)

NOTICE: The purpose of this power of attorney is to give the person you designate (your "agent") broad powers to make health care decisions for you, including power to require, consent to, or withdraw any type of personal care or medical treatment for any physical or mental condition, and to admit you to or discharge you from any hospital, home, or other institution. This form does not impose a duty on your agent to exercise granted powers; but when powers are exercised, your agent will have to use due care to act for your benefit and in accordance with this form and keep a record of receipts, disbursements, and significant actions taken as agent. A court can take away the powers of your agent if it finds the agent is not acting properly. Unless you expressly limit the duration of this power in the manner provided below, until you revoke this power or a court acting on your behalf terminates it, your agent may exercise the powers given here throughout your lifetime, even after you become disabled. The powers you give your agent, your right to revoke those powers, and the penalties for violating the law are explained more fully in sections 4-5, 4-6, 4-9, and 4-10[b] of the Illinois "Powers of Attorney for Health Care Law" of which this form is a part. That law expressly permits the use of any different form of power of attorney you may desire. If there is anything about this form that you do not understand, you should ask a lawyer to explain it to you.

Durable Power of Attorney for Financial Affairs

A Durable Power of Attorney for Financial Affairs allows you to appoint an agent (referred to as an 'attorney-in-fact') to handle your financial affairs during a period that you are unable to handle them yourself. With this form, you are giving another person the right to manage your financial and business matters on your behalf. They are given the power to act as you could, if you were able.

You do not have to appoint someone to handle your financial affairs. It is, however, often useful to do so. If there is someone available who can be trusted implicitly to act on your behalf, the appointment of such a person can eliminate many problems that may arise if you are unable to handle your own affairs. The appointment of an agent for your financial affairs allows for the paying of bills, writing of checks, etc. while you are unable to do so yourself.

You should appoint someone whom you trust completely. With the form included in the Advance Health Care Directive in this book, you are granting the appointed agent very broad powers to handle your affairs. You will give your agent the maximum power under law to perform the following specific acts on your behalf: all acts relating to any and all of your financial and/or business affairs, including all banking and financial institution transactions, all real estate transactions, all insurance and annuity transactions, all claims and litigation, and all

---

Sample Official Notice for Durable Power of Attorney for Financial Affairs

NOTICE: This is an important document. Before signing this document, you should know these important facts. By signing this document, you are not giving up any powers or rights to control your finances and property yourself. In addition to your own powers and rights, you are giving another person, your attorney-in-fact, broad powers to handle your finances and property. This unlimited durable power of attorney gives the person whom you designate (your "attorney-in-fact") broad powers to handle your finances and property, which includes powers to encumber, sell, or otherwise dispose of any real or personal property without advance notice to you or approval by you. The powers will exist after you become disabled or incapacitated. This document does not authorize anyone to make medical or other health care decisions for you. If you own complex or special assets such as a business or if there is anything about this form that you do not understand, you should ask a lawyer to explain this form to you before you sign it. If you wish to change your unlimited durable power of attorney, you must complete a new document and revoke this one. You may revoke this document at any time by destroying it, directing another person to destroy it in your presence, or signing a written and dated statement expressing your intent to revoke this document. If you revoke this document, you should notify your attorney-in-fact and any other person to whom you have given a copy of the form. You should also notify all parties having custody of your assets. These parties have no responsibility to you unless you actually notify them of the revocation. If your attorney-in-fact is your spouse and your marriage is annulled, or you are divorced after signing this document, this document is invalid. Since some third parties or transactions may not permit use of this document, it is advisable to check in advance if possible, for any special requirements that may be imposed. You should sign this form only if the attorney-in-fact you name is reliable, trustworthy, and competent to manage your affairs.

business transactions. Your attorney-in-fact (agent) is granted full power to act on your behalf in the same manner as if you were personally present.

The Durable Power of Attorney for Financial Affairs will become effective upon your disability, as certified by your primary physician or, if your primary physician is not available, by any other attending physician. This power of attorney grants no power or authority to your designated attorney-in-fact regarding health care decisions. Only the Durable Power of Attorney for Health Care can confer those powers. You may, of course, choose to select the very same person to act as both your Health Care Agent and your Agent for financial affairs.

By accepting their appointment, your agent agrees to act in your best interest as he or she considers advisable. The Durable Power of Attorney for Financial Matters may be revoked at any time and is automatically revoked on your death.

Many states provide for a notice to persons signing a Durable Powers of Attorney for Financial Affairs. Above is an sample of a standard notice of this type. You should read this notice carefully in order to understand the gravity and possible consequences of signing a document of this type.

Designation of Primary Physician

This form allows you to make known your personal choice of the doctor whom you would like to care for you should you be unable to make known your choice. Generally, people desire that their personal family physician be designated as their primary physician since this person is most aware of their personal wishes and desires concerning health care issues. The use of this form is optional.

Organ Donation

The use of a form of this type allows you to make a donation of your organs. Several states include such decisions in either their Living Will form or their Durable Power of Attorney for Health Care form. In the Advance Health Care Directives provided in this book however, the Organ Donation form is a separate section. Using this form, you may make choices about whether and how you may wish any of your organs to be donated for medical, scientific, or educational uses after your death. All states have versions of a state law usually referred to as an "Anatomical Gift Act," which provides that individuals may make personal choices about whether and how to provide for the gift of their organs after death. Because of the many lives that can be saved though the use of transplanted donated organs, many states actually actively encourage such donations. Please read through this section of the Directive carefully and make your appropriate decisions.

Preparing and Signing Your Advance Health Care Directive

(1) Select the appropriate form for your state from the included forms. Carefully read through each section of your Advance Health Care Directive. You may wish to make two copies of your state's Advance Health Care Directive. This will allow you to use one form as a draft copy and the other form for a final copy that you and your witnesses will sign.

(2) You will need to initial your choices in the first section of the form as to which sections of the entire Advance Health Care Directive you wish to be effective. The choices are:

- Living Will
- Selection of Health Care Agent
- Durable Power of Attorney for Financial Affairs
- Designation of Primary Physician
- Organ Donation

Please note that you may choose to exclude any of the above portions of your form and the remaining portions will be valid. If you wish to exclude one or more portions, DO NOT place your initials in the space before the section that you wish to exclude. Be careful so that you are certain you are expressing your desires exactly as you wish on these very important matters. If you do not wish to use a particular main section of the entire form, cross out that section of the form clearly and do not initial that section in either the first paragraph of the Directive or in the paragraph directly before your signature near the end of the Directive. If you do not wish to use a particular paragraph within one of the five main sections of the form, cross out that paragraph also.

(3) Make the appropriate choices in each section where indicated by initialing the designated place. Depending on which state form that you use, you may have many choices to initial or you may have no choices to initial. Please carefully read through the paragraphs and clauses that require choices to be certain that you understand the choices that you will be making. If you wish to add additional instructions or limitations in the places indicated on the form, please type or clearly print your instructions. If you need to add additional pages, please use the form titled "Additional Information for Advance Health Care Directive" which is provided on page 19. If you need and use additional pages, be certain that you initial and date each added page and that you clearly label each additional page regarding which paragraph or section of the form to which it pertains.

(4) In the section on Organ Donations, you may choose to either donate all of your organs or limit your donation to certain specific organs. Likewise, you may provide that the organs be used for any purposes or you may limit their use to certain purposes.

(5) Finally, you will need to complete the signature and witness/notary sections of your forms. When you have a completed original with no erasures or corrections, staple all of the pages together in the upper left-hand corner. Do not sign this document or fill in the date yet. You should now assemble your witnesses and/or a Notary Public to witness your signature. As noted in the Appendix, be certain that your witnesses meet your specific state requirements.

In addition, please note that several states and the District of Columbia have laws in effect regarding witnesses when the declarant is a patient in a nursing home, boarding facility, hospital, or skilled or intermediate health care facility. In those situations, it is advisable to have a patient ombudsman, patient advocate, or the director of the health care facility to act as the third witness to the signing of an Advance Health Care Directive.

If you are unable to have a Notary Public present, the witnessing of your Advance Health Care Directive will still be valid, except for the Durable Power of Attorney for Financial Affairs section. This section requires that a Notary Public witness your signature. Also, if you are unable to assemble the appropriate witnesses who meet your state's requirements, your signature on your Advance Health Care Directive may be witnessed solely by a Notary Public. However, in order that your Advance Health Care Directive be accepted by all legal and medical authorities with as little difficulty as possible, it is highly recommended that you have your signing of this important document witnessed by both your appropriate witnesses and a Notary Public.

(6) In front of all of the witnesses and the Notary Public, the following should take place in the order shown:

(a) There is no requirement that the witnesses know any of the terms of your Advance Health Care Directive or that they read any of your Advance Health Care Directive. All that is necessary is that they observe you sign your Advance Health Care Directive and that they also sign the Advance Health Care Directive as witnesses in each other's presence.

(b) You will sign your Advance Health Care Directive at the end where indicated, exactly as your name is written on your Advance Health Care Directive, in ink using a pen. At this time, you should also again initial your choices as to which sections you have chosen (directly before your signature space). You will also need to fill in the date on the first page of the Directive, date and initial each Additional Information Page (if you used any), and fill in your address after your signature. Once you have signed and completed all of the necessary information, pass your Advance Health Care Directive to the first witness, who should sign and date the acknowledgment where indicated and also print his or her name.

(c) After the first witness has signed, have the Advance Health Care Directive passed to the second witness, who should also sign and date the acknowledgment where indicated and print his or her name.

(d) Throughout this ceremony, you and all of the witnesses must remain together. The final step, if required in your state or if you are completing the Durable Power of Attorney for Financial Affairs, is for the Notary Public to sign in the space where indicated. You must have your Advance Health Care Directive notarized if you are completing the section of the document for Durable Power of Attorney for Financial Affairs.

(e) If you have chosen individuals to act as either your Health Care Agent (Durable Power of Attorney for Health Care) or as your Attorney-in-fact for Financial Affairs (Durable

Additional Information for Advance Health Care Directive

of _____ (name)

The following information is to be considered as a part of my Advance Health Care Directive (*insert additional information*):

Initials of Declarant _____   Date _____

Power of Attorney for Financial Affairs), you should have them sign the form at the end where shown acknowledging that they accept their appointment.

(7) When this step is completed, your Advance Health Care Directive that you have signed is a valid legal document. Have several copies made and, if appropriate, deliver a copy to your attending physician to have placed in your medical records file. You should also provide a copy to any person who was selected as either your Health Care Agent or your Agent for Financial Affairs. You may also desire to give a copy to the person you have chosen as the executor of your will, your clergy, and your spouse or other trusted relative.

Revoking Your Advance Health Care Directive

All states have provided methods for the easy revocation of Advance Health Care Directives and the forms that they contain. Since such forms provide authority to medical personnel to withhold life-support technology that will likely result in death to the patient, great care must be taken to insure that a change of mind by the patient is heeded. If revocation of your Advance Health Care Directive is an important issue, please consult your state's laws directly. For the revocation of an Advance Health Care Directive, any one of the following methods of revocation is generally acceptable:

- Physical destruction of the Advance Health Care Directive, such as tearing, burning, or mutilating the document
- A written revocation of the Advance Health Care Directive by you or by a person acting at your direction. A form for this is provided at the end of this section. You may use two witnesses and the notary acknowledgment on this form, although most states do not require the use of witnesses for the written revocation of an Advance Health Care Directive to be valid
- An oral revocation in the presence of a witness who signs and dates an affidavit confirming a revocation. This oral declaration may take any manner. Most states allow for a person to revoke such a document by any indication (even non-verbal) of the intent to revoke an Advance Health Care Directive, regardless of his or her physical or mental condition. A form for this effect is included, titled "Witness Affidavit of Oral Revocation of Advance Health Care Directive"

To use the Revocation of Advance Health Care Directive form provided on the next page, simply fill in the appropriate information and sign it in front of your witnesses and a notary public. In addition, your two witnesses should sign it at the same time, although this is not a requirement for the revocation to be effective. You may have this form notarized, but this is also not a requirement for the revocation to be effective.

If it is necessary to use the Witness Affidavit of Oral Revocation of Advance Health Care Directive form, the witness should actually observe your indication of an intention to revoke your Advance Health Care Directive. This may take the form of any verbal or non-verbal direction, as long as your intent to revoke is clearly and unmistakably evident to the witness. This form does not need to be notarized to be effective.

Revocation of
Advance Health Care Directive

I, _____ , am the maker and signatory of an Advance Health Care Directive which was dated _____ , and which was executed by me for use in the State of _____ .

By this written revocation, I hereby entirely revoke such Advance Health Care Directive, any Living Will, any Durable Power of Attorney for Health Care, any Durable Power of Attorney for Financial Affairs, any Organ Donation, or any other appointment or designation of a person to make any health care or financial decisions on my behalf. I intend that all of the above-mentioned documents no longer have any force or effect whatsoever.

BY SIGNING HERE I INDICATE THAT I UNDERSTAND THE PURPOSE AND EFFECT OF THIS DOCUMENT.

Signature _____   Date _____

City, County, and State of Residence _____

Notary Acknowledgment

State of _____
County of _____
On _____ , _____ came before me personally and, under oath, stated that he or she is the person described in the above document and he or she signed the above document in my presence. I declare under penalty of perjury that the person whose name is subscribed to this instrument appears to be of sound mind and under no duress, fraud, or undue influence.

_____
Notary Public
My commission expires _____

Witness Acknowledgment

The declarant is personally known to me and I believe him or her to be of sound mind and under no duress, fraud, or undue influence.

Witness Signature _____   Date _____
Printed Name of Witness _____

Witness Signature _____   Date _____
Printed Name of Witness _____

Witness Affidavit of Oral Revocation of Advance Health Care Directive

_____ , herein referred to as the declarant, was the maker and signatory of an Advance Health Care Directive which was dated _____ , and which was executed by him or her for use in the State of _____ .

By this written affidavit, I, _____ , the witness, hereby affirm that on the date of _____ , I personally witnessed the above-named declarant make known to me, through verbal and/or non-verbal methods, their clear and unmistakable intent to entirely revoke such Advance Health Care Directive, any Living Will, any Durable Power of Attorney for Health Care, any Durable Power of Attorney for Financial Affairs, any Organ Donation, or any other appointment or designation of a person to make any health care or financial decisions on his or her behalf. It is my belief that the above-named declarant fully intended that all of the above-mentioned documents no longer have any force or effect whatsoever.

Witness Acknowledgment

The declarant is personally known to me and I believe him or her to be of sound mind and under no duress, fraud, or undue influence.

Witness Signature _____   Date _____

Printed Name of Witness _____

Alabama Advance Health Care Directive

On this date of _____ , I, _____ , do hereby sign, execute, and adopt the following as my Advance Health Care Directive. I direct any and all persons or entities involved with my health care in any manner that these decisions are my wishes and were adopted without duress or force and of my own free will. I have placed my *initials* next to the sections of this Directive that I have adopted:

[   ] Living Will

[   ] Selection of Health Care Agent (Health Care Proxy)

[   ] Durable Power of Attorney for Financial Affairs

[   ] Designation of Primary Physician

[   ] Organ Donation

Living Will

I, _____ , being nineteen (19) years of age or older, of sound mind, hereby revoke any prior advance directive for health care, and in lieu thereof hereby willfully and voluntarily make known my desires by my instructions to others through my living will, or by my appointment of a health care proxy, or both, that my dying shall not be artificially prolonged under the circumstances set forth below, and do hereby declare:

LIVING WILL: If my attending physician determines that I am no longer able to give directions to my health care providers regarding my medical treatment, I direct my attending physician and other health care providers to provide, withhold, or withdraw certain treatment from me under the circumstances I have indicated below by my initials. I understand that by initialing any of the paragraphs in this Living Will I am authorizing the withholding or withdrawal of certain treatments and this may lead to my death. I understand that I will be given treatment that is necessary for comfort or to alleviate my pain except where I specifically request otherwise.

(1) TERMINAL ILLNESS OR INJURY.

(a) If my attending physician and another physician determine that I have an incurable terminal illness or injury which will lead to my death within six (6) months or less (*initial your choice*):

[   ] I DO want medically-indicated life-sustaining treatment, even if it will not cure me and will only prolong the dying process.

[   ] I do NOT want life-sustaining treatment which would not cure me but which would only prolong the dying process.

In addition, before life-sustaining treatment is withheld or withdrawn as directed above, I direct that my attending physician shall discuss with the following person(s), if they are available, the benefits and burdens of taking such action and my stated wishes in this advance directive (*insert name[s] and address[es] of person[s] chosen*):

_____ (name), of _____
_____ (address)

_____ (name), of _____
_____ (address)

_____ (name), of _____
_____ (address)

(b) I understand that artificially-provided nutrition and hydration (tube feeding of food and water) may be necessary to preserve my life (*initial your choice*):

[   ] I DO want medically-indicated artificially-provided nutrition and hydration, even if it will only prolong the dying process.

[   ] I do NOT want artificially-provided nutrition and hydration under the circumstance initialed below (*add other medical directives, if any. If none, state "none"*):

In addition, before artificially-provided nutrition and hydration are withheld or withdrawn as directed above, I direct that my attending physician shall discuss with the following persons, if they are available, the benefits and burdens of taking such action and my stated wishes in this advance directive:

(2) PERMANENT UNCONSCIOUSNESS.

(a) If in the judgment of my attending physician and another physician, I am in a condition of permanent unconsciousness (*initial your choice*):

[   ] I DO want medically-indicated life-sustaining treatment, even if it will not cure me and will only maintain me in a condition of permanent unconsciousness.

[   ] I do NOT want life-sustaining treatment which would not cure me but which would only maintain me in a condition of permanent unconsciousness.

In addition, before life-sustaining treatment is withheld or withdrawn as directed above, I direct that my attending physician shall discuss with the following person(s), if they are available, the benefits and burdens of taking such action and my stated wishes in this advance directive (*insert name[s] and address[es] of person[s] chosen*):

_____ (name), of _____
_____ (address)

_____ (name), of _____
_____ (address)

_____ (name), of _____
_____ (address)

(b) I understand that artificially-provided nutrition and hydration (tube feeding of food and water) may be necessary to preserve my life (*initial your choice*):

[   ] I DO want medically-indicated artificially-provided nutrition and hydration, even if it will only maintain me in a condition of permanent unconsciousness.

[   ] I do NOT want artificially-provided nutrition and hydration under the circumstance initialed below (*add other medical directives, if any. If none, state "none"*):

In addition, before artificially-provided nutrition and hydration are withheld or withdrawn as directed above, I direct that my attending physician shall discuss with the following persons, if they are available, the benefits and burdens of taking such action and my stated wishes in this advance directive:

(3) OTHER DIRECTIVES. I direct that (*add other medical directives, if any. If none, state "none"*):

Selection of Health Care Agent (Health Care Proxy)

(4) HEALTH CARE PROXY.

(a) I understand that my health care proxy is a person whom I may choose here to make medical treatment decisions for me as described below (*initial your choice*):

[   ] I do NOT want to appoint a health care proxy.

[   ] I DO want to appoint a health care proxy.

If my attending physician determines that I am no longer able to give directions to my health care providers regarding my medical treatment, I direct my attending physician and other health care providers to follow the instructions of _____ (name), whom I appoint as my health care proxy. My health care proxy is authorized to make whatever medical treatment decisions I could make if I were able, including decisions regarding the withholding or withdrawing of life-sustaining treatment.

(b) (*Initial your choice*):

[   ] I do NOT authorize my health care proxy to make decisions regarding whether artificially-provided nutrition and hydration be withheld or withdrawn.

[   ] I DO authorize my health care proxy to make decisions regarding whether artificially-provided nutrition and hydration be withheld or withdrawn.

(c) I specifically direct my health care proxy to (*add other medical directives, if any. If none, state "none"*):

(5) CONFLICTING PROVISIONS. If the decisions made by the person I have appointed as my health care proxy disagree with the instructions in my Living Will (*initial your choice*):

[   ] I want the instructions in my Living Will to be followed.

[   ] I want the person I have appointed as health care proxy to make the final decisions.

I understand that if I do not initial either of the above, then my health care proxy will make the final decisions.

(6) DEFINITIONS. As used in this advance directive for health care, the following terms have the meaning set forth below:

(a)   Artificially-provided nutrition and hydration. A medical treatment consisting of the administration of food and water through a tube or intravenous line, where I am not required to chew or swallow voluntarily. Artificially-provided nutrition and hydration does not include assisted feeding, such as spoon or bottle feeding.

(b)   Life-sustaining treatment. Any medical treatment, procedure, or intervention that, in the judgment of the attending physician, when applied to me, would serve only to prolong the dying process where I have a terminal illness or injury, or would serve only to maintain me in a condition of permanent unconsciousness. These procedures shall include, but are not limited to, assisted ventilation, cardiopulmonary resuscitation, renal dialysis, surgical procedures, blood transfusions, and the administration of drugs and antibiotics. Life-sustaining treatment shall not include the administration of medication or the performance of any medical treatment where, in the opinion of the attending physician, the medication or treatment is necessary to provide comfort or to alleviate pain.

(c) Permanent unconsciousness. A condition that, to a reasonable degree of medical certainty:
    (i) Will last permanently, without improvement; and
    (ii) In which thought, sensation, purposeful action, social interaction, and awareness of self and environment are absent; and
    (iii) Which condition has existed for a period of time sufficient, in accordance with applicable professional standards, to make such a diagnosis; and
    (iv) Which condition is confirmed by a physician who is qualified and experienced in making such a diagnosis.
(d) Terminally-ill or injured patient. A patient whose death is imminent or whose condition, to a reasonable degree of medical certainty, is hopeless unless he or she is artificially-supported through the use of life-sustaining procedures.

(7) OTHER PROVISIONS.
(a) I understand that if I have been diagnosed as pregnant and that diagnosis is known to my attending physician, directions in this advance directive for health care concerning the providing, withholding, and withdrawal of life-sustaining treatment and artificially-provided nutrition and hydration shall have no force or effect during the course of my pregnancy.
(b) In the absence of my ability to give directions regarding the use of life-sustaining treatment, it is my intention that this advance directive for health care shall be honored by my family, my physician(s), and health care provider(s) as the final expression of my legal right to refuse medical or surgical treatment and accept the consequences from such refusal.
(c) I understand the full import of this declaration and I am emotionally and mentally competent to make this advance directive for health care.
(d) Nothing herein shall be construed as a directive to exclude from consultation or notification any relative of mine about my health condition or dying. Written directives by me as to whether to notify or consult with certain family members shall be respected by health care workers, attorneys-in-fact, or surrogates.
(e) I understand that I may revoke this directive at any time.

Durable Power of Attorney for Financial Affairs

I, _____ , grant a durable power of attorney for financial affairs to _____ (name), of _____ _____ (address), to act as my attorney-in-fact. This power of attorney shall become effective upon my disability, as certified by my primary physician or, if my primary physician is not available, by any other attending physician. This power of attorney grants no power or authority regarding health care decisions to my designated attorney-in-fact.

I give my attorney-in-fact the maximum power under law to perform the following specific acts on my behalf: all acts relating to any and all of my financial and/or business affairs, including all banking and financial institution transactions, all real estate transactions, all insurance and annuity transactions, all claims and litigation, and all business transactions. My attorney-in-fact is granted full power to act on my behalf in the same manner as if I were personally present.

My attorney-in-fact accepts this appointment and agrees to act in my best interest as he or she considers advisable. This power of attorney may be revoked by me at any time and is automatically revoked on my death. This power of attorney shall not be affected by my present or future disability or incapacity. My attorney-in-fact shall not be compensated for his or her services nor shall my attorney-in-fact be liable to me, my estate, heirs, successors, or assigns for acting or refraining from acting under this document, except for willful misconduct or gross negligence. Any third party who receives a signed copy of this document may act under it. Revocation of this document is not effective unless a third party has actual knowledge of such revocation.

Designation of Primary Physician

I designate the following physician as my primary physician: _____ (name), of _____ (address).

Organ Donation

In the event of my death, I have placed my initials next to the following part(s) of my body that I wish donated for the purposes that I have *initialed* below:

[   ] any organs or parts **OR**

[ ] eyes		[ ] bone and connective tissue		[ ] skin	
[ ] heart		[ ] kidney(s)		[ ] liver	
[ ] lung(s)		[ ] pancreas		[ ] other _____	

for the purposes of:

[   ] any purpose authorized by law **OR**

[ ] transplantation		[ ] research		[ ] therapy
[ ] medical education		[ ] other limitations _____		

Signature

I sign this Advance Health Care Directive, consisting of the following sections, which I have *initialed* below and have elected to adopt:

[   ] Living Will
[   ] Selection of Health Care Agent (Health Care Proxy)
[   ] Durable Power of Attorney for Financial Affairs
[   ] Designation of Primary Physician
[   ] Organ Donation

BY SIGNING HERE I INDICATE THAT I UNDERSTAND THE PURPOSE AND EFFECT OF THIS DOCUMENT.

Signature _____   Date _____

City, County, and State of Residence _____

Notary Acknowledgment

State of _____

County of _____

On _____ , _____ came before me personally and, under oath, stated that he or she is the person described in the above document and he or she signed the above document in my presence. I declare under penalty of perjury that the person whose name is subscribed to this instrument appears to be of sound mind and under no duress, fraud, or undue influence.

_____
Notary Public

My commission expires _____

Witness Acknowledgment

The declarant is personally known to me and I believe him or her to be of sound mind and under no duress, fraud, or undue influence. I did not sign the declarant's signature above for or at the direction of the declarant and I am not appointed as the health care agent or attorney-in-fact herein. I am at least eighteen (18) years of age and I am not related to the declarant by blood, adoption, or marriage, entitled to any portion of the estate of the declarant according to the laws of intestate succession or under any will of declarant or codicil thereto, or directly financially responsible for declarant's medical care. I am not a health care provider of the declarant or an employee of the health facility in which the declarant is a patient.

Witness Signature _____ Date _____

Printed Name of Witness _____

Witness Signature _____ Date _____

Printed Name of Witness _____

Acceptance of Health Care Agent and Financial Attorney-in-Fact

I accept my appointment as Health Care Agent:

Signature _____ Date _____

I accept my appointment as Attorney-in-Fact for Financial Affairs:

Signature _____ Date _____

Alaska Advance Health Care Directive

On this date of _____ , I, _____ , do hereby sign, execute, and adopt the following as my Advance Health Care Directive. I direct any and all persons or entities involved with my health care in any manner that these decisions are my wishes and were adopted without duress or force and of my own free will. I have placed my *initials* next to the sections of this Directive that I have adopted:

[   ]   Living Will
[   ]   Selection of Health Care Agent (Durable Power of Attorney for Health Care)
[   ]   Durable Power of Attorney for Financial Affairs
[   ]   Designation of Primary Physician
[   ]   Organ Donation

Living Will

If I should have an incurable or irreversible condition that will cause my death within a relatively short time, it is my desire that my life not be prolonged by administration of life-sustaining procedures. If my condition is terminal and I am unable to participate in decisions regarding my medical treatment, I direct my attending physician to withhold or withdraw procedures that merely prolong the dying process and are not necessary to my comfort or to alleviate pain (*initial your choice*):

[   ] I DO desire that nutrition or hydration (food and water) be provided by gastric tube or intravenously if necessary.

[   ] I do NOT desire that nutrition or hydration (food and water) be provided by gastric tube or intravenously if necessary.

Notwithstanding the other provisions of this declaration, if I have donated an organ under this declaration or by another method, and if I am in a hospital when a do-not-resuscitate order is to be implemented for me, I do NOT want the do-not-resuscitate order to take effect until the donated organ can be evaluated to determine if the organ is suitable for donation.

Selection of Health Care Agent
(Durable Power of Attorney for Health Care)

The powers granted from the principal to the agent or agents in the following document are limited to the power to make your health care decisions. The following document should be used only after careful consideration. If you have any questions about this document, you should seek competent legal advice. You may revoke this power of attorney at any time.

Pursuant to AS 13.26.338 - 13.26.353, I, _____ , of
_____ (address), do hereby
appoint _____ (name), _____
_____ (address), as my attorney-in-fact to act concerning my
health care services in my name, place, and stead in any way which I myself could do, if I were
personally present, with respect to the following matters, as defined in AS 13.26.344, to the
full extent that I am permitted by law to act through an agent.

This document shall become effective upon the date of my disability and shall not otherwise be
affected by my disability.

Durable Power of Attorney for Financial Affairs

I, _____ , grant a durable power of attorney for financial
affairs to _____ (name), of _____
_____ (address), to act as my attorney-in-fact. This power of attorney
shall become effective upon my disability, as certified by my primary physician or, if my primary
physician is not available, by any other attending physician. This power of attorney grants no
power or authority regarding health care decisions to my designated attorney-in-fact.

I give my attorney-in-fact the maximum power under law to perform the following specific
acts on my behalf: all acts relating to any and all of my financial and/or business affairs,
including all banking and financial institution transactions, all real estate transactions, all insurance and annuity transactions, all claims and litigation, and all business transactions. My
attorney-in-fact is granted full power to act on my behalf in the same manner as if I were
personally present.

My attorney-in-fact accepts this appointment and agrees to act in my best interest as he or she
considers advisable. This power of attorney may be revoked by me at any time and is automatically revoked on my death. This power of attorney shall not be affected by my present or
future disability or incapacity. My attorney-in-fact shall not be compensated for his or her
services nor shall my attorney-in-fact be liable to me, my estate, heirs, successors, or assigns
for acting or refraining from acting under this document, except for willful misconduct or
gross negligence. Any third party who receives a signed copy of this document may act under
it. Revocation of this document is not effective unless a third party has actual knowledge of
such revocation.

Designation of Primary Physician

I designate the following physician as my primary physician: _____
(name), of _____ (address).

Organ Donation

In the event of my death, I have placed my initials next to the following part(s) of my body that I wish donated for the purposes that I have *initialed* below:

[   ] any organs or parts **OR**

[   ] eyes   [   ] bone and connective tissue   [   ] skin

[   ] heart   [   ] kidney(s)   [   ] liver

[   ] lung(s)   [   ] pancreas   [   ] other _____

for the purposes of:

[   ] any purpose authorized by law **OR**

[   ] transplantation   [   ] research   [   ] therapy

[   ] medical education   [   ] other limitations _____

Signature

I sign this Advance Health Care Directive, consisting of the following sections, which I have *initialed* below and have elected to adopt:

[   ] Living Will

[   ] Selection of Health Care Agent (Durable Power of Attorney for Health Care)

[   ] Durable Power of Attorney for Financial Affairs

[   ] Designation of Primary Physician

[   ] Organ Donation

BY SIGNING HERE I INDICATE THAT I UNDERSTAND THE PURPOSE AND EFFECT OF THIS DOCUMENT.

Signature _____   Date _____

City, County, and State of Residence _____

Notary Acknowledgment

State of _____

County of _____

On _____ , _____ came before me personally and, under oath, stated that he or she is the person described in the above document and he or she signed the above document in my presence. I declare under penalty of perjury that the person whose name is subscribed to this instrument appears to be of sound mind and under no duress, fraud, or undue influence.

_____

Notary Public

My commission expires _____

Witness Acknowledgment

The declarant is personally known to me and I believe him or her to be of sound mind and under no duress, fraud, or undue influence. I did not sign the declarant's signature above for or at the direction of the declarant and I am not appointed as the health care agent or attorney-in-fact herein. I am at least eighteen (18) years of age and I am not related to the declarant by blood, adoption, or marriage, entitled to any portion of the estate of the declarant according to the laws of intestate succession or under any will of declarant or codicil thereto, or directly financially responsible for declarant's medical care. I am not a health care provider of the declarant or an employee of the health facility in which the declarant is a patient.

Witness Signature _____ Date _____

Printed Name of Witness _____

Witness Signature _____ Date _____

Printed Name of Witness _____

Acceptance of Health Care Agent and Financial Attorney-in-Fact

I accept my appointment as Health Care Agent:

Signature _____ Date _____

I accept my appointment as Attorney-in-Fact for Financial Affairs:

Signature _____ Date _____

Arizona Advance Health Care Directive

On this date of _____ , I, _____ , do hereby sign, execute, and adopt the following as my Advance Health Care Directive. I direct any and all persons or entities involved with my health care in any manner that these decisions are my wishes and were adopted without duress or force and of my own free will. I have placed my *initials* next to the sections of this Directive that I have adopted:

[   ] Living Will
[   ] Selection of Health Care Agent (Health Care Power of Attorney)
[   ] Durable Power of Attorney for Financial Affairs
[   ] Designation of Primary Physician
[   ] Organ Donation

Living Will

Some general statements concerning your health care options are outlined below. If you agree with one of the statements, you should *initial* that statement. Read all of these statements carefully before you initial your selection. You can also write your own statement concerning life-sustaining treatment and other matters relating to your health care. You may *initial* any combination of paragraphs (1), (2), (3), and (4), but if you *initial* paragraph (5), the others should not be *initialed*.

[   ] 1. If I have a terminal condition I do NOT want my life to be prolonged and I do NOT want life-sustaining treatment, beyond comfort care, that would serve only to artificially delay the moment of my death.

[   ] 2. If I am in a terminal condition or an irreversible coma or a persistent vegetative state that my doctors reasonably feel to be irreversible or incurable, I DO want the medical treatment necessary to provide care that would keep me comfortable, but I do NOT want the following:

    [   ] (a) Cardiopulmonary resuscitation, for example, the use of drugs, electric shock, and artificial breathing.

    [   ] (b) Artificially-administered food and fluids.

    [   ] (c) To be taken to a hospital if at all avoidable.

[   ] 3. Notwithstanding my other directions, if I am known to be pregnant, I do NOT want life-sustaining treatment withheld or withdrawn if it is possible that the embryo/fetus will develop to the point of live birth with the continued application of life-sustaining treatment.

[   ] 4. Notwithstanding my other directions, I DO want the use of all medical care necessary to treat my condition until my doctors reasonably conclude that my condition is terminal or is irreversible and incurable or I am in a persistent vegetative state.

[   ] 5. I want my life to be prolonged to the greatest extent possible.

Other or Additional Statements of Desires (*add other statements, if any. If none, state "none"*):

Selection of Health Care Agent (Health Care Power of Attorney)

I, _____ , as principal, designate _____
(name), of _____ (address), as
my agent for all matters relating to my health care, including, without limitation, full power to
give or refuse consent to all medical, surgical, hospital, and related health care. This power of
attorney is effective on my inability to make or communicate health care decisions. All of my
agent's actions under this power during any period when I am unable to make or communicate
health care decisions or when there is uncertainty whether I am dead or alive have the same
effect on my heirs, devisees and personal representatives as if I were alive, competent, and
acting for myself (*initial your choice*):
I have [   ] **OR**   I have NOT [   ] completed and attached a living will for purposes
of providing specific direction to my agent in situations that may occur during any period
when I am unable to make or communicate health care decisions or after my death. My agent
is directed to implement those choices I have initialed in the living will.
This health care directive is made under Section 36-3221, Arizona Revised Statutes, and continues
in effect for all who may rely on it except those to whom I have given notice of its revocation.

Durable Power of Attorney for Financial Affairs

I, _____ , grant a durable power of attorney for financial affairs to _____ (name), of _____
_____ (address), to act as my attorney-in-fact. This power of attorney
shall become effective upon my disability, as certified by my primary physician or, if my primary
physician is not available, by any other attending physician. This power of attorney grants no
power or authority regarding health care decisions to my designated attorney-in-fact.

I give my attorney-in-fact the maximum power under law to perform the following specific
acts on my behalf: all acts relating to any and all of my financial and/or business affairs,
including all banking and financial institution transactions, real estate transactions, insurance
and annuity transactions, claims and litigation, and business transactions. My attorney-in-fact
is granted full power to act on my behalf in the same manner as if I were personally present.

My attorney-in-fact accepts this appointment and agrees to act in my best interest as he or she considers advisable. This power of attorney may be revoked by me at any time and is automatically revoked on my death. This power of attorney shall not be affected by my present or future disability or incapacity. My attorney-in-fact shall not be compensated for his or her services nor shall my attorney-in-fact be liable to me, my estate, heirs, successors, or assigns for acting or refraining from acting under this document, except for willful misconduct or gross negligence. Any third party who receives a signed copy of this document may act under it. Revocation of this document is not effective unless a third party has actual knowledge of such revocation.

Designation of Primary Physician

I designate the following physician as my primary physician: _____
(name), of _____ (address).

Organ Donation

In the event of my death, I have placed my initials next to the following part(s) of my body that I wish donated for the purposes that I have *initialed* below:

[   ] any organs or parts **OR**

[   ] eyes   [   ] bone and connective tissue   [   ] skin
[   ] heart   [   ] kidney(s)   [   ] liver
[   ] lung(s)   [   ] pancreas   [   ]other _____

for the purposes of:

[   ] any purpose authorized by law **OR**

[   ] transplantation   [   ] research   [   ] therapy
[   ] medical education   [   ] other limitations _____

Signature

I sign this Advance Health Care Directive, consisting of the following sections, which I have *initialed* below and have elected to adopt:

[   ] Living Will
[   ] Selection of Health Care Agent (Health Care Power of Attorney)
[   ] Durable Power of Attorney for Financial Affairs
[   ] Designation of Primary Physician
[   ] Organ Donation

BY SIGNING HERE I INDICATE THAT I UNDERSTAND THE PURPOSE AND EFFECT OF THIS DOCUMENT.

Signature _____   Date _____

City, County, and State of Residence _____

Notary Acknowledgment

State of _____

County of _____

On _____ , _____ came before me personally and, under oath, stated that he or she is the person described in the above document and he or she signed the above document in my presence. I declare under penalty of perjury that the person whose name is subscribed to this instrument appears to be of sound mind and under no duress, fraud, or undue influence.

_____
Notary Public
My commission expires _____

Witness Acknowledgment

The declarant has been personally known to me and I believe him or her to be of sound mind. I did not sign the declarant's signature above for or at the direction of the declarant and I am not appointed as the health care proxy or attorney-in-fact therein. I am at least eighteen (18) years of age and I am not related to the declarant by blood, adoption, or marriage, entitled to any portion of the estate of the declarant according to the laws of intestate succession or under any will of declarant or codicil thereto, or directly financially responsible for declarant's medical care.

Witness Signature _____   Date _____

Printed Name of Witness _____

Witness Signature _____   Date _____

Printed Name of Witness _____

Acceptance of Health Care Agent and Financial Attorney-in-Fact

I accept my appointment as Health Care Agent:

Signature _____   Date _____

I accept my appointment as Attorney-in-Fact for Financial Affairs:

Signature _____   Date _____

Arkansas Advance Health Care Directive

On this date of _____ , I, _____ , do hereby sign, execute, and adopt the following as my Advance Health Care Directive. I direct any and all persons or entities involved with my health care in any manner that these decisions are my wishes and were adopted without duress or force and of my own free will. I have placed my *initials* next to the sections of this Directive that I have adopted:

[   ]   Living Will
[   ]   Selection of Health Care Agent (Durable Power of Attorney for Health Care)
[   ]   Durable Power of Attorney for Financial Affairs
[   ]   Designation of Primary Physician
[   ]   Organ Donation

Living Will Declaration

If I should have an incurable or irreversible condition that will cause my death within a relatively short time, and I am no longer able to make decisions regarding my medical treatment, **OR** if I should become permanently unconscious, I direct my attending physician, pursuant to the Arkansas Rights of the Terminally Ill or Permanently Unconscious Act (*initial your choice*):
[   ]   to withhold or withdraw treatment that only prolongs the process of dying and is not necessary to my comfort or to alleviate pain.
Other directions (*add any additional directions*):

I direct my attending physician, pursuant to the Arkansas Rights of the Terminally Ill or Permanently Unconscious Act (*initial your choice*):
[   ]   to follow the instructions of _____ (name), whom I appoint below as my Health Care Attorney-in-Fact to decide whether life-sustaining treatment should be withheld or withdrawn.

Pursuant to state law: A physician or other health care provider who is furnished a copy of the declaration shall make it a part of the declarant's medical record and, if unwilling to comply with the declaration, promptly so advise the declarant. In the case of a qualified patient, the patient's health care attorney-in-fact, in consultation with the attending physician, shall have the authority to make treatment decisions for the patient including the withholding or withdrawal of life-sustaining procedures.

Selection of Health Care Agent
(Durable Power of Attorney for Health Care)

I, _____ , hereby appoint _____
(name), of _____ (address), as my health care agent to make any and all health care decisions for me, except to the extent that I state otherwise. This Durable Power of Attorney for Health Care shall take effect in the event I become unable to make my own health care decisions. My health care agent and any alternate health care agent shall have the authority to make all health care decisions regarding any care, treatment, service, or procedure to maintain, diagnose, treat, or provide for my physical or mental health or personal care. My health care agent and any alternate agent shall also have the authority to make decisions regarding the providing, withholding, or withdrawing of life-sustaining treatment pursuant to the Arkansas Rights of the Terminally Ill or Permanently Unconscious Act.

Optional Instructions (*insert any additional instructions*):

Durable Power of Attorney for Financial Affairs

I, _____ , grant a durable power of attorney for financial affairs to _____ (name), of _____ _____ (address), to act as my attorney-in-fact. This power of attorney shall become effective upon my disability, as certified by my primary physician or, if my primary physician is not available, by any other attending physician. This power of attorney grants no power or authority regarding health care decisions to my designated attorney-in-fact.

I give my attorney-in-fact the maximum power under law to perform the following specific acts on my behalf: all acts relating to any and all of my financial and/or business affairs, including all banking and financial institution transactions, all real estate transactions, all insurance

and annuity transactions, all claims and litigation, and all business transactions. My attorney-in-fact is granted full power to act on my behalf in the same manner as if I were personally present.

My attorney-in-fact accepts this appointment and agrees to act in my best interest as he or she considers advisable. This power of attorney may be revoked by me at any time and is automatically revoked on my death. This power of attorney shall not be affected by my present or future disability or incapacity. My attorney-in-fact shall not be compensated for his or her services nor shall my attorney-in-fact be liable to me, my estate, heirs, successors, or assigns for acting or refraining from acting under this document, except for willful misconduct or gross negligence. Any third party who receives a signed copy of this document may act under it. Revocation of this document is not effective unless a third party has actual knowledge of such revocation.

Designation of Primary Physician

I designate the following physician as my primary physician: _____
(name), of _____ (address).

Organ Donation

In the event of my death, I have placed my initials next to the following part(s) of my body that I wish donated for the purposes that I have *initialed* below:
[   ] any organs or parts **OR**
[   ] eyes   [   ] bone and connective tissue   [   ] skin
[   ] heart   [   ] kidney(s)   [   ] liver
[   ] lung(s)   [   ] pancreas   [   ] other _____
for the purposes of:
[   ] any purpose authorized by law **OR**
[   ] transplantation   [   ] research   [   ] therapy
[   ] medical education   [   ] other limitations _____

Signature

I sign this Advance Health Care Directive, consisting of the following sections, which I have *initialed* below and have elected to adopt:
[   ] Living Will
[   ] Selection of Health Care Agent (Durable Power of Attorney for Health Care)
[   ] Durable Power of Attorney for Financial Affairs
[   ] Designation of Primary Physician
[   ] Organ Donation
BY SIGNING HERE I INDICATE THAT I UNDERSTAND THE PURPOSE AND EFFECT OF THIS DOCUMENT.

Signature _____   Date _____

City, County, and State of Residence _____

Notary Acknowledgment

State of _____

County of _____

On _____ , _____ came before me personally and, under oath, stated that he or she is the person described in the above document and he or she signed the above document in my presence. I declare under penalty of perjury that the person whose name is subscribed to this instrument appears to be of sound mind and under no duress, fraud, or undue influence.

_____
Notary Public
My commission expires _____

Witness Acknowledgment

The declarant is personally known to me and I believe him or her to be of sound mind and under no duress, fraud, or undue influence. I did not sign the declarant's signature above for or at the direction of the declarant and I am not appointed as the health care agent or attorney-in-fact herein. I am at least eighteen (18) years of age and I am not related to the declarant by blood, adoption, or marriage, entitled to any portion of the estate of the declarant according to the laws of intestate succession or under any will of declarant or codicil thereto, or directly financially responsible for declarant's medical care. I am not a health care provider of the declarant or an employee of the health facility in which the declarant is a patient.

Witness Signature _____   Date _____

Printed Name of Witness _____

Witness Signature _____   Date _____

Printed Name of Witness _____

Acceptance of Health Care Agent and Financial Attorney-in-Fact

I accept my appointment as Health Care Agent:

Signature _____   Date _____

I accept my appointment as Attorney-in-Fact for Financial Affairs:

Signature _____   Date _____

California Advance Health Care Directive

On this date of _____ , I, _____ , do hereby sign, execute, and adopt the following as my Advance Health Care Directive. I direct any and all persons or entities involved with my health care in any manner that these decisions are my wishes and were adopted without duress or force and of my own free will. I have placed my *initials* next to the sections of this Directive that I have adopted:

[   ]   Living Will (Instructions for Health Care)
[   ]   Selection of Health Care Agent (Power of Attorney for Health Care)
[   ]   Durable Power of Attorney for Financial Affairs
[   ]   Designation of Primary Physician
[   ]   Organ Donation

You have the right to give instructions about your own health care. You also have the right to name someone else to make health care decisions for you. This form lets you do either or both of these things. It also lets you express your wishes regarding dona-tion of organs and the designation of your primary physician. If you use this form, you may complete or modify all or any part of it. You are free to use a different form.

PART 1 of this form lets you give specific instructions about any aspect of your health care, whether or not you appoint an agent. Choices are provided for you to express your wishes regarding the provision, withholding, or withdrawal of treatment to keep you alive, as well as the provision of pain relief. Space is provided for you to add to the choices you have made or for you to write out any additional wishes.

PART 2 of this form is a Power of Attorney for Health Care. Part 2 lets you name another individual as agent to make health care decisions for you if you become incapable of making your own decisions or if you want someone else to make those decisions for you now even though you are still capable. (Your agent may not be an operator or employee of a community care facility or a residential care facility where you are receiving care, or your supervising health care provider or employee of the health care institution where you are receiving care, unless your agent is related to you or is a co-worker.) Unless the form you sign limits the authority of your agent, your agent may make all health care decisions for you. This form has a place for you to limit the authority of your agent. You need not limit the authority of your agent if you wish to rely on your agent for all health care decisions that may have to be made. If you choose not to limit the authority of your agent, your agent will have the right to:

(1) Consent or refuse consent to any care, treatment, service, or procedure to main-tain, diagnose, or otherwise affect a physical or mental condition;

(2) Select or discharge health care providers and institutions;

(3) Approve or disapprove diagnostic tests, surgical procedures, and programs of medication;

(4) Direct the provision, withholding, or withdrawal of artificial nutrition and hydration and all other forms of health care, including cardiopulmonary resuscitation; and

(5) Make anatomical gifts, authorize an autopsy, and direct the disposition of your remains.

PART 3 of this form lets you designate a person to handle financial matters during the time that you are disabled. This does not have to be the same person whom you appointed as your Power of Attorney for Health Care.

PART 4 of this form lets you designate a physician to have primary responsibility for your health care.

PART 5 of this form lets you express an intention to donate your bodily organs and tissues following your death.

After completing this form, sign and date the form at the end. The form must be signed by two (2) qualified witnesses or acknowledged before a notary public. Give a copy of the signed and completed form to your physician, any other health care providers you may have, any health care institution at which you are receiving care, and any health care agents you have named. You should talk to the person you have named as agent to make sure that he or she understands your wishes and is willing to take the responsibility.

You have the right to revoke this advance health care directive or replace this form at any time.

Part 1: Living Will (Instructions for Health Care)

If you fill out this part of the form, you may strike any wording you do not want.

END-OF-LIFE DECISIONS: I direct that my health care providers and others involved in my care provide, withhold, or withdraw treatment in accordance with the choice I have marked below (*initial only one box*):

[　　] (a) Choice NOT To Prolong Life. I do NOT want my life to be prolonged if:

(i) I have an incurable and irreversible condition that will result in my death within a relatively short time,

(ii) I become unconscious and, to a reasonable degree of medical certainty, I will not regain consciousness, **OR**

(iii) the likely risks and burdens of treatment would outweigh the expected benefits, **OR**

[　　] (b) Choice TO Prolong Life. I DO want my life to be prolonged as long as possible within the limits of generally-accepted health care standards.

RELIEF FROM PAIN (*initial if this is your choice*): [　　] Except as I state in the following space, I direct that treatment for alleviation of pain or discomfort should be provided at all times even if it hastens my death (*add exceptions and additional sheets as needed*):

OTHER WISHES: (*If you do not agree with any of the optional choices above and wish to write your own, or if you wish to add to the instructions you have given above, you may do so here. Add additional sheets if needed.*) I direct that:

Part 2: Selection of Health Care Agent
(Power of Attorney for Health Care)

DESIGNATION OF AGENT: I designate the following individual as my agent to make health care decisions for me: _____ (name), of _____
_____ (address).

AGENT'S AUTHORITY: My agent is authorized to make all health care decisions for me, including decisions to provide, withhold, or withdraw artificial nutrition and hydration, and all other forms of healthcare to keep me alive, except as I state here (*add additional sheets if needed*):

WHEN AGENT'S AUTHORITY BECOMES EFFECTIVE: My agent's authority becomes effective when my primary physician determines that I am unable to make my own health care decisions unless I *initial* the following box. If I *initial* this box [   ], my agent's authority to make health care decisions for me takes effect immediately.

AGENT'S OBLIGATION: My agent shall make health care decisions for me in accordance with this power of attorney for health care, any instructions I give in Part 1 of this form, and my other wishes to the extent known to my agent. To the extent my wishes are unknown, my agent shall make health care decisions for me in accordance with what my agent determines to be in my best interest. In determining my best interest, my agent shall consider my personal values to the extent known to my agent.

AGENT'S POSTDEATH AUTHORITY: My agent is authorized to make anatomical gifts, authorize an autopsy, and direct disposition of my remains, except as I state here or in Part 4 of this form (*insert exceptions and additional sheets if needed*):

NOMINATION OF CONSERVATOR: If a conservator of my person needs to be appointed for me by a court, I nominate the agent designated in this form.

Part 3: Durable Power of Attorney for Financial Affairs

I, _____ , grant a durable power of attorney for financial affairs to _____ (name), of _____ _____ (address), to act as my attorney-in-fact. This power of attorney shall become effective upon my disability, as certified by my primary physician or, if my primary physician is not available, by any other attending physician. This power of attorney grants no power or authority regarding health care decisions to my designated attorney-in-fact.

I give my attorney-in-fact the maximum power under law to perform the following specific acts on my behalf: all acts relating to any and all of my financial and/or business affairs, including all banking and financial institution transactions, all real estate transactions, all insurance and annuity transactions, all claims and litigation, and all business transactions. My attorney-in-fact is granted full power to act on my behalf in the same manner as if I were personally present.

My attorney-in-fact accepts this appointment and agrees to act in my best interest as he or she considers advisable. This power of attorney may be revoked by me at any time and is automatically revoked on my death. This power of attorney shall not be affected by my present or future disability or incapacity. My attorney-in-fact shall not be compensated for his or her services nor shall my attorney-in-fact be liable to me, my estate, heirs, successors, or assigns for acting or refraining from acting under this document, except for willful misconduct or gross negligence. Any third party who receives a signed copy of this document may act under it. Revocation of this document is not effective unless a third party has actual knowledge of such revocation.

Part 4: Designation of Primary Physician

I designate the following physician as my primary physician: _____ (name), of _____ (address).

Part 5: Organ Donation

In the event of my death, I have placed my initials next to the following part(s) of my body that I wish donated for the purposes that I have *initialed* below:

[   ] any organs or parts **OR**

[ ] eyes	[ ] bone and connective tissue	[ ] skin
[ ] heart	[ ] kidney(s)	[ ] liver
[ ] lung(s)	[ ] pancreas	[ ] other _____

for the purposes of:

[   ] any purpose authorized by law **OR**

[   ] transplantation   [   ] research   [   ] therapy

[   ] medical education   [   ] other limitations _____

Signature

I sign this Advance Health Care Directive, consisting of the following sections, which I have *initialed* below and have elected to adopt:

[   ] Living Will (Instructions for Health Care)

[   ] Selection of Health Care Agent (Power of Attorney for Health Care)

[   ] Durable Power of Attorney for Financial Affairs

[   ] Designation of Primary Physician

[   ] Organ Donation

BY SIGNING HERE I INDICATE THAT I UNDERSTAND THE PURPOSE AND EFFECT OF THIS DOCUMENT.

Signature _____   Date _____

City, County, and State of Residence _____

Notary Acknowledgment

State of _____

County of _____

On _____ , _____ came before me personally and, under oath, stated that he or she is the person described in the above document and he or she signed the above document in my presence. I declare under penalty of perjury that the person whose name is subscribed to this instrument appears to be of sound mind and under no duress, fraud, or undue influence.

_____

Notary Public

My commission expires _____

Witness Acknowledgment

Witness #1 Statement: I declare under penalty of perjury under the laws of California that:
(1) the individual who signed or acknowledged this advance health care directive is personally known to me, or that the individual's identity was proven to me by convincing evidence;
(2) the individual signed or acknowledged this advance directive in my presence;
(3) the individual appears to be of sound mind and under no duress, fraud, or undue influence;
(4) I am not a person appointed as an agent by this advance directive; and
(5) I am at least eighteen (18) years of age and I am not the individual's health care provider, an employee of the individual's health care provider, the operator of of a community care facility, an employee of an operator of a community care facility, the operator of a residential care facility for the elderly, or an employee of an operator of a residential care facility for the elderly.

Signature _____ Date _____

Printed Name of Witness _____

Witness #2 Statement: I declare under penalty of perjury under the laws of California that:
(1) the individual who signed or acknowledged this advance health care directive is personally known to me, or that the individual's identity was proven to me by convincing evidence;
(2) the individual signed or acknowledged this advance directive in my presence;
(3) the individual appears to be of sound mind and under no duress, fraud, or undue influence;
(4) I am not a person appointed as an agent by this advance directive; and
(5) I am not the individual's health care provider, an employee of the individual's health care provider, the operator of a community care facility, an employee of an operator of a community care facility, the operator of a residential care facility for the elderly, nor an employee of an operator of a residential care facility for the elderly.
I further declare under penalty of perjury under the laws of California that I am at least eighteen (18) years of age and I am not related to the individual executing this advance health care directive by blood, marriage, or adoption, and, to the best of my knowledge, am not entitled to any part of the individual's estate upon his or her death under a will now existing or by operation of law.

Witness Signature _____ Date _____

Printed Name of Witness _____

Acceptance of Health Care Agent and Financial Attorney-in-Fact

I accept my appointment as Health Care Agent:

Signature _____ Date _____

I accept my appointment as Attorney-in-Fact for Financial Affairs:

Signature _____ Date _____

Colorado Advance Health Care Directive

On this date of _____ , I, _____ , do hereby sign, execute, and adopt the following as my Advance Health Care Directive. I direct any and all persons or entities involved with my health care in any manner that these decisions are my wishes and were adopted without duress or force and of my own free will. I have placed my *signature* next to the sections of this Directive that I have adopted:

[   ] Living Will (Declaration as to Medical or Surgical Treatment)

[   ] Selection of Health Care Agent (Medical Durable Power of Attorney for Health Care)

[   ] Durable Power of Attorney for Financial Affairs

[   ] Designation of Primary Physician

[   ] Organ Donation

Living Will (Declaration as to Medical or Surgical Treatment)

I, _____ , being of sound mind and at least eighteen (18) years of age, direct that my life shall not be artificially-prolonged under the circumstances set forth below and hereby declare that:

(1) If at any time my attending physician and one (1) other qualified physician certify in writing that:

   (a) I have an injury, disease, or illness which is not curable or reversible and which, in their judgment, is a terminal condition, and

   (b) For a period of seven (7) consecutive days or more, I have been unconscious, comatose, or otherwise incompetent so as to be unable to make or communicate responsible decisions concerning my person, then:

I direct that, in accordance with Colorado law, life-sustaining procedures shall be withdrawn and withheld pursuant to the terms of this declaration, it being understood that life-sustaining procedures shall not include any medical procedure or intervention for nourishment considered necessary by the attending physician to provide comfort or alleviate pain. However, I may specifically direct, in accordance with Colorado law, that artificial nourishment be withdrawn or withheld pursuant to the terms of this declaration.

(2) In the event that the only procedure I am being provided is artificial nourishment, I direct that one of the following actions be taken (*initial your choice*):

[   ] (a) Artificial nourishment SHALL NOT be continued when it is the only procedure being provided; **OR**

[   ] (b) Artificial nourishment SHALL be continued for _____ days when it is the only procedure being provided; **OR**

[   ] (c) Artificial nourishment SHALL be continued when it is the only procedure being provided.

Selection of Health Care Agent
(Medical Durable Power of Attorney for Health Care)

I, _____ , hereby appoint _____ (name),
of _____ (address), as my
agent to make health care decisions for me if and when I am unable to make my own health care
decisions. This gives my agent the power to consent to giving, withholding, or stopping any health
care, treatment, service, or diagnostic procedure. My agent also has the authority to talk with
health care personnel, get information, and sign forms necessary to carry out those decisions.
By this document I intend to create a Medical Durable Power of Attorney which shall take effect
upon my incapacity to make my own health care decisions and shall continue during that incapacity. My agent shall make health care decisions as I may direct below or as I make known to him or
her in some other way. If I have not expressed a choice about the health care in question, my
agent shall base his or her decisions on what he or she believes to be in my best interest.
(1) Statement of desires concerning life-prolonging care, treatment, services, and procedures
(*insert your wishes. Attach additional sheets if necessary*):

(2) Special provisions and limitations (*add any provisions and limitations*):

Durable Power of Attorney for Financial Affairs

I, _____ , grant a durable power of attorney for financial affairs
to _____ (name), of _____
_____ (address), to act as my attorney-in-fact. This power of attorney shall
become effective upon my disability, as certified by my primary physician or, if my primary
physician is not available, by any other attending physician. This power of attorney grants no
power or authority regarding health care decisions to my designated attorney-in-fact.

I give my attorney-in-fact the maximum power under law to perform the following specific
acts on my behalf: all acts relating to any and all of my financial and/or business affairs,

including all banking and financial institution transactions, all real estate transactions, all insurance and annuity transactions, all claims and litigation, and all business transactions. My attorney-in-fact is granted full power to act on my behalf in the same manner as if I were personally present.

My attorney-in-fact accepts this appointment and agrees to act in my best interest as he or she considers advisable. This power of attorney may be revoked by me at any time and is automatically revoked on my death. This power of attorney shall not be affected by my present or future disability or incapacity. My attorney-in-fact shall not be compensated for his or her services nor shall my attorney-in-fact be liable to me, my estate, heirs, successors, or assigns for acting or refraining from acting under this document, except for willful misconduct or gross negligence. Any third party who receives a signed copy of this document may act under it. Revocation of this document is not effective unless a third party has actual knowledge of such revocation.

Designation of Primary Physician

I designate the following physician as my primary physician: _____
(name), of _____ (address).

Organ Donation

[   ] any organs or parts **OR**

[   ] eyes   [   ] bone and connective tissue   [   ] skin

[   ] heart   [   ] kidney(s)   [   ] liver

[   ] lung(s)   [   ] pancreas   [   ] other _____

for the purposes of:

[   ] any purpose authorized by law **OR**

[   ] transplantation   [   ] research   [   ] therapy

[   ] medical education   [   ] other limitations _____

Signature

I sign this Advance Health Care Directive, consisting of the following sections, which I have *initialed* below and have elected to adopt:

[   ] Living Will (Declaration as to Medical or Surgical Treatment)

[   ] Selection of Health Care Agent (Medical Durable Power of Attorney for Health Care)

[   ] Durable Power of Attorney for Financial Affairs

[   ] Designation of Primary Physician

[   ] Organ Donation

BY SIGNING HERE I INDICATE THAT I UNDERSTAND THE PURPOSE AND EFFECT OF THIS DOCUMENT.

Signature _____   Date _____

City, County, and State of Residence _____

Notary Acknowledgment

State of _____

County of _____

On _____ , _____ came before me personally and, under oath, stated that he or she is the person described in the above document and he or she signed the above document in my presence. I declare under penalty of perjury that the person whose name is subscribed to this instrument appears to be of sound mind and under no duress, fraud, or undue influence.

_____

Notary Public

My commission expires _____

Witness Acknowledgment

The declarant is personally known to me and I believe him or her to be of sound mind and under no duress, fraud, or undue influence. I did not sign the declarant's signature above for or at the direction of the declarant and I am not appointed as the health care agent or attorney-in-fact herein. I am at least eighteen (18) years of age and I am not related to the declarant by blood, adoption, or marriage, entitled to any portion of the estate of the declarant according to the laws of intestate succession or under any will of declarant or codicil thereto, or directly financially responsible for declarant's medical care. I am not a health care provider of the declarant or an employee of the health facility in which the declarant is a patient.

Witness Signature _____   Date _____

Printed Name of Witness _____

Witness Signature _____   Date _____

Printed Name of Witness _____

Acceptance of Health Care Agent and Financial Attorney-in-Fact

I accept my appointment as Health Care Agent:

Signature _____   Date _____

I accept my appointment as Attorney-in-Fact for Financial Affairs:

Signature _____   Date _____

Connecticut Advance Health Care Directive

On this date of _____ , I, _____ , do hereby sign, execute, and adopt the following as my Advance Health Care Directive. I direct any and all persons or entities involved with my health care in any manner that these decisions are my wishes and were adopted without duress or force and of my own free will. I have placed my *initials* next to the sections of this Directive that I have adopted:

[   ] Living Will (Health Care Instructions)

[   ] Selection of My Health Care Agent (Attorney-in-Fact for Health Care Decisions)

[   ] Durable Power of Attorney for Financial Affairs

[   ] Designation of Primary Physician

[   ] Organ Donation

NOTICE TO ANY ATTENDING PHYSICIAN: These are my health care instructions. As my physician, you may rely on any decision made by my health care agent, attorney-in-fact for health care decisions, or conservator of my person, if I am unable to make a decision for myself.

Living Will (Health Care Instructions)

I, _____ , the author of this document, request that, if my condition is deemed terminal or if I am determined to be permanently unconscious, I be allowed to die and not be kept alive through life support systems. By terminal condition, I mean that I have an incurable or irreversible medical condition which, without the administration of life support systems, will, in the opinion of my attending physician, result in death within a relatively short time. By permanently unconscious I mean that I am in a permanent coma or persistent vegetative state which is an irreversible condition in which I am at no time aware of myself or the environment and show no behavioral response to the environment. The life support systems which I do not want include, but are not limited to: Artificial respiration, cardiopulmonary resuscitation, and artificial means of providing nutrition and hydration. I do want sufficient pain medication to maintain my physical comfort. I do not intend any direct taking of my life, but only that my dying not be unreasonably prolonged.

Selection of My Health Care Agent
(Attorney-in-Fact for Health Care Decisions)

I appoint _____ (name), of _____
_____ (address), to be my health care agent and my attorney-in-fact for health care decisions. If my attending physician determines that I am unable to under-

stand and appreciate the nature and consequences of health care decisions and am unable to reach and communicate an informed decision regarding treatment, my health care agent and attorney-in-fact for health care decisions is authorized to:

(1) Convey to my physician my wishes concerning the withholding or removal of life support systems;

(2) Take whatever actions are necessary to ensure that any wishes are given effect;

(3) Consent, refuse, or withdraw consent to any medical treatment as long as such action is consistent with my wishes concerning the withholding or removal of life support systems; and

(4) Consent to any medical treatment designed solely for the purpose of maintaining physical comfort.

If a conservator of my person should need to be appointed, I designate that the person above whom I have designated as my health care agent also be appointed my conservator.

Durable Power of Attorney for Financial Affairs

I, _____ , grant a durable power of attorney for financial affairs to _____ (name), of _____ _____ (address), to act as my attorney-in-fact. This power of attorney shall become effective upon my disability, as certified by my primary physician or, if my primary physician is not available, by any other attending physician. This power of attorney grants no power or authority regarding health care decisions to my designated attorney-in-fact.

I give my attorney-in-fact the maximum power under law to perform the following specific acts on my behalf: all acts relating to any and all of my financial and/or business affairs, including all banking and financial institution transactions, all real estate transactions, all insurance and annuity transactions, all claims and litigation, and all business transactions. My attorney-in-fact is granted full power to act on my behalf in the same manner as if I were personally present.

My attorney-in-fact accepts this appointment and agrees to act in my best interest as he or she considers advisable. This power of attorney may be revoked by me at any time and is automatically revoked on my death. This power of attorney shall not be affected by my present or future disability or incapacity. My attorney-in-fact shall not be compensated for his or her services nor shall my attorney-in-fact be liable to me, my estate, heirs, successors, or assigns for acting or refraining from acting under this document, except for willful misconduct or gross negligence. Any third party who receives a signed copy of this document may act under it. Revocation of this document is not effective unless a third party has actual knowledge of such revocation.

Designation of Primary Physician

I designate the following physician as my primary physician: _____ (name), of _____ (address).

Organ Donation

[   ] any organs or parts **OR**
[   ] eyes   [   ] bone and connective tissue   [   ] skin
[   ] heart   [   ] kidney(s)   [   ] liver
[   ] lung(s)   [   ] pancreas   [   ] other _____
for the purposes of:
[   ] any purpose authorized by law **OR**
[   ] transplantation   [   ] research   [   ] therapy
[   ] medical education   [   ] other limitations _____

Signature

I sign this Advance Health Care Directive, consisting of the following sections, which I have *initialed* below and have elected to adopt:
[   ] Living Will (Health Care Instructions)
[   ] Selection of My Health Care Agent (Attorney-in-Fact for Health Care Decisions)
[   ] Durable Power of Attorney for Financial Affairs
[   ] Designation of Primary Physician
[   ] Organ Donation
BY SIGNING HERE I INDICATE THAT I UNDERSTAND THE PURPOSE AND EF-FECT OF THIS DOCUMENT.

Signature _____   Date _____

City, County, and State of Residence _____

Notary Acknowledgment

State of _____
County of _____
On _____ , _____ came before me per-sonally and, under oath, stated that he or she is the person described in the above document and he or she signed the above document in my presence. I declare under penalty of perjury that the person whose name is subscribed to this instrument appears to be of sound mind and under no duress, fraud, or undue influence.

_____
Notary Public
My commission expires _____

Witness Acknowledgment

We, the subscribing witnesses, being duly sworn, say that we witnessed the execution of these health care instructions, the appointments of a health care agent and an attorney-in-fact, the designation of a conservator for future incapacity, the designation of a primary physician, and a document of anatomical gift by the author of this document; that the author subscribed, published, and declared the same to be the author's instructions, appointments, and designation in our presence; that we thereafter subscribed the document as witnesses in the author's presence, at the author's request, and in the presence of each other; that at the time of the execution of said document the author appeared to us to be eighteen (18) years of age or older, of sound mind, able to understand the nature and consequences of said document, and under no improper influence, and we make this affidavit at the author's request. The author has been personally known to us and we believe him or her to be of sound mind. We did not sign the author's signature above for or at the direction of the author and we are not appointed as the health care agent or attorney-in-fact therein. We are not related to the author by blood, adoption, or marriage, entitled to any portion of the estate of the author according to the laws of intestate succession or under any will of author or codicil thereto, or directly financially responsible for author's medical care.

Witness Signature _____ Date _____

Printed Name of Witness _____

Witness Signature _____ Date _____

Printed Name of Witness _____

Acceptance of Health Care Agent and Financial Attorney-in-Fact

I accept my appointment as Health Care Agent:

Signature _____ Date _____

I accept my appointment as Attorney-in-Fact for Financial Affairs:

Signature _____ Date _____

Delaware Advance Health Care Directive

On this date of _____ , I, _____ , do hereby sign, execute, and adopt the following as my Advance Health Care Directive. I direct any and all persons or entities involved with my health care in any manner that these decisions are my wishes and were adopted without duress or force and of my own free will. I have placed my *initials* next to the sections of this Directive that I have adopted:

[   ] Living Will (Instructions for Health Care)
[   ] Selection of Health Care Agent (Power of Attorney for Health Care)
[   ] Durable Power of Attorney for Financial Affairs
[   ] Designation of Primary Physician
[   ] Organ Donation

Living Will (Instructions for Health Care)

If you are satisfied to allow your agent to determine what is best for you in making end-of-life decisions, you need not fill out this part of the form. If you do fill out this part of the form, you may strike any wording you do not want.

END-OF-LIFE DECISIONS: If I am in a qualifying condition, I direct that my health care providers and others involved in my care provide, withhold, or withdraw treatment in accordance with the choice I have marked below:

Choice NOT To Prolong Life. I do NOT want my life to be prolonged if (*initial all that apply*):
[   ] (1) I have a terminal condition (an incurable condition caused by injury, disease, or illness which, to a reasonable degree of medical certainty, makes death imminent and from which, despite the application of life-sustaining procedures, there can be no recovery) and regarding artificial nutrition and hydration, I make the following specific directions (*please initial your choices*):
Artificial nutrition through a conduit:
[   ] yes, I want it used, **OR**   [   ] no, I do NOT want it used
Hydration through a conduit:
[   ] yes, I want it used, **OR**   [   ] no, I do NOT want it used

[   ] (2) I become permanently unconscious (a medical condition that has been diagnosed in accordance with currently-accepted medical standards that has lasted at least four (4) weeks and with reasonable medical certainty as total and irreversible loss of consciousness and capacity for interaction with the environment. The term includes, without limitation, a persistent

vegetative state or irreversible coma) and regarding artificial nutrition and hydration, I make the following specific directions (*please initial your choices*):
Artificial nutrition through a conduit:
[   ] yes, I want it used, **OR**   [   ] no, I do NOT want it used
Hydration through a conduit:
[   ] yes, I want it used, **OR**   [   ] no, I do NOT want it used

Choice TO Prolong Life. (*Please initial if you choose*):
[   ] I want my life TO be prolonged as long as possible within the limits of generally-accepted health care standards.
RELIEF FROM PAIN: Except as I state in the following space, I direct treatment for alleviation of pain or discomfort be provided at all times, even if it hastens my death (*insert exceptions and additional sheets if needed*):

OTHER MEDICAL INSTRUCTIONS: (*If you do not agree with any of the optional choices above and wish to write your own, or if you wish to add to the instructions you have given above, you may do so here. Add additional sheets if necessary.*) I direct that:

Selection of Health Care Agent (Power of Attorney for Health Care)

DESIGNATION OF AGENT: I designate the following individual as my agent to make health care decisions for me _____ (name), of _____
_____ (address).
AGENT'S AUTHORITY: If I am not in a qualifying condition, my agent is authorized to make all health care decisions for me, except decisions about life-sustaining procedures and as I state here; and if I am in a qualifying condition, my agent is authorized to make all health care decisions for me, except as I state here (*add additional sheets if necessary*):

WHEN AGENT'S AUTHORITY BECOMES EFFECTIVE: My agent's authority becomes effective when my primary physician determines I lack the capacity to make my own health care decisions. As to decisions concerning the providing, withholding, and withdrawal of life-sustaining procedures, my agent's authority becomes effective when my primary physician determines I lack the capacity to make my own health care decisions and my primary physician and another physician determine I am in a terminal condition or permanently unconscious.

AGENT'S OBLIGATION: My agent shall make health care decisions for me in accordance with this power of attorney for health care, any instructions I give in this form, and my other wishes to the extent known to my agent. To the extent my wishes are unknown, my agent shall make health care decisions for me in accordance with what my agent determines to be in my best interest. In determining my best interest, my agent shall consider my personal values to the extent known to my agent.

NOMINATION OF GUARDIAN: If a guardian of my person needs to be appointed for me by a court (*please initial one*):

[   ] I nominate the agent whom I named in this form to act as guardian.

[   ] I nominate the following to be my guardian (*insert name and address*):

_____ (name), of _____
_____ (address)

[   ] I do NOT nominate anyone to be my guardian.

Durable Power of Attorney for Financial Affairs

I, _____ , grant a durable power of attorney for financial affairs to _____ (name), of _____
_____ (address), to act as my attorney-in-fact. This power of attorney shall become effective upon my disability, as certified by my primary physician or, if my primary physician is not available, by any other attending physician. This power of attorney grants no power or authority regarding health care decisions to my designated attorney-in-fact.

I give my attorney-in-fact the maximum power under law to perform the following specific acts on my behalf: all acts relating to any and all of my financial and/or business affairs, including all banking and financial institution transactions, all real estate transactions, all insurance and annuity transactions, all claims and litigation, and all business transactions. My attorney-in-fact is granted full power to act on my behalf in the same manner as if I were personally present.

My attorney-in-fact accepts this appointment and agrees to act in my best interest as he or she considers advisable. This power of attorney may be revoked by me at any time and is automatically revoked on my death. This power of attorney shall not be affected by my present or future disability or incapacity. My attorney-in-fact shall not be compensated for his or her services nor shall my attorney-in-fact be liable to me, my estate, heirs, successors, or assigns for acting or refraining from acting under this document, except for willful misconduct or gross negligence. Any third party who receives a signed copy of this document may act under it. Revocation of this document is not effective unless a third party has actual knowledge of such revocation.

Designation of Primary Physician

I designate the following physician as my primary physician: _____
(name), of _____ (address).

Organ Donation

In the event of my death, I have placed my initials next to the following part(s) of my body that I wish donated for the purposes that I have *initialed* below:

[   ] any organs or parts **OR**

[   ] eyes   [   ] bone and connective tissue   [   ] skin

[   ] heart   [   ] kidney(s)   [   ] liver

[   ] lung(s)   [   ] pancreas   [   ] other _____

for the purposes of:

[   ] any purpose authorized by law **OR**

[   ] transplantation   [   ] research   [   ] therapy

[   ] medical education   [   ] other limitations _____

Signature

I sign this Advance Health Care Directive, consisting of the following sections, which I have *initialed* below and have elected to adopt:

[   ] Living Will (Instructions for Health Care)

[   ] Selection of Health Care Agent (Power of Attorney for Health Care)

[   ] Durable Power of Attorney for Financial Affairs

[   ] Designation of Primary Physician

[   ] Organ Donation

BY SIGNING HERE I INDICATE THAT I UNDERSTAND THE PURPOSE AND EFFECT OF THIS DOCUMENT.

Signature _____ Date _____

City, County, and State of Residence _____

Notary Acknowledgment

State of _____

County of _____

On _____ , _____ came before me personally and, under oath, stated that he or she is the person described in the above document and he or she signed the above document in my presence. I declare under penalty of perjury that the person whose name is subscribed to this instrument appears to be of sound mind and under no duress, fraud, or undue influence.

_____

Notary Public

My commission expires _____

Witness Acknowledgment

STATEMENTS OF WITNESSES: SIGNED AND DECLARED by the above-named declarant as and for his or her written declaration under 16 Del. C. §§ 2502 and 2503, in our presence, who in his or her presence, at his or her request, and in the presence of each other, have hereunto subscribed our names as witnesses, and state that:

(1) The Declarant is mentally competent.

(2) Neither of the witnesses:

(a) Is related to the declarant by blood, marriage, or adoption;

(b) Is entitled to any portion of the estate of the declarant under any will of the declarant or codicil thereto then existing nor, at the time of the executing of the advance health care directive, is so entitled by operation of law then existing;

(c) Has, at the time of the execution of the advance health care directive, a present or inchoate claim against any portion of the estate of the declarant;

(d) Has a direct financial responsibility for the declarant's medical care;

(e) Has a controlling interest in or is an operator or an employee of a residential long-term health care institution in which the declarant is a resident; **OR**

(f) Is under eighteen (18) years of age.

(3) If the declarant is a resident of a sanitarium, rest home, nursing home, boarding home, or related institution, one of the witnesses, _____(name), is, at the time of the execution of the advance health care directive, a patient advocate or ombudsman designated by the Division of Services for Aging and Adults with Physical Disabilities, or the Public Guardian.

Witness Signature _____   Date _____

Printed Name of Witness _____

Witness Signature _____   Date _____

Printed Name of Witness _____

Acceptance of Health Care Agent and Financial Attorney-in-Fact

I accept my appointment as Health Care Agent:

Signature _____   Date _____

I accept my appointment as Attorney-in-Fact for Financial Affairs:

Signature _____   Date _____

District of Columbia (Washington D.C.) Advance Health Care Directive

On this date of _____ , I, _____ , do hereby sign, execute, and adopt the following as my Advance Health Care Directive. I direct any and all persons or entities involved with my health care in any manner that these decisions are my wishes and were adopted without duress or force and of my own free will. I have placed my *initials* next to the sections of this Directive that I have adopted:

[   ]   Living Will
[   ]   Selection of Health Care Agent (Power of Attorney for Health Care)
[   ]   Durable Power of Attorney for Financial Affairs
[   ]   Designation of Primary Physician
[   ]   Organ Donation

Living Will

I, _____ , being of sound mind, willfully and voluntarily make known my desires that my dying shall not be artificially prolonged under the circumstances set forth below and do declare: If at any time I should have an incurable injury, disease, or illness certified to be a terminal condition by two (2) physicians who have personally examined me, one (1) of whom shall be my attending physician, and the physicians have determined that my death will occur whether or not life-sustaining procedures are utilized and where the application of life-sustaining procedures would serve only to artificially prolong the dying process, I direct that such procedures be withheld or withdrawn, and that I be permitted to die naturally with only the administration of medication or the performance of any medical procedure deemed necessary to provide me with comfort care or to alleviate pain.

Other directions (*insert other instructions*):

In the absence of my ability to give directions regarding the use of such life-sustaining procedures, it is my intention that this declaration shall be honored by my family and physician(s) as the final expression of my legal right to refuse medical or surgical treatment and to accept the consequences from such refusal.

I understand the full import of this declaration and I am emotionally and mentally competent to make this declaration.

Selection of Health Care Agent (Power of Attorney for Health Care)

INFORMATION ABOUT THIS DOCUMENT: This is an important legal document. Before signing this document, it is vital for you to know and understand these facts: This document gives the person you name as your attorney-in-fact the power to make health care decisions for you if you cannot make the decisions for yourself. After you have signed this document, you have the right to make health care decisions for yourself if you are mentally competent to do so. In addition, after you have signed this document, no treatment may be given to you or stopped over your objection if you are mentally competent to make that decision. You may state in this document any type of treatment that you do not desire and any that you want to make sure you receive. You have the right to take away the authority of your attorney-in-fact, unless you have been adjudicated incompetent, by notifying your attorney-in-fact or health care provider either orally or in writing. Should you revoke the authority of your attorney-in-fact, it is advisable to revoke in writing and to place copies of the revocation wherever this document is located. If there is anything in this document that you do not understand, you should ask a social worker, lawyer, or other person to explain it to you. You should keep a copy of this document after you have signed it. Give a copy to the person you name as your attorney-in-fact. If you are in a health care facility, a copy of this document should be included in your medical record.

I, _____ , hereby appoint _____
(name), of _____
(address), as my attorney-in-fact to make health care decisions for me if I become unable to make my own health care decisions. This gives my attorney-in-fact the power to grant, refuse, or withdraw consent on my behalf for any health care service, treatment, or procedure. My attorney-in-fact also has the authority to talk to health care personnel, get information, and sign forms necessary to carry out these decisions.

With this document, I intend to create a power of attorney for health care, which shall take effect if I become incapable of making my own health care decisions and shall continue during that incapacity. My attorney-in-fact shall make health care decisions as I direct below or as I make known to my attorney-in-fact in some other way.

Statement of directives concerning life-prolonging care, treatment, services and procedures (*insert statement. Attach additional sheets if necessary*):

Special provisions and limitations (*add any provisions and limitations*):

Durable Power of Attorney for Financial Affairs

I, _____ , grant a durable power of attorney for financial affairs to _____ (name), of _____ (address), to act as my attorney-in-fact. This power of attorney shall become effective upon my disability, as certified by my primary physician or, if my primary physician is not available, by any other attending physician. This power of attorney grants no power or authority regarding health care decisions to my designated attorney-in-fact.

I give my attorney-in-fact the maximum power under law to perform the following specific acts on my behalf: all acts relating to any and all of my financial and/or business affairs, including all banking and financial institution transactions, all real estate transactions, all insurance and annuity transactions, all claims and litigation, and all business transactions. My attorney-in-fact is granted full power to act on my behalf in the same manner as if I were personally present.

My attorney-in-fact accepts this appointment and agrees to act in my best interest as he or she considers advisable. This power of attorney may be revoked by me at any time and is automatically revoked on my death. This power of attorney shall not be affected by my present or future disability or incapacity. My attorney-in-fact shall not be compensated for his or her services nor shall my attorney-in-fact be liable to me, my estate, heirs, successors, or assigns for acting or refraining from acting under this document, except for willful misconduct or gross negligence. Any third party who receives a signed copy of this document may act under it. Revocation of this document is not effective unless a third party has actual knowledge of such revocation.

Designation of Primary Physician

I designate the following physician as my primary physician: _____
(name), of _____ (address).

Organ Donation

In the event of my death, I have placed my initials next to the following part(s) of my body that
I wish donated for the purposes that I have *initialed* below:

[   ] any organs or parts **OR**

[   ] eyes   [   ] bone and connective tissue   [   ] skin

[   ] heart   [   ] kidney(s)   [   ] liver

[   ] lung(s)   [   ] pancreas   [   ] other _____

for the purposes of:

[   ] any purpose authorized by law **OR**

[   ] transplantation   [   ] research   [   ] therapy

[   ] medical education   [   ] other limitations _____

Signature

I sign this Advance Health Care Directive, consisting of the following sections, which I have
initialed below and have elected to adopt:

[   ]   Living Will

[   ]   Selection of Health Care Agent (Power of Attorney for Health Care)

[   ]   Durable Power of Attorney for Financial Affairs

[   ]   Designation of Primary Physician

[   ]   Organ Donation

BY SIGNING HERE I INDICATE THAT I UNDERSTAND THE PURPOSE AND EF-
FECT OF THIS DOCUMENT.

Signature _____   Date _____

City, County, and State of Residence _____

Notary Acknowledgment

State of _____

County of _____

On _____ , _____ came before me personally and, under oath, stated that he or she is the person described in the above document and he or she signed the above document in my presence. I declare under penalty of perjury that the person whose name is subscribed to this instrument appears to be of sound mind and under no duress, fraud, or undue influence.

_____
Notary Public
My commission expires _____

Witness Acknowledgment

The declarant is personally known to me and I believe him or her to be of sound mind and under no duress, fraud, or undue influence. I did not sign the declarant's signature above for or at the direction of the declarant and I am not appointed as the health care agent or attorney-in-fact herein. I am at least eighteen (18) years of age and I am not related to the declarant by blood, adoption, or marriage, entitled to any portion of the estate of the declarant according to the laws of intestate succession or under any will of declarant or codicil thereto, or directly financially responsible for declarant's medical care. I am not a health care provider of the declarant or an employee of the health facility in which the declarant is a patient.

Witness Signature _____   Date _____

Printed Name of Witness _____

Witness Signature _____   Date _____

Printed Name of Witness _____

Acceptance of Health Care Agent and Financial Attorney-in-Fact

I accept my appointment as Health Care Agent:

Signature _____   Date _____

I accept my appointment as Attorney-in-Fact for Financial Affairs:

Signature _____   Date _____

Florida Advance Health Care Directive

On this date of _____ , I, _____ , do hereby sign, execute, and adopt the following as my Advance Health Care Directive. I direct any and all persons or entities involved with my health care in any manner that these decisions are my wishes and were adopted without duress or force and of my own free will. I have placed my *initials* next to the sections of this Directive that I have adopted:

[   ] Living Will
[   ] Selection of Health Care Agent (Designation of Health Care Surrogate)
[   ] Durable Power of Attorney for Financial Affairs
[   ] Designation of Primary Physician
[   ] Organ Donation

Living Will

I, _____ , willfully and voluntarily make known my desire that my dying not be artificially prolonged under the circumstances set forth below, and I do hereby declare that, if at any time I am incapacitated and (*initial one*):

[   ] I have a terminal condition, **OR**
[   ] I have an end-stage condition, **OR**
[   ] I am in a persistent vegetative state,

and if my attending or treating physician and another consulting physician have determined that there is no reasonable medical probability of my recovery from such condition, I direct that life-prolonging procedures be withheld or withdrawn when the application of such procedures would serve only to prolong artificially the process of dying, and that I be permitted to die naturally with only the administration of medication or the performance of any medical procedure deemed necessary to provide me with comfort care or to alleviate pain. It is my intention that this declaration be honored by my family and physician as the final expression of my legal right to refuse medical or surgical treatment and to accept the consequences for such refusal. Additional Instructions (*optional*):

Selection of Health Care Agent
(Designation of Health Care Surrogate)

In the event that I have been determined to be incapacitated to provide express and informed consent to withholding, withdrawal, or continuation of life-prolonging procedures or to provide informed consent for medical treatment and surgical and diagnostic procedures, I wish to designate as my surrogate for health care decisions and to carry out the provisions of my living will (if I have adopted one [1]) _____ (name), of _____ (address).

I fully understand that this designation will permit my designee to make health care decisions, except for anatomical gifts, unless I have executed an anatomical gift declaration pursuant to law, and to provide, withhold, or withdraw consent on my behalf; to apply for public benefits to defray the cost of health care; and to authorize my admission to or transfer from a health care facility. Additional instructions (*optional*):

I further affirm that this designation is not being made as a condition of treatment or admission to a health care facility.

Durable Power of Attorney for Financial Affairs

I, _____ , grant a durable power of attorney for financial affairs to _____ (name), of _____ _____ (address), to act as my attorney-in-fact. This power of attorney shall become effective upon my disability, as certified by my primary physician or, if my primary physician is not available, by any other attending physician. This power of attorney grants no power or authority regarding health care decisions to my designated attorney-in-fact.

I give my attorney-in-fact the maximum power under law to perform the following specific acts on my behalf: all acts relating to any and all of my financial and/or business affairs, including all banking and financial institution transactions, all real estate transactions, all insurance and annuity transactions, all claims and litigation, and all business transactions. My attorney-in-fact is granted full power to act on my behalf in the same manner as if I were personally present.

My attorney-in-fact accepts this appointment and agrees to act in my best interest as he or she considers advisable. This power of attorney may be revoked by me at any time and is automatically revoked on my death. This power of attorney shall not be affected by my present or future disability or incapacity. My attorney-in-fact shall not be compensated for his or her services nor shall my attorney-in-fact be liable to me, my estate, heirs, successors, or assigns for acting or refraining from acting under this document, except for willful misconduct or gross negligence. Any third party who receives a signed copy of this document may act under it. Revocation of this document is not effective unless a third party has actual knowledge of such revocation.

Designation of Primary Physician

I designate the following physician as my primary physician: _____
(name), of _____ (address).

Organ Donation

In the event of my death, I have placed my initials next to the following part(s) of my body that I wish donated for the purposes that I have *initialed* below:

[   ] any organs or parts **OR**

[   ] eyes   [   ] bone and connective tissue   [   ] skin

[   ] heart   [   ] kidney(s)   [   ] liver

[   ] lung(s)   [   ] pancreas   [   ] other _____

for the purposes of:

[   ] any purpose authorized by law **OR**

[   ] transplantation   [   ] research   [   ] therapy

[   ] medical education   [   ] other limitations _____

Signature

I sign this Advance Health Care Directive, consisting of the following sections, which I have *initialed* below and have elected to adopt:

[   ] Living Will

[   ] Selection of Health Care Agent (Designation of Health Care Surrogate)

[   ] Durable Power of Attorney for Financial Affairs

[   ] Designation of Primary Physician

[   ] Organ Donation

BY SIGNING HERE I INDICATE THAT I UNDERSTAND THE PURPOSE AND EFFECT OF THIS DOCUMENT.

Signature _____   Date _____

City, County, and State of Residence _____

Notary Acknowledgment

State of _____

County of _____

On _____ , _____ came before me personally and, under oath, stated that he or she is the person described in the above document and he or she signed the above document in my presence. I declare under penalty of perjury that the person whose name is subscribed to this instrument appears to be of sound mind and under no duress, fraud, or undue influence.

_____

Notary Public

My commission expires _____

Witness Acknowledgment

The declarant is personally known to me and I believe him or her to be of sound mind and under no duress, fraud, or undue influence. I did not sign the declarant's signature above for or at the direction of the declarant and I am not appointed as the health care agent or attorney-in-fact herein. I am at least eighteen (18) years of age and I am not related to the declarant by blood, adoption, or marriage, entitled to any portion of the estate of the declarant according to the laws of intestate succession or under any will of declarant or codicil thereto, or directly financially responsible for declarant's medical care. I am not a health care provider of the declarant or an employee of the health facility in which the declarant is a patient.

Witness Signature _____ Date _____

Printed Name of Witness _____

Witness Signature _____ Date _____

Printed Name of Witness _____

Acceptance of Health Care Agent and Financial Attorney-in-Fact

I accept my appointment as Health Care Agent:

Signature _____ Date _____

I accept my appointment as Attorney-in-Fact for Financial Affairs:

Signature _____ Date _____

Georgia Advance Health Care Directive

On this date of _____ , I, _____ , do hereby sign, execute, and adopt the following as my Advance Health Care Directive. I direct any and all persons or entities involved with my health care in any manner that these decisions are my wishes and were adopted without duress or force and of my own free will. I have placed my *initials* next to the sections of this Directive that I have adopted:

[   ] Living Will
[   ] Selection of Health Care Agent (Durable Power of Attorney for Health Care)
[   ] Durable Power of Attorney for Financial Affairs
[   ] Designation of Primary Physician
[   ] Organ Donation

Living Will

I, _____ , being of sound mind, willfully and voluntarily make known my desire that my life shall not be prolonged under the circumstances set forth below and do declare:

If at any time I should (*initial each option desired*):

[   ] have a terminal condition,
[   ] be in a coma with no reasonable expectation of regaining consciousness, **OR**
[   ] be in a persistent vegetative state with no reasonable expectation of regaining significant cognitive function, as defined in and established in accordance with the procedures set forth in paragraphs (2), (9), and (13) of Code Section 31-32-2 of the Official Code of Georgia Annotated, I direct that the application of life-sustaining procedures to my body be withheld or withdrawn and that I be permitted to die.

With regard to artificially supplied nutrition and hydration, I direct that (*initial the option desired*):

[   ] artificial nutrition be provided.
[   ] artificial nutrition be withheld or withdrawn.

If I am a female and I have been diagnosed as pregnant, I want this living will to be carried out despite my pregnancy (*initial if desired*):   [   ]

70

Other directions (*insert any other instructions*):

In the absence of my ability to give directions regarding the use of such life-sustaining procedures, it is my intention that this living will shall be honored by my family and physician(s) as the final expression of my legal right to refuse medical or surgical treatment and to accept the consequences from such refusal. I understand that I may revoke this living will at any time. I understand the full import of this living will, and I am at least eighteen (18) years of age and am emotionally and mentally competent to make this living will.

Selection of Health Care Agent
(Durable Power of Attorney for Health Care)

I, _____ , hereby appoint _____
(name), of _____ (address), as my attorney-in-fact (my agent) to act for me and in my name in any way I could act in person to make any and all decisions for me concerning my personal care, medical treatment, hospitalization, and health care and to require, withhold, or withdraw any type of medical treatment or procedure, even though my death may ensue. My agent shall have the same access to my medical records that I have, including the right to disclose the contents to others. My agent shall also have full power to make a disposition of any part or all of my body for medical purposes, authorize an autopsy of my body, and direct the disposition of my remains.

The powers granted above shall not include the following powers or shall be subject to the following rules or limitations (*here you may include any specific limitations you deem appropriate, such as your own definition of when life-sustaining or death-delaying measures should be withheld; a direction to continue nourishment and fluids or other life-sustaining or death-delaying treatment in all events; or instructions to refuse any specific types of treatment that are inconsistent with your religious beliefs or unacceptable to you for any other reason, such as blood transfusion, electroconvulsive therapy, or amputation*):

The subject of life-sustaining or death-delaying treatment is of particular importance. (*If you agree with one of these statements, you may initial that statement, but do not initial more than one*):

[   ] *Initialed*. I do NOT want my life to be prolonged nor do I want life-sustaining or death-delaying treatment to be provided or continued if my agent believes the burdens of the treatment outweigh the expected benefits. I want my agent to consider the relief of suffering, the expense involved, and the quality as well as the possible extension of my life in making decisions concerning life-sustaining or death-delaying treatment.

[   ] *Initialed*. I DO want my life to be prolonged and I want life-sustaining or death-delaying treatment to be provided or continued unless I am in a coma, including a persistent vegetative state, which my attending physician believes to be irreversible, in accordance with reasonable medical standards at the time of reference. If and when I have suffered such an irreversible coma, I want life-sustaining or death-delaying treatment to be withheld or discontinued.

[   ] *Initialed*. I DO want my life to be prolonged to the greatest extent possible without regard to my condition, the chances I have for recovery, or the cost of the procedures.

This power of attorney shall become effective on my disability, incapacity, or incompetency. I am fully informed as to all the contents of this form and understand the full import of this grant of powers to my agent.

Durable Power of Attorney for Financial Affairs

I, _____ , grant a durable power of attorney for financial affairs to _____ (name), of _____ _____ (address), to act as my attorney-in-fact. This power of attorney shall become effective upon my disability, as certified by my primary physician or, if my primary physician is not available, by any other attending physician. This power of attorney grants no power or authority regarding health care decisions to my designated attorney-in-fact.

I give my attorney-in-fact the maximum power under law to perform the following specific acts on my behalf: all acts relating to any and all of my financial and/or business affairs, including all banking and financial institution transactions, all real estate transactions, all insurance and annuity transactions, all claims and litigation, and all business transactions. My attorney-in-fact is granted full power to act on my behalf in the same manner as if I were personally present.

My attorney-in-fact accepts this appointment and agrees to act in my best interest as he or she considers advisable. This power of attorney may be revoked by me at any time and is automatically revoked on my death. This power of attorney shall not be affected by my present or future disability or incapacity. My attorney-in-fact shall not be compensated for his or her services nor shall my attorney-in-fact be liable to me, my estate, heirs, successors, or assigns for acting or refraining from acting under this document, except for willful misconduct or gross negligence. Any third party who receives a signed copy of this document may act under it. Revocation of this document is not effective unless a third party has actual knowledge of such revocation.

Designation of Primary Physician

I designate the following physician as my primary physician: _____ (name), of _____ (address).

Organ Donation

In the event of my death, I have placed my initials next to the following part(s) of my body that I wish donated for the purposes that I have *initialed* below:

[   ] any organs or parts **OR**

[   ] eyes   [   ] bone and connective tissue   [   ] skin

[   ] heart   [   ] kidney(s)   [   ] liver

[   ] lung(s)   [   ] pancreas   [   ] other _____

for the purposes of:

[   ] any purpose authorized by law **OR**

[   ] transplantation   [   ] research   [   ] therapy

[   ] medical education   [   ] other limitations _____

Signature

I sign this Advance Health Care Directive, consisting of the following sections, which I have *initialed* below and have elected to adopt:

[   ]   Living Will

[   ]   Selection of Health Care Agent (Durable Power of Attorney for Health Care)

[   ]   Durable Power of Attorney for Financial Affairs

[   ]   Designation of Primary Physician

[   ]   Organ Donation

BY SIGNING HERE I INDICATE THAT I UNDERSTAND THE PURPOSE AND EFFECT OF THIS DOCUMENT.

Signature _____   Date _____

City, County, and State of Residence _____

Notary Acknowledgment

State of _____

County of _____

On _____ , _____ came before me personally and, under oath, stated that he or she is the person described in the above document and he or she signed the above document in my presence. I declare under penalty of perjury that the person whose name is subscribed to this instrument appears to be of sound mind and under no duress, fraud, or undue influence.

_____

Notary Public

My commission expires _____

Witness Acknowledgment

The declarant is personally known to me and I believe him or her to be of sound mind and under no duress, fraud, or undue influence. I did not sign the declarant's signature above for or at the direction of the declarant and I am not appointed as the health care agent or attorney-in-fact herein. I am at least eighteen (18) years of age and I am not related to the declarant by blood, adoption, or marriage, entitled to any portion of the estate of the declarant according to the laws of intestate succession or under any will of declarant or codicil thereto, or directly financially responsible for declarant's medical care. I am not a health care provider of the declarant or an employee of the health facility in which the declarant is a patient.

Witness Signature _____   Date _____

Printed Name of Witness _____

Witness Signature _____   Date _____

Printed Name of Witness _____

An additional witness is required when this document is signed by a patient in a hospital or skilled nursing facility. I hereby witness this living will and attest that I believe the declarant to be of sound mind and to have made this living will willingly and voluntarily.

Witness Signature _____   Date _____

Printed Name of Witness _____
(Medical director of skilled nursing facility or staff physician not participating in care of the patient, or chief of the hospital medical staff, staff physician, or hospital designee not participating in care of the patient.)

Acceptance of Health Care Agent and Financial Attorney-in-Fact

I accept my appointment as Health Care Agent:

Signature _____   Date _____

I accept my appointment as Attorney-in-Fact for Financial Affairs:

Signature _____   Date _____

Hawaii Advance Health Care Directive

On this date of _____ , I, _____ , do hereby sign, execute, and adopt the following as my Advance Health Care Directive. I direct any and all persons or entities involved with my health care in any manner that these decisions are my wishes and were adopted without duress or force and of my own free will. I have placed my *initials* next to the sections of this Directive that I have adopted:

[   ] Living Will (Instructions for Health Care)
[   ] Selection of Health Care Agent (Power of Attorney for Health Care)
[   ] Durable Power of Attorney for Financial Affairs
[   ] Designation of Primary Physician
[   ] Organ Donation

You have the right to give instructions about your own health care. You also have the right to name someone else to make health care decisions for you. This form lets you do either or both of these things. It also lets you express your wishes regarding donation of organs and the designation of your primary physician. If you use this form, you may complete or modify all or any part of it. You are free to use a different form.

PART 1 of this form lets you give specific instructions about any aspect of your health care, whether or not you appoint an agent. Choices are provided for you to express your wishes regarding the provision, withholding, or withdrawal of treatment to keep you alive, as well as the provision of pain relief. Space is provided for you to add to the choices you have made or for you to write out any additional wishes. If you are satisfied to allow your agent to determine what is best for you in making end-of-life decisions, you need not fill out Part 1 of this form.

PART 2 of this form is a Power of Attorney for Health Care. Part 2 lets you name another individual as your agent to make health care decisions for you if you become incapable of making your own decisions or if you want someone else to make those decisions for you now even though you are still capable. Your agent may not be an operator or employee of a community care facility or a residential care facility where you are receiving care, or your supervising health care provider or employee of the health care institution where you are receiving care, unless your agent is related to you or is a co-worker. Unless the form you sign limits the authority of your agent, your agent may make all health care decisions for you. This form has a place for you to limit the authority of your agent. You need not limit the authority of your agent if you wish to rely on your agent for all health care decisions that may have to be made. If you choose not to limit the authority of your agent, your agent will have the right to:

(a) Consent or refuse consent to any care, treatment, service, or procedure to maintain, diagnose, or otherwise affect a physical or mental condition;

(b) Select or discharge health care providers and institutions;

(c) Approve or disapprove diagnostic tests, surgical procedures, and programs of medication;

(d) Direct the provision, withholding, or withdrawal of artificial nutrition and hydration and all other forms of health care, including cardiopulmonary resuscitation; and

(e) Make anatomical gifts, authorize an autopsy, and direct the disposition of your remains.

PART 3 of this form lets you designate a person to handle your financial affairs while you are unable to do so.

PART 4 of this form lets you designate a physician to have primary responsibility for your health care.

PART 5 of this form lets you express an intention to donate your bodily organs and tissues following your death.

After completing this form, sign and date the form at the end. The form must be signed by two (2) qualified witnesses or acknowledged before a notary public. Give a copy of the signed and completed form to your physician, any other health care providers you may have, any health care institution at which you are receiving care, and any health care agents you have named. You should talk to the person you have named as agent to make sure that he or she understands your wishes and is willing to take the responsibility. You have the right to revoke this advance health care directive or replace this form at any time.

Part 1: Living Will (Instructions for Health Care)

END-OF-LIFE DECISIONS: I direct that my health care providers and others involved in my care provide, withhold, or withdraw treatment in accordance with the choice I have marked below (*initial only one box*):

[   ] (1) Choice NOT To Prolong Life. I do not want my life to be prolonged if:

(a) I have an incurable and irreversible condition that will result in my death within a relatively short time;

(b) I become unconscious and, to a reasonable degree of medical certainty, I will not regain consciousness; **OR**

(c) the likely risks and burdens of treatment would outweigh the expected benefits; **OR**

[   ] (2) Choice TO Prolong Life. I want my life to be prolonged as long as possible within the limits of generally accepted health care standards.

RELIEF FROM PAIN: Except as I state in the following space, I direct that treatment for alleviation of pain or discomfort should be provided at all times even if it hastens my death (*insert exceptions*):

OTHER WISHES: (*If you do not agree with any of the optional choices above and wish to write your own, or if you wish to add to the instructions you have given above, you may do so here.*) I direct that (*add additional sheets if needed*):

Part 2: Selection of Health Care Agent (Power of Attorney for Health Care)

DESIGNATION OF AGENT: I designate the following individual as my agent to make health care decisions for me _____ (name), of _____ _____ (address).

AGENT'S AUTHORITY: My agent is authorized to make all health care decisions for me, including decisions to provide, withhold, or withdraw artificial nutrition and hydration, and all other forms of healthcare to keep me alive, except as I state here (*add additional sheets if needed*):

WHEN AGENT'S AUTHORITY BECOMES EFFECTIVE: My agent's authority becomes effective when my primary physician determines that I am unable to make my own health care decisions unless I mark the following box. If I *initial* this box   [   ], my agent's authority to make health care decisions for me takes effect immediately.

AGENT'S OBLIGATION: My agent shall make health care decisions for me in accordance with this power of attorney for health care, any instructions I give in Part 2 of this form, and my other wishes to the extent known to my agent. To the extent my wishes are unknown, my agent shall make health care decisions for me in accordance with what my agent determines to be in my best interest. In determining my best interest, my agent shall consider my personal values to the extent known to my agent.

AGENT'S POSTDEATH AUTHORITY: My agent is authorized to make anatomical gifts, authorize an autopsy, and direct disposition of my remains, except as I state here or in Part 5 of this form (*insert any exceptions*):

NOMINATION OF CONSERVATOR: If a conservator of my person needs to be appointed for me by a court, I nominate the agent designated in this form.

Part 3: Durable Power of Attorney for Financial Affairs

I, _____ , grant a durable power of attorney for financial affairs to _____ (name), of _____ ; _____ (address), to act as my attorney-in-fact. This power of attorney shall become effective upon my disability, as certified by my primary physician or, if my primary physician is not available, by any other attending physician. This power of attorney grants no power or authority regarding health care decisions to my designated attorney-in-fact.

I give my attorney-in-fact the maximum power under law to perform the following specific acts on my behalf: all acts relating to any and all of my financial and/or business affairs, including all banking and financial institution transactions, all real estate transactions, all insurance and annuity transactions, all claims and litigation, and all business transactions. My attorney-in-fact is granted full power to act on my behalf in the same manner as if I were personally present.

My attorney-in-fact accepts this appointment and agrees to act in my best interest as he or she considers advisable. This power of attorney may be revoked by me at any time and is automatically revoked on my death. This power of attorney shall not be affected by my present or future disability or incapacity. My attorney-in-fact shall not be compensated for his or her services nor shall my attorney-in-fact be liable to me, my estate, heirs, successors, or assigns for acting or refraining from acting under this document, except for willful misconduct or gross negligence. Any third party who receives a signed copy of this document may act under it. Revocation of this document is not effective unless a third party has actual knowledge of such revocation.

Part 4: Designation of Primary Physician

I designate the following physician as my primary physician: _____
(name), of _____ (address).

Part 5: Organ Donation

In the event of my death, I have placed my initials next to the following part(s) of my body that I wish donated for the purposes that I have *initialed* below:
[   ] any organs or parts **OR**
[   ] eyes   [   ] bone and connective tissue   [   ] skin
[   ] heart   [   ] kidney(s)   [   ] liver
[   ] lung(s)   [   ] pancreas   [   ] other _____
for the purposes of:
[   ] any purpose authorized by law **OR**
[   ] transplantation   [   ] research   [   ] therapy
[   ] medical education   [   ] other limitations _____

Signature

I sign this Advance Health Care Directive, consisting of the following sections, which I have *initialed* below and have elected to adopt:
[   ] Living Will (Instructions for Health Care)
[   ] Selection of Health Care Agent (Power of Attorney for Health Care)
[   ] Durable Power of Attorney for Financial Affairs
[   ] Designation of Primary Physician
[   ] Organ Donation
BY SIGNING HERE I INDICATE THAT I UNDERSTAND THE PURPOSE AND EFFECT OF THIS DOCUMENT.

Signature _____ Date _____

City, County, and State of Residence _____

Notary Acknowledgment

State of _____

County of _____

On _____ , _____ came before me per-
sonally and, under oath, stated that he or she is the person described in the above document
and he or she signed the above document in my presence. I declare under penalty of perjury
that the person whose name is subscribed to this instrument appears to be of sound mind and
under no duress, fraud, or undue influence.

Notary Public
My commission expires _____

Witness Acknowledgment

The declarant is personally known to me and I believe him or her to be of sound mind and
under no duress, fraud, or undue influence. I did not sign the declarant's signature above for
or at the direction of the declarant and I am not appointed as the health care agent or attorney-
in-fact herein. I am at least eighteen (18) eyears of age and I am not related to the declarant by
blood, adoption, or marriage, entitled to any portion of the estate of the declarant according
to the laws of intestate succession or under any will of declarant or codicil thereto, or directly
financially responsible for declarant's medical care. I am not a health care provider of the
declarant or an employee of the health facility in which the declarant is a patient.

Witness Signature _____   Date _____

Printed Name of Witness _____

Witness Signature _____   Date _____

Printed Name of Witness _____

Acceptance of Health Care Agent and Financial Attorney-in-Fact

I accept my appointment as Health Care Agent:

Signature _____   Date _____

I accept my appointment as Attorney-in-Fact for Financial Affairs:

Signature _____   Date _____

Idaho Advance Health Care Directive

On this date of _____ , I, _____ , do hereby sign, execute, and adopt the following as my Advance Health Care Directive. I direct any and all persons or entities involved with my health care in any manner that these decisions are my wishes and were adopted without duress or force and of my own free will. I have placed my *initials* next to the sections of this Directive that I have adopted:

[   ] Living Will (Directive to Withhold or to Provide Treatment)
[   ] Selection of Health Care Agent (Durable Power of Attorney for Health Care)
[   ] Durable Power of Attorney for Financial Affairs
[   ] Designation of Primary Physician
[   ] Organ Donation

Living Will (Directive to Withhold or to Provide Treatment)

(1) If at any time I should have an incurable injury, disease, illness, or condition certified to be terminal by two (2) medical doctors who have examined me, and where the application of life-sustaining procedures of any kind would serve only to prolong artificially the moment of my death, and where a medical doctor determines that my death is imminent, whether or not life-sustaining procedures are utilized, or I have been diagnosed as being in a persistent vegetative state, I direct that the following marked expression of my intent be followed, that I be permitted to die naturally, and that I receive any medical treatment or care that may be required to keep me free of pain or distress *(initial one):*

[   ] If at any time I should become unable to communicate my instructions, then I direct that all medical treatment, care, nutrition, and hydration necessary to restore my health, sustain my life, and abolish or alleviate pain or distress be provided to me. Nutrition and hydration shall not be withheld or withdrawn from me if I would die from malnutrition or dehydration rather than from my injury, disease, illness, or condition.

[   ] If at any time I should become unable to communicate my instructions and where the application of artificial life-sustaining procedures shall serve only to prolong artificially the moment of my death, I direct such procedures be withheld or withdrawn except for the administration of nutrition and hydration.

[   ] If at any time I should become unable to communicate my instructions and where the application of artificial life-sustaining procedures shall serve only to prolong artificially the moment of death, I direct such procedures be withheld or withdrawn including withdrawal of the administration of nutrition and hydration.

(2) In the absence of my ability to give directions regarding the use of life-sustaining procedures, I hereby appoint _____ (name), of _____ _____ (address), as my attorney-in-fact/proxy for

the making of decisions relating to my health care in my place; and it is my intention that this appointment shall be honored by him or her, my family, relatives, friends, physicians, and lawyer as the final expression of my legal right to refuse medical or surgical treatment; and I accept the consequences of such a decision. I have duly executed a Durable Power of Attorney for health care decisions on this date.

(3) In the absence of my ability to give further directions regarding my treatment, including life-sustaining procedures, it is my intention that this directive shall be honored by my family and physicians as the final expression of my legal right to refuse or accept medical and surgical treatment, and I accept the consequences of such refusal.

(4) If I have been diagnosed as pregnant and that diagnosis is known to any interested person, this directive shall have no force during the course of my pregnancy.

(5) I understand the full importance of this directive and am emotionally and mentally competent to make this directive. No participant in the making of this directive or in its being carried into effect, whether it be a medical doctor, my spouse, a relative, friend, or any other person, shall be held responsible in any way, legally, professionally, or socially, for complying with my directions.

Selection of Health Care Agent
(Durable Power of Attorney for Health Care)

(1) DESIGNATION OF HEALTH CARE AGENT. I, _____ , do hereby designate and appoint _____ (name), of _____ _____ (address), as my attorney-in-fact (agent) to make health care decisions for me as authorized in this document. For the purposes of this document, "health care decision" means consent, refusal of consent, or withdrawal of consent to any care, treatment, service, or procedure to maintain, diagnose, or treat an individual's physical condition.

(2) CREATION OF DURABLE POWER OF ATTORNEY FOR HEALTH CARE. By this document I intend to create a durable power of attorney for health care. This power of attorney shall not be affected by my subsequent incapacity.

(3) GENERAL STATEMENT OF AUTHORITY GRANTED. Subject to any limitations in this document, I hereby grant to my agent full power and authority to make health care decisions for me to the same extent that I could make such decisions for myself if I had the capacity to do so. In exercising this authority, my agent shall make health care decisions that are consistent with my desires as stated in this document or otherwise made known to my agent, including, but not limited to, my desires concerning obtaining or refusing or withdrawing life-prolonging care, treatment, services, and procedures. (If *you want to limit the authority of your agent to make health care decisions for you, you can state the limitations in paragraph [4], "Statement of Desires, Special Provisions, and Limitations" below. You can indicate your desires by including a statement of your desires in the same paragraph.*)

(4) STATEMENT OF DESIRES, SPECIAL PROVISIONS, AND LIMITATIONS. (*If there are any types of treatment that you do not want to be used, you should state them in the space on the next page. If you want to limit in any other way the authority given your agent by this document, you should state the limits in the space below. If you do not state any limits, your agent will have broad powers to make health care decisions for you, except to the extent that there are limits provided by law.*) In exercising the authority under this durable power of

attorney for health care, my agent shall act consistently with my desires as stated below and is subject to the special provisions and limitations stated in the living will.

Additional statement of desires, special provisions, and limitations (*attach additional pages if you need more space to complete your statement. If you attach additional pages, you must date and sign each of the additional pages at the same time you date and sign this document*):

(5) INSPECTION AND DISCLOSURE OF INFORMATION RELATING TO MY PHYSICAL OR MENTAL HEALTH. Subject to any limitations in this document, my agent has the power and authority to do all of the following:

(a) Request, review, and receive any information, verbal or written, regarding my physical or mental health, including, but not limited to, medical and hospital records;

(b) Execute on my behalf any releases or other documents that may be required in order to obtain this information;

(c) Consent to the disclosure of this information; and

(d) Consent to the donation of any of my organs for medical purposes. (*If you want to limit the authority of your agent to receive and disclose information relating to your health, you must state the limitations in paragraph [4] "Statement of Desires, Special Provisions, and Limitations" above.*)

(6) SIGNING DOCUMENTS, WAIVERS, AND RELEASES. Where necessary to implement the health care decisions that my agent is authorized by this document to make, my agent has the power and authority to execute on my behalf all of the following:

(a) Documents titled or purporting to be a "Refusal to Permit Treatment" and "Leaving Hospital Against Medical Advice;" and

(b) Any necessary waiver or release from liability required by a hospital or physician.

(7) PRIOR DESIGNATIONS REVOKED. I revoke any prior durable power of attorney for health care.

Durable Power of Attorney for Financial Affairs

I, _____ , grant a durable power of attorney for financial affairs to _____ (name), of _____ _____ (address), to act as my attorney-in-fact. This power of attorney shall become effective upon my disability, as certified by my primary physician or, if my primary physician is not available, by any other attending physician. This power of attorney grants no power or authority regarding health care decisions to my designated attorney-in-fact.

I give my attorney-in-fact the maximum power under law to perform the following specific acts on my behalf: all acts relating to any and all of my financial and/or business affairs, including all banking and financial institution transactions, all real estate transactions, all insurance

and annuity transactions, all claims and litigation, and all business transactions. My attorney-in-fact is granted full power to act on my behalf in the same manner as if I were personally present.

My attorney-in-fact accepts this appointment and agrees to act in my best interest as he or she considers advisable. This power of attorney may be revoked by me at any time and is automatically revoked on my death. This power of attorney shall not be affected by my present or future disability or incapacity. My attorney-in-fact shall not be compensated for his or her services nor shall my attorney-in-fact be liable to me, my estate, heirs, successors, or assigns for acting or refraining from acting under this document, except for willful misconduct or gross negligence. Any third party who receives a signed copy of this document may act under it. Revocation of this document is not effective unless a third party has actual knowledge of such revocation.

Designation of Primary Physician

I designate the following physician as my primary physician: _____
(name), of _____ (address).

Organ Donation

In the event of my death, I have placed my initials next to the following part(s) of my body that I wish donated for the purposes that I have *initialed* below:
[   ] any organs or parts **OR**
[   ] eyes   [   ] bone and connective tissue   [   ] skin
[   ] heart   [   ] kidney(s)   [   ] liver
[   ] lung(s)   [   ] pancreas   [   ] other _____
for the purposes of:
[   ] any purpose authorized by law **OR**
[   ] transplantation   [   ] research   [   ] therapy
[   ] medical education   [   ] other limitations _____

Signature

I sign this Advance Health Care Directive, consisting of the following sections, which I have *initialed* below and have elected to adopt:
[   ] Living Will (Directive to Withhold or to Provide Treatment)
[   ] Selection of Health Care Agent (Durable Power of Attorney for Health Care)
[   ] Durable Power of Attorney for Financial Affairs
[   ] Designation of Primary Physician
[   ] Organ Donation
BY SIGNING HERE I INDICATE THAT I UNDERSTAND THE PURPOSE AND EFFECT OF THIS DOCUMENT.

Signature _____   Date _____

City, County, and State of Residence _____

Notary Acknowledgment

State of _____

County of _____

On _____ , _____ came before me personally and, under oath, stated that he or she is the person described in the above document and he or she signed the above document in my presence. I declare under penalty of perjury that the person whose name is subscribed to this instrument appears to be of sound mind and under no duress, fraud, or undue influence.

Notary Public
My commission expires _____

Witness Acknowledgment

The declarant is personally known to me and I believe him or her to be of sound mind and under no duress, fraud, or undue influence. I did not sign the declarant's signature above for or at the direction of the declarant and I am not appointed as the health care agent or attorney-in-fact herein. I am at least eighteen (18) years of age and I am not related to the declarant by blood, adoption, or marriage, entitled to any portion of the estate of the declarant according to the laws of intestate succession or under any will of declarant or codicil thereto, or directly financially responsible for declarant's medical care. I am not a health care provider of the declarant or an employee of the health facility in which the declarant is a patient.

Witness Signature _____ Date _____

Printed Name of Witness _____

Witness Signature _____ Date _____

Printed Name of Witness _____

Acceptance of Health Care Agent and Financial Attorney-in-Fact

I accept my appointment as Health Care Agent:

Signature _____ Date _____

I accept my appointment as Attorney-in-Fact for Financial Affairs:

Signature _____ Date _____

Illinois Advance Health Care Directive

On this date of _____ , I, _____ , do hereby sign, execute, and adopt the following as my Advance Health Care Directive. I direct any and all persons or entities involved with my health care in any manner that these decisions are my wishes and were adopted without duress or force and of my own free will. I have placed my *initials* next to the sections of this Directive that I have adopted:

[   ] Living Will
[   ] Selection of Health Care Agent (Power of Attorney for Health Care)
[   ] Durable Power of Attorney for Financial Affairs
[   ] Designation of Primary Physician
[   ] Organ Donation

Living Will Declaration

If at any time I should have an incurable and irreversible injury, disease, or illness judged to be a terminal condition by my attending physician who has personally examined me and has determined that my death is imminent except for death-delaying procedures, I direct that such procedures which would only prolong the dying process be withheld or withdrawn, and that I be permitted to die naturally with only the administration of medication, sustenance, or the performance of any medical procedure deemed necessary by my attending physician to provide me with comfort care.

In the absence of my ability to give directions regarding the use of such death-delaying procedures, it is my intention that this declaration shall be honored by my family and physician as the final expression of my legal right to refuse medical or surgical treatment and accept the consequences from such refusal.

Selection of Health Care Agent (Power of Attorney for Health Care)

NOTICE: The purpose of this power of attorney is to give the person you designate (your "agent") broad powers to make health care decisions for you, including power to require, consent to, or withdraw any type of personal care or medical treatment for any physical or mental condition, and to admit you to or discharge you from any hospital, home, or other institution. This form does not impose a duty on your agent to exercise granted powers; but when powers are exercised, your agent will have to use due care to act for your benefit and in accordance with this form and keep a record of receipts, disbursements, and significant actions taken as agent. A court can take away the powers of your agent if it finds the agent is not acting properly. Unless you expressly limit the duration of this power in the manner provided below, until you revoke this power or a court acting on your behalf terminates it, your agent may exercise the powers given here throughout your lifetime, even after you become disabled. The powers you give your agent, your right to revoke those powers, and the penalties for violating the law are explained more fully in Sections 4-5, 4-6, 4-9, and 4-10[b] of the Illinois "Powers of Attorney for Health Care Law" of which this form is a part. That law expressly permits the use of any different form of power of attorney you may desire. If there is anything about this form that you do not understand, you should ask a lawyer to explain it to you.

I, _____ , hereby appoint _____
(name), of _____ (address), as my attorney-in-fact (my "agent") to act for me and in my name (in any way I could act in person) to make any and all decisions for me concerning my personal care, medical treatment, hospitalization, and health care and to require, withhold, or withdraw any type of medical treatment or procedure, even though my death may ensue. My agent shall have the same access to my medical records that I have, including the right to disclose the contents to others. My agent shall also have full power to authorize an autopsy and direct the disposition of my remains. Effective upon my death, my agent has the full power to make an anatomical gift of the following:

[   ] Any organ
[   ] Specific organs (*list the specific organs*):

The powers granted above shall not include the following powers or shall be subject to the following rules or limitations (*here you may include any specific limitations you deem appropriate, such as: your own definition of when life-sustaining measures should be withheld; a direction to continue food and fluids or life-sustaining treatment in all events; or instructions to refuse any specific types of treatment that are inconsistent with your religious beliefs or unacceptable to you for any other reason, such as blood transfusion, electro-convulsive therapy, amputation, psychosurgery, voluntary admission to a mental institution, etc.*):

(*The subject of life-sustaining treatment is of particular importance. For your convenience in dealing with that subject, some general statements concerning the withholding or removal of life-sustaining treatment are set forth on the following pages. If you agree with one of these statements, you may initial that statement; but do not initial more than one.*)

[   ] *Initialed.* I do NOT want my life to be prolonged nor do I want life-sustaining treatment to be provided or continued if my agent believes the burdens of the treatment outweigh the expected benefits. I want my agent to consider the relief of suffering, the expense involved, and the quality as well as the possible extension of my life in making decisions concerning life-sustaining treatment.

[   ] *Initialed.* I DO want my life to be prolonged and I want life-sustaining treatment to be provided or continued unless I am in a coma which my attending physician believes to be irreversible, in accordance with reasonable medical standards at the time of reference. If and when I have suffered irreversible coma, I want life-sustaining treatment to be withheld or discontinued.

[   ] *Initialed.* I DO want my life to be prolonged to the greatest extent possible without regard to my condition, the chances I have for recovery, or the cost of the procedures.

This power of attorney shall become effective on my primary or attending doctor's determination of my disability. If a guardian of my person is to be appointed, I nominate the agent acting under this power of attorney as such guardian, to serve without bond or security. I am fully informed as to all the contents of this form and understand the full import of this grant of powers to my agent.

Durable Power of Attorney for Financial Affairs

I, _____ , grant a durable power of attorney for financial affairs to _____ (name), of _____ _____ (address), to act as my attorney-in-fact. This power of attorney shall become effective upon my disability, as certified by my primary physician or, if my primary physician is not available, by any other attending physician. This power of attorney grants no power or authority regarding health care decisions to my designated attorney-in-fact.

I give my attorney-in-fact the maximum power under law to perform the following specific acts on my behalf: all acts relating to any and all of my financial and/or business affairs, including all banking and financial institution transactions, all real estate transactions, all insurance and annuity transactions, all claims and litigation, and all business transactions. My attorney-in-fact is granted full power to act on my behalf in the same manner as if I were personally present.

My attorney-in-fact accepts this appointment and agrees to act in my best interest as he or she considers advisable. This power of attorney may be revoked by me at any time and is automatically revoked on my death. This power of attorney shall not be affected by my present or future disability or incapacity. My attorney-in-fact shall not be compensated for his or her services nor shall my attorney-in-fact be liable to me, my estate, heirs, successors, or assigns for acting or refraining from acting under this document, except for willful misconduct or gross negligence. Any third party who receives a signed copy of this document may act under it. Revocation of this document is not effective unless a third party has actual knowledge of such revocation.

Designation of Primary Physician

I designate the following physician as my primary physician: _____
(name), of _____ (address).

Organ Donation

In the event of my death, I have placed my initials next to the following part(s) of my body that I wish donated for the purposes that I have *initialed* below:

[   ] any organs or parts **OR**

[   ] eyes   [   ] bone and connective tissue   [   ] skin

[   ] heart   [   ] kidney(s)   [   ] liver

[   ] lung(s)   [   ] pancreas   [   ] other _____

for the purposes of:

[   ] any purpose authorized by law **OR**

[   ] transplantation   [   ] research   [   ] therapy

[   ] medical education   [   ] other limitations _____

Signature

I sign this Advance Health Care Directive, consisting of the following sections, which I have *initialed* below and have elected to adopt:

[   ]   Living Will

[   ]   Selection of Health Care Agent (Power of Attorney for Health Care)

[   ]   Durable Power of Attorney for Financial Affairs

[   ]   Designation of Primary Physician

[   ]   Organ Donation

BY SIGNING HERE I INDICATE THAT I UNDERSTAND THE PURPOSE AND EFFECT OF THIS DOCUMENT.

Signature _____   Date _____

City, County, and State of Residence _____

Notary Acknowledgment

State of _____
County of _____

On _____ , _____ came before me personally and, under oath, stated that he or she is the person described in the above document and he or she signed the above document in my presence. I declare under penalty of perjury that the person whose name is subscribed to this instrument appears to be of sound mind and under no duress, fraud, or undue influence.

_____
Notary Public
My commission expires _____

Witness Acknowledgment

The declarant is personally known to me and I believe him or her to be of sound mind and under no duress, fraud, or undue influence. I did not sign the declarant's signature above for or at the direction of the declarant and I am not appointed as the health care agent or attorney-in-fact herein. I am at least eighteen (18) years of age and I am not related to the declarant by blood, adoption, or marriage, entitled to any portion of the estate of the declarant according to the laws of intestate succession or under any will of declarant or codicil thereto, or directly financially responsible for declarant's medical care. I am not a health care provider of the declarant or an employee of the health facility in which the declarant is a patient.

Witness Signature _____   Date _____

Printed Name of Witness _____

Witness Signature _____   Date _____

Printed Name of Witness _____

Acceptance of Health Care Agent and Financial Attorney-in-Fact

I accept my appointment as Health Care Agent:

Signature _____   Date _____

I accept my appointment as Attorney-in-Fact for Financial Affairs:

Signature _____   Date _____

Indiana Advance Health Care Directive

On this date of _____ , I, _____ , do hereby sign, execute, and adopt the following as my Advance Health Care Directive. I direct any and all persons or entities involved with my health care in any manner that these decisions are my wishes and were adopted without duress or force and of my own free will. I have placed my *initials* next to the sections of this Directive that I have adopted:

[   ] Living Will or Life-Prolonging Procedures Declaration
[   ] Selection of Health Care Agent
[   ] Durable Power of Attorney for Financial Affairs
[   ] Designation of Primary Physician
[   ] Organ Donation

Living Will Declaration or Life-Prolonging Procedures Declaration

You may select either a Living Will Declaration OR a Life-Prolonging Procedures Declaration, but not both.

LIVING WILL DECLARATION
[   ] (*Initial if you choose this option.*) If at any time my attending physician certifies in writing that:
(1) I have an incurable injury, disease, or illness,
(2) my death will occur within a short time, and
(3) the use of life-prolonging procedures would serve only to artificially prolong the dying process, I direct that such procedures be withheld or withdrawn, and that I be permitted to die naturally with only the performance or provision of any medical procedure or medication necessary to provide me with comfort care or to alleviate pain, and, if I have so indicated below, the provision of artificially-supplied nutrition and hydration (*indicate your choice by initialing only one of the following*):

[   ] I DO wish to receive artificially-supplied nutrition and hydration, even if the effort to sustain life is futile or excessively burdensome to me.

[   ] I do NOT wish to receive artificially-supplied nutrition and hydration, if the effort to sustain life is futile or excessively burdensome to me.

[   ] I intentionally make no decision concerning artificially-supplied nutrition and hydration, leaving the decision to my health care representative appointed under IC 16-36-1-7 or my attorney-in-fact with health care powers under IC 30-5-5.

In the absence of my ability to give directions regarding the use of life-prolonging procedures, it is my intention that this declaration be honored by my family and physician as the final expression of my legal right to refuse medical or surgical treatment and accept the consequences of the refusal. I understand the full import of this declaration.

OR

LIFE-PROLONGING PROCEDURES DECLARATION

[   ] (*Initial if you choose this option.*) If at any time I have an incurable injury, disease, or illness determined to be a terminal condition, I request the use of life-prolonging procedures that would extend my life. This includes appropriate nutrition and hydration, the administration of medication, and the performance of all other medical procedures necessary to extend my life, to provide comfort care, or to alleviate pain.

In the absence of my ability to give directions regarding the use of life-prolonging procedures, it is my intention that this declaration be honored by my family and physician as the final expression of my legal right to request medical or surgical treatment and accept the consequences of the request. I understand the full import of this declaration.

Selection of Health Care Agent

I, _____ , hereby appoint _____
(name), of _____ (address), as my attorney-in-fact to make health care decisions on my behalf whenever I am incapable of making my own health care decisions. I grant my attorney-in-fact the following powers in matters affecting my health care to:
(1) employ or contract with servants, companions, or health care providers involved in my health care,
(2) admit or release me from a hospital or health care facility,
(3) have access to my records, including medical records,
(4) make anatomical gifts on my behalf,
(5) request an autopsy, and
(6) make plans for the disposition of my body.

APPOINTMENT OF MY ATTORNEY-IN-FACT AS MY HEALTH CARE REPRESENTATIVE: In addition to the powers granted above, I appoint my attorney-in-fact as my health care representative to make decisions in my best interest concerning the consent, withdrawal, or withholding of health care. I understand health care to include any medical care, treatment, service, or procedure to maintain, diagnose, treat, or provide for my physical or mental well-being. Health care also includes the providing of nutrition and hydration. If at any time, based on my previously-expressed preferences and the diagnosis and prognosis, my health care representative is satisfied that certain health care is not or would not be beneficial, or that such health care is or would be excessively burdensome, then my health care representative may express my will that such health care be withheld or withdrawn and may consent on my behalf that any or all health care be discontinued or not instituted, even if death may result. My health care representative must try to discuss this decision with me. However, if I am unable to communicate, my health care representative may make such a decision for me, after consultation with my physician or physicians and other relevant health care givers. To the extent appropriate, my health care representative may also discuss this decision with my family and others, to the extent they are available.

Durable Power of Attorney for Financial Affairs

I, _____ , grant a durable power of attorney for financial affairs to _____ (name), of _____ _____ (address), to act as my attorney-in-fact. This power of attorney shall become effective upon my disability, as certified by my primary physician or, if my primary physician is not available, by any other attending physician. This power of attorney grants no power or authority regarding health care decisions to my designated attorney-in-fact.

I give my attorney-in-fact the maximum power under law to perform the following specific acts on my behalf: all acts relating to any and all of my financial and/or business affairs, including all banking and financial institution transactions, all real estate transactions, all insurance and annuity transactions, all claims and litigation, and all business transactions. My attorney-in-fact is granted full power to act on my behalf in the same manner as if I were personally present.

My attorney-in-fact accepts this appointment and agrees to act in my best interest as he or she considers advisable. This power of attorney may be revoked by me at any time and is automatically revoked on my death. This power of attorney shall not be affected by my present or future disability or incapacity. My attorney-in-fact shall not be compensated for his or her services nor shall my attorney-in-fact be liable to me, my estate, heirs, successors, or assigns for acting or refraining from acting under this document, except for willful misconduct or gross negligence. Any third party who receives a signed copy of this document may act under it. Revocation of this document is not effective unless a third party has actual knowledge of such revocation.

Designation of Primary Physician

I designate the following physician as my primary physician: _____ (name), of _____ (address).

Organ Donation

In the event of my death, I have placed my initials next to the following part(s) of my body that I wish donated for the purposes that I have *initialed* below:

[   ] any organs or parts **OR**

[   ] eyes   [   ] bone and connective tissue   [   ] skin

[   ] heart   [   ] kidney(s)   [   ] liver

[   ] lung(s)   [   ] pancreas   [   ] other _____

for the purposes of:

[   ] any purpose authorized by law **OR**

[   ] transplantation   [   ] research   [   ] therapy

[   ] medical education   [   ] other limitations _____

Signature

I sign this Advance Health Care Directive, consisting of the following sections, which I have *initialed* below and have elected to adopt:

[   ] Living Will or Life-Prolonging Procedures Declaration

[   ] Selection of Health Care Agent

[   ] Durable Power of Attorney for Financial Affairs

[   ] Designation of Primary Physician

[   ] Organ Donation

BY SIGNING HERE I INDICATE THAT I UNDERSTAND THE PURPOSE AND EFFECT OF THIS DOCUMENT.

Signature _____ Date _____

City, County, and State of Residence _____

Notary Acknowledgment

State of _____

County of _____

On _____ , _____ came before me personally and, under oath, stated that he or she is the person described in the above document and he or she signed the above document in my presence. I declare under penalty of perjury that the person whose name is subscribed to this instrument appears to be of sound mind and under no duress, fraud, or undue influence.

_____

Notary Public

My commission expires _____

Witness Acknowledgment

The declarant is personally known to me and I believe him or her to be of sound mind and under no duress, fraud, or undue influence. I did not sign the declarant's signature above for or at the direction of the declarant and I am not appointed as the health care agent or attorney-in-fact herein. I am at least eighteen (18) years of age and I am not related to the declarant by blood, adoption, or marriage, entitled to any portion of the estate of the declarant according to the laws of intestate succession or under any will of declarant or codicil thereto, or directly financially responsible for declarant's medical care. I am not a health care provider of the declarant or an employee of the health facility in which the declarant is a patient.

Witness Signature _____ Date _____

Printed Name of Witness _____

Witness Signature _____ Date _____

Printed Name of Witness _____

Acceptance of Health Care Agent and Financial Attorney-in-Fact

I accept my appointment as Health Care Agent:

Signature _____ Date _____

I accept my appointment as Attorney-in-Fact for Financial Affairs:

Signature _____ Date _____

Iowa Advance Health Care Directive

On this date of _____ , I, _____ , do hereby sign, execute, and adopt the following as my Advance Health Care Directive. I direct any and all persons or entities involved with my health care in any manner that these decisions are my wishes and were adopted without duress or force and of my own free will. I have placed my *initials* next to the sections of this Directive that I have adopted:

[   ] Living Will
[   ] Selection of Health Care Agent (Durable Power of Attorney for Health Care)
[   ] Durable Power of Attorney for Financial Affairs
[   ] Designation of Primary Physician
[   ] Organ Donation

Living Will

If I should have an incurable or irreversible condition that will result either in death within a relatively short period of time or a state of permanent unconsciousness from which, to a reasonable degree of medical certainty, there can be no recovery, it is my desire that my life not be prolonged by the administration of life-sustaining procedures. If I am unable to participate in my health care decisions, I direct my attending physician to withhold or withdraw life-sustaining procedures that merely prolong the dying process and are not necessary to my comfort or freedom from pain.

Selection of Health Care Agent
(Durable Power of Attorney for Health Care)

I hereby appoint _____ (name), of _____
_____ (address), as my attorney-in-fact (my agent) and give to my agent the power to make health care decisions for me. This power exists only when I am unable, in the judgment of my attending physician, to make those health care decisions. The attorney-in-fact must act consistently with my desires as stated in this document or otherwise made known.

Except as otherwise specified in this document, this document gives my agent the power, where otherwise consistent with the law of this state, to consent to my physician not giving health care or stopping health care which is necessary to keep me alive. This document gives my agent power to make health care decisions on my behalf, including the power to consent, refuse to consent, or withdraw consent to the provision of any care, treatment, service, or procedure to maintain, diagnose, or treat a physical or mental condition. This power is subject to any statement of my desires and any limitations included in this document. My agent has the right to examine my medical records and to consent to disclosure of such records.

Optional instructions (*include additional instructions, if any*):

Durable Power of Attorney for Financial Affairs

I, _____ , grant a durable power of attorney for financial affairs to _____ (name), of _____
_____ (address), to act as my attorney-in-fact. This power of attorney shall become effective upon my disability, as certified by my primary physician or, if my primary physician is not available, by any other attending physician. This power of attorney grants no power or authority regarding health care decisions to my designated attorney-in-fact.

I give my attorney-in-fact the maximum power under law to perform the following specific acts on my behalf: all acts relating to any and all of my financial and/or business affairs, including all banking and financial institution transactions, all real estate transactions, all insurance and annuity transactions, all claims and litigation, and all business transactions. My attorney-in-fact is granted full power to act on my behalf in the same manner as if I were personally present.

My attorney-in-fact accepts this appointment and agrees to act in my best interest as he or she considers advisable. This power of attorney may be revoked by me at any time and is automatically revoked on my death. This power of attorney shall not be affected by my present or future disability or incapacity. My attorney-in-fact shall not be compensated for his or her services nor shall my attorney-in-fact be liable to me, my estate, heirs, successors, or assigns for acting or refraining from acting under this document, except for willful misconduct or gross negligence. Any third party who receives a signed copy of this document may act under it. Revocation of this document is not effective unless a third party has actual knowledge of such revocation.

Designation of Primary Physician

I designate the following physician as my primary physician: _____
(name), of _____ (address).

Organ Donation

In the event of my death, I have placed my initials next to the following part(s) of my body that I wish donated for the purposes that I have *initialed* below:

[   ] any organs or parts **OR**

[   ] eyes   [   ] bone and connective tissue   [   ] skin

[   ] heart   [   ] kidney(s)   [   ] liver

[   ] lung(s)   [   ] pancreas   [   ] other _____

for the purposes of:

[   ] any purpose authorized by law **OR**

[   ] transplantation   [   ] research   [   ] therapy

[   ] medical education   [   ] other limitations _____

Signature

I sign this Advance Health Care Directive, consisting of the following sections, which I have *initialed* below and have elected to adopt:

[   ]   Living Will

[   ]   Selection of Health Care Agent (Durable Power of Attorney for Health Care)

[   ]   Durable Power of Attorney for Financial Affairs

[   ]   Designation of Primary Physician

[   ]   Organ Donation

BY SIGNING HERE I INDICATE THAT I UNDERSTAND THE PURPOSE AND EF-FECT OF THIS DOCUMENT.

Signature _____   Date _____

City, County, and State of Residence _____

Notary Acknowledgment

State of _____

County of _____

On _____ , _____ came before me per-sonally and, under oath, stated that he or she is the person described in the above document and he or she signed the above document in my presence. I declare under penalty of perjury that the person whose name is subscribed to this instrument appears to be of sound mind and under no duress, fraud, or undue influence.

_____

Notary Public

My commission expires _____

Witness Acknowledgment

The declarant is personally known to me and I believe him or her to be of sound mind and under no duress, fraud, or undue influence. I did not sign the declarant's signature above for or at the direction of the declarant and I am not appointed as the health care agent or attorney-in-fact herein. I am at least eighteen (18) years of age and I am not related to the declarant by blood, adoption, or marriage, entitled to any portion of the estate of the declarant according to the laws of intestate succession or under any will of declarant or codicil thereto, or directly financially responsible for declarant's medical care. I am not a health care provider of the declarant or an employee of the health facility in which the declarant is a patient.

Witness Signature _____ Date _____

Printed Name of Witness _____

Witness Signature _____ Date _____

Printed Name of Witness _____

Acceptance of Health Care Agent and Financial Attorney-in-Fact

I accept my appointment as Health Care Agent:

Signature _____ Date _____

I accept my appointment as Attorney-in-Fact for Financial Affairs:

Signature _____ Date _____

Kansas Advance Health Care Directive

On this date of _____ , I, _____ , do hereby sign, execute, and adopt the following as my Advance Health Care Directive. I direct any and all persons or entities involved with my health care in any manner that these decisions are my wishes and were adopted without duress or force and of my own free will. I have placed my *initials* next to the sections of this Directive that I have adopted:

[　　] Living Will
[　　] Selection of Health Care Agent (Durable Power of Attorney for Health Care)
[　　] Durable Power of Attorney for Financial Affairs
[　　] Designation of Primary Physician
[　　] Organ Donation

Living Will

I, _____ (name), being of sound mind, willfully and voluntarily make known my desire that my dying shall not be artificially prolonged under the circumstances set forth below, and do hereby declare: If at any time I should have an incurable injury, disease, or illness certified to be a terminal condition by two physicians who have personally examined me, one of whom shall be my attending physician, and the physicians have determined that my death will occur whether or not life-sustaining procedures are utilized and where the application of life-sustaining procedures would serve only to artificially prolong the dying process, I direct that such procedures be withheld or withdrawn, and that I be permitted to die naturally with only the administration of medication or the performance of any medical procedure deemed necessary to provide me with comfort care. In the absence of my ability to give directions regarding the use of such life-sustaining procedures, it is my intention that this declaration shall be honored by my family and physician(s) as the final expression of my legal right to refuse medical or surgical treatment and accept the consequences from such refusal. I understand the full import of this declaration and I am emotionally and mentally competent to make this declaration.

OTHER DIRECTIONS (*attach additional sheets if needed*):

Selection of Health Care Agent
(Durable Power of Attorney for Health Care)

I, _____ , designate and appoint _____
_____ (name), of _____
_____ (address), to be my agent for health care decisions and pursuant to the language stated below, on my behalf to:

(1) Consent, refuse consent, or withdraw consent to any care, treatment, service, or procedure to maintain, diagnose, or treat a physical or mental condition, and to make decisions about organ donation, autopsy, and disposition of the body;

(2) Make all necessary arrangements at any hospital, psychiatric hospital, psychiatric treatment facility, hospice, nursing home, or similar institution;

(3) Employ or discharge health care personnel to include physicians, psychiatrists, psychologists, dentists, nurses, therapists, or any other person who is licensed, certified, or otherwise authorized or permitted by the laws of this state to administer health care as the agent shall deem necessary for my physical, mental, and emotional well-being; and

(4) Request, receive, and review any information, verbal or written, regarding my personal affairs or physical or mental health including medical and hospital records and to execute any releases of other documents that may be required in order to obtain such information.

In exercising the grant of authority set forth above my agent for health care decisions shall (*here may be inserted any special instructions or statement of the principal's desires to be followed by the agent in exercising the authority granted*):

The powers of the agent herein shall be limited to the extent set out in writing in this durable power of attorney for health care decisions and shall not include the power to revoke or invalidate any previously existing declaration made in accordance with the natural death act.

The agent shall be prohibited from authorizing consent for the following items (*insert any prohibitions on agent's authority to give consent*):

This durable power of attorney for health care decisions shall be subject to the additional following limitations (*insert any limitations on the agent's authority*):

This power of attorney for health care decisions shall become effective immediately and shall not be affected by my subsequent disability or incapacity or upon the occurrence of my disability or incapacity. Any durable power of attorney for health care decisions I have previously made is hereby revoked. This durable power of attorney for health care decisions shall be revoked by an instrument in writing executed, witnessed, or acknowledged in the same manner as required herein.

Durable Power of Attorney for Financial Affairs

I, _____ , grant a durable power of attorney for financial affairs to _____ (name), of _____ _____ (address), to act as my attorney-in-fact. This power of attorney shall become effective upon my disability, as certified by my primary physician or, if my primary physician is not available, by any other attending physician. This power of attorney grants no power or authority regarding health care decisions to my designated attorney-in-fact.

I give my attorney-in-fact the maximum power under law to perform the following specific acts on my behalf: all acts relating to any and all of my financial and/or business affairs, including all banking and financial institution transactions, all real estate transactions, all insurance and annuity transactions, all claims and litigation, and all business transactions. My attorney-in-fact is granted full power to act on my behalf in the same manner as if I were personally present.

My attorney-in-fact accepts this appointment and agrees to act in my best interest as he or she considers advisable. This power of attorney may be revoked by me at any time and is automatically revoked on my death. This power of attorney shall not be affected by my present or future disability or incapacity. My attorney-in-fact shall not be compensated for his or her services nor shall my attorney-in-fact be liable to me, my estate, heirs, successors, or assigns for acting or refraining from acting under this document, except for willful misconduct or gross negligence. Any third party who receives a signed copy of this document may act under it. Revocation of this document is not effective unless a third party has actual knowledge of such revocation.

Designation of Primary Physician

I designate the following physician as my primary physician: _____
(name), of _____ (address).

Organ Donation

In the event of my death, I have placed my initials next to the following part(s) of my body that I wish donated for the purposes that I have *initialed* below:

[   ] any organs or parts **OR**

[   ] eyes   [   ] bone and connective tissue   [   ] skin

[   ] heart   [   ] kidney(s)   [   ] liver

[   ] lung(s)   [   ] pancreas   [   ] other _____

for the purposes of:

[   ] any purpose authorized by law **OR**

[   ] transplantation   [   ] research   [   ] therapy

[   ] medical education   [   ] other limitations _____

Signature

I sign this Advance Health Care Directive, consisting of the following sections, which I have *initialed* below and have elected to adopt:

[   ] Living Will

[   ] Selection of Health Care Agent (Durable Power of Attorney for Health Care)

[   ] Durable Power of Attorney for Financial Affairs

[   ] Designation of Primary Physician

[   ] Organ Donation

BY SIGNING HERE I INDICATE THAT I UNDERSTAND THE PURPOSE AND EFFECT OF THIS DOCUMENT.

Signature _____ Date _____

City, County, and State of Residence _____

Notary Acknowledgment

State of _____

County of _____

On _____ , _____ came before me per-
sonally and, under oath, stated that he or she is the person described in the above document
and he or she signed the above document in my presence. I declare under penalty of perjury
that the person whose name is subscribed to this instrument appears to be of sound mind and
under no duress, fraud, or undue influence.

_____

Notary Public
My commission expires _____

Witness Acknowledgment

The declarant is personally known to me and I believe him or her to be of sound mind and
under no duress, fraud, or undue influence. I did not sign the declarant's signature above for
or at the direction of the declarant and I am not appointed as the health care agent or attorney-
in-fact herein. I am at least eighteen (18) years of age and I am not related to the declarant by
blood, adoption, or marriage, entitled to any portion of the estate of the declarant according
to the laws of intestate succession or under any will of declarant or codicil thereto, or directly
financially responsible for declarant's medical care. I am not a health care provider of the
declarant or an employee of the health facility in which the declarant is a patient.

Witness Signature _____   Date _____

Printed Name of Witness _____

Witness Signature _____   Date _____

Printed Name of Witness _____

Acceptance of Health Care Agent and Financial Attorney-in-Fact

I accept my appointment as Health Care Agent:

Signature _____   Date _____

I accept my appointment as Attorney-in-Fact for Financial Affairs:

Signature _____   Date _____

Kentucky Advance Health Care Directive

On this date of _____ , I, _____ , do hereby sign, execute, and adopt the following as my Advance Health Care Directive. I direct any and all persons or entities involved with my health care in any manner that these decisions are my wishes and were adopted without duress or force and of my own free will. I have placed my *initials* next to the sections of this Directive that I have adopted:

[   ]   Living Will
[   ]   Selection of Health Care Agent
[   ]   Durable Power of Attorney for Financial Affairs
[   ]   Designation of Primary Physician
[   ]   Organ Donation

Living Will

My wishes regarding life-prolonging treatment and artificially-provided nutrition and hydration to be provided to me if I no longer have decisional capacity, have a terminal condition, or become permanently unconscious have been indicated by checking and initialing the appropriate lines below. By checking and *initialing* the appropriate lines, I specifically:

(*Initial one*)

[   ]   Direct that treatment be withheld or withdrawn, and that I be permitted to die naturally with only the administration of medication or the performance of any medical treatment deemed necessary to alleviate pain.

[   ]   Do NOT authorize that life-prolonging treatment be withheld or withdrawn.

(*Initial one*)

[   ]   Authorize the withholding or withdrawal of artificially-provided food, water, or other artificially-provided nourishment or fluids.

[   ]   Do NOT authorize the withholding or withdrawal of artificially-provided food, water, or other artificially-provided nourishment or fluids.

[   ]   Authorize my surrogate, designated on the following page, to withhold or withdraw artificially-provided nourishment or fluids, or other treatment if the surrogate determines that withholding or withdrawing is in my best interest; but I do not mandate that withholding or withdrawing.

In the absence of my ability to give directions regarding the use of life-prolonging treatment and artificially-provided nutrition and hydration, it is my intention that this directive shall be honored by my attending physician, my family, and any surrogate designated pursuant to this directive as the final expression of my legal right to refuse medical or surgical treatment and I accept the consequences of the refusal. If I have been diagnosed as pregnant and that diagnosis is known to my attending physician, this directive shall have no force or effect during the course of my pregnancy.

Selection of Health Care Agent

I designate _____ (name), of _____
_____ (address), as my health care surrogate to make health care decisions for me in accordance with this directive when I no longer have decisional capacity. Any prior designation is revoked. If I do not designate a surrogate, the above instructions indicated in my living will are my directions to my attending physician. If I have designated a surrogate, my surrogate shall comply with my wishes as indicated above in my living will.

Durable Power of Attorney for Financial Affairs

I, _____ , grant a durable power of attorney for financial affairs to _____ (name), of _____
_____ (address), to act as my attorney-in-fact. This power of attorney shall become effective upon my disability, as certified by my primary physician or, if my primary physician is not available, by any other attending physician. This power of attorney grants no power or authority regarding health care decisions to my designated attorney-in-fact.

I give my attorney-in-fact the maximum power under law to perform the following specific acts on my behalf: all acts relating to any and all of my financial and/or business affairs, including all banking and financial institution transactions, all real estate transactions, all insurance and annuity transactions, all claims and litigation, and all business transactions. My attorney-in-fact is granted full power to act on my behalf in the same manner as if I were personally present.

My attorney-in-fact accepts this appointment and agrees to act in my best interest as he or she considers advisable. This power of attorney may be revoked by me at any time and is automatically revoked on my death. This power of attorney shall not be affected by my present or future disability or incapacity. My attorney-in-fact shall not be compensated for his or her services nor shall my attorney-in-fact be liable to me, my estate, heirs, successors, or assigns for acting or refraining from acting under this document, except for willful misconduct or gross negligence. Any third party who receives a signed copy of this document may act under it. Revocation of this document is not effective unless a third party has actual knowledge of such revocation.

Designation of Primary Physician

I designate the following physician as my primary physician: _____
(name), of _____ (address).

Organ Donation

In the event of my death, I have placed my initials next to the following part(s) of my body that I wish donated for the purposes that I have *initialed* below:

[   ] any organs or parts **OR**

[   ] eyes   [   ] bone and connective tissue   [   ] skin

[   ] heart   [   ] kidney(s)   [   ] liver

[   ] lung(s)   [   ] pancreas   [   ] other _____

for the purposes of:

[   ] any purpose authorized by law **OR**

[   ] transplantation   [   ] research   [   ] therapy

[   ] medical education   [   ] other limitations _____

Signature

I sign this Advance Health Care Directive, consisting of the following sections, which I have *initialed* below and have elected to adopt:

[   ] Living Will

[   ] Selection of Health Care Agent

[   ] Durable Power of Attorney for Financial Affairs

[   ] Designation of Primary Physician

[   ] Organ Donation

BY SIGNING HERE I INDICATE THAT I UNDERSTAND THE PURPOSE AND EFFECT OF THIS DOCUMENT.

Signature _____   Date _____

City, County, and State of Residence _____

Notary Acknowledgment

State of _____

County of _____

On _____ , _____ came before me personally and, under oath, stated that he or she is the person described in the above document and he or she signed the above document in my presence. I declare under penalty of perjury that the person whose name is subscribed to this instrument appears to be of sound mind and under no duress, fraud, or undue influence.

_____

Notary Public

My commission expires _____

Witness Acknowledgment

The declarant is personally known to me and I believe him or her to be of sound mind and under no duress, fraud, or undue influence. I did not sign the declarant's signature above for or at the direction of the declarant and I am not appointed as the health care agent or attorney-in-fact herein. I am at least eighteen (18) years of age and I am not related to the declarant by blood, adoption, or marriage, entitled to any portion of the estate of the declarant according to the laws of intestate succession or under any will of declarant or codicil thereto, or directly financially responsible for declarant's medical care. I am not a health care provider of the declarant or an employee of the health facility in which the declarant is a patient.

Witness Signature _____ Date _____

Printed Name of Witness _____

Witness Signature _____ Date _____

Printed Name of Witness _____

Acceptance of Health Care Agent and Financial Attorney-in-Fact

I accept my appointment as Health Care Agent:

Signature _____ Date _____

I accept my appointment as Attorney-in-Fact for Financial Affairs:

Signature _____ Date _____

Louisiana Advance Health Care Directive

On this date of _____ , I, _____ , do hereby sign, execute, and adopt the following as my Advance Health Care Directive. I direct any and all persons or entities involved with my health care in any manner that these decisions are my wishes and were adopted without duress or force and of my own free will. I have placed my *initials* next to the sections of this Directive that I have adopted:

[   ]   Living Will
[   ]   Selection of Health Care Agent
[   ]   Durable Power of Attorney for Financial Affairs
[   ]   Designation of Primary Physician
[   ]   Organ Donation

Living Will Declaration

If at any time I should have an incurable injury, disease or illness, be in a continual profound comatose state with no reasonable chance of recovery, or am certified to be in a terminal and irreversible condition by two (2) physicians who have personally examined me, one (1) of whom shall be my attending physician, and the physicians have determined that my death will occur whether or not life-sustaining procedures are utilized and where the application of life-sustaining procedures would serve only to prolong artificially the dying process, I direct that such procedures be withheld or withdrawn and that I be permitted to die naturally with only the administration of medication or the performance of any medical procedure deemed necessary to provide me with comfort care.

In the absence of my ability to give directions regarding the use of such life-sustaining procedures, it is my intention that this declaration shall be honored by my family and physician(s) as the final expression of my legal right to refuse medical or surgical treatment and accept the consequences from such refusal.

Selection of Health Care Agent

I, _____ , authorize _____
(name), of _____ (address), to make all medical treatment decisions for me, including decisions to withhold or withdraw any form of life-sustaining procedure on my behalf should I be:

(1) diagnosed as suffering from a terminal and irreversible condition, and

(2) comatose, incompetent, or otherwise mentally or physically incapable of communication.

I have discussed my desires concerning terminal care with my agent named previously, and I trust his or her judgment on my behalf. I understand that if I have not filled in any name in this clause or if the agent I have chosen is unavailable or unwilling to act on my behalf, my living will declaration will nevertheless be given effect should the above-discussed circumstance arise.

Durable Power of Attorney for Financial Affairs

I, _____ , grant a durable power of attorney for financial affairs to _____ (name), of _____ _____ (address), to act as my attorney-in-fact. This power of attorney shall become effective upon my disability, as certified by my primary physician or, if my primary physician is not available, by any other attending physician. This power of attorney grants no power or authority regarding health care decisions to my designated attorney-in-fact.

I give my attorney-in-fact the maximum power under law to perform the following specific acts on my behalf: all acts relating to any and all of my financial and/or business affairs, including all banking and financial institution transactions, all real estate transactions, all insurance and annuity transactions, all claims and litigation, and all business transactions. My attorney-in-fact is granted full power to act on my behalf in the same manner as if I were personally present.

My attorney-in-fact accepts this appointment and agrees to act in my best interest as he or she considers advisable. This power of attorney may be revoked by me at any time and is automatically revoked on my death. This power of attorney shall not be affected by my present or future disability or incapacity. My attorney-in-fact shall not be compensated for his or her services nor shall my attorney-in-fact be liable to me, my estate, heirs, successors, or assigns for acting or refraining from acting under this document, except for willful misconduct or gross negligence. Any third party who receives a signed copy of this document may act under it. Revocation of this document is not effective unless a third party has actual knowledge of such revocation.

Designation of Primary Physician

I designate the following physician as my primary physician: _____ (name), of _____ (address).

Organ Donation

In the event of my death, I have placed my initials next to the following part(s) of my body that I wish donated for the purposes that I have *initialed* below:

[   ] any organs or parts **OR**

[   ] eyes   [   ] bone and connective tissue   [   ] skin

[   ] heart   [   ] kidney(s)   [   ] liver

[   ] lung(s)   [   ] pancreas   [   ] other _____

for the purposes of:

[   ] any purpose authorized by law **OR**

[   ] transplantation   [   ] research   [   ] therapy

[   ] medical education   [   ] other limitations _____

Signature

I sign this Advance Health Care Directive, consisting of the following sections, which I have *initialed* below and have elected to adopt:

[   ] Living Will

[   ] Selection of Health Care Agent

[   ] Durable Power of Attorney for Financial Affairs

[   ] Designation of Primary Physician

[   ] Organ Donation

BY SIGNING HERE I INDICATE THAT I UNDERSTAND THE PURPOSE AND EFFECT OF THIS DOCUMENT.

Signature _____   Date _____

City, County, and State of Residence _____

Notary Acknowledgment

State of _____

County of _____

On _____ , _____ came before me personally and, under oath, stated that he or she is the person described in the above document and he or she signed the above document in my presence. I declare under penalty of perjury that the person whose name is subscribed to this instrument appears to be of sound mind and under no duress, fraud, or undue influence.

_____

Notary Public

My commission expires _____

Witness Acknowledgment

The declarant is personally known to me and I believe him or her to be of sound mind and under no duress, fraud, or undue influence. I did not sign the declarant's signature above for or at the direction of the declarant and I am not appointed as the health care agent or attorney-in-fact herein. I am at least eighteen (18) years of age and I am not related to the declarant by blood, adoption, or marriage, entitled to any portion of the estate of the declarant according to the laws of intestate succession or under any will of declarant or codicil thereto, or directly financially responsible for declarant's medical care. I am not a health care provider of the declarant or an employee of the health facility in which the declarant is a patient.

Witness Signature _____   Date _____

Printed Name of Witness _____

Witness Signature _____   Date _____

Printed Name of Witness _____

Acceptance of Health Care Agent and Financial Attorney-in-Fact

I accept my appointment as Health Care Agent:

Signature _____   Date _____

I accept my appointment as Attorney-in-Fact for Financial Affairs:

Signature _____   Date _____

Maine Advance Health Care Directive

On this date of _____ , I, _____ , do hereby sign, execute, and adopt the following as my Advance Health Care Directive. I direct any and all persons or entities involved with my health care in any manner that these decisions are my wishes and were adopted without duress or force and of my own free will. I have placed my *initials* next to the sections of this Directive that I have adopted:

[   ]   Living Will (Instructions for Health Care)

[   ]   Selection of Health Care Agent (Power of Attorney for Health Care)

[   ]   Durable Power of Attorney for Financial Affairs

[   ]   Designation of Primary Physician

[   ]   Organ Donation

Living Will Declaration (Instructions for Health Care)

(If you are satisfied to allow your agent to determine what is best for you in making end-of-life decisions, you need not fill out this part of the form. If you do fill out this part of the form, you may strike any wording you do not want.)

END-OF-LIFE DECISIONS: I direct that my health care providers and others involved in my care provide, withhold, or withdraw treatment in accordance with the choice I have *initialed* below:

[   ]   (1) Choice NOT To Prolong Life: I do NOT want my life to be prolonged if:

  (a) I have an incurable and irreversible condition that will result in my death within a relatively short time;

  (b) I become unconscious and, to a reasonable degree of medical certainty, I will not regain consciousness; **OR**

  (c) the likely risks and burdens of treatment would outweigh the expected benefits.

  OR

[   ]   (2) Choice TO Prolong Life: I DO want my life to be prolonged as long as possible within the limits of generally-accepted health care standards.

ARTIFICIAL NUTRITION AND HYDRATION: Artificial nutrition and hydration must be provided, withheld, or withdrawn in accordance with the choice I have made in paragraph (6) unless I mark the following box:

If I *initial* this box [   ], artificial nutrition and hydration must be provided regardless of my condition and regardless of the choice I have made in paragraph (6).

RELIEF FROM PAIN: Except as I state in the following space, I direct that treatment for alleviation of pain or discomfort be provided at all times, even if it hastens my death (*list any exceptions*):

OTHER WISHES: (*If you do not agree with any of the optional choices above and wish to write your own, or if you wish to add to the instructions you have given above, you may do so here.*) I direct that (*add additional sheets if needed*):

Selection of Health Care Agent (Power of Attorney for Health Care)

DESIGNATION OF AGENT: I designate the following individual as my agent to make health care decisions for me _____ (name), of _____
_____ (address).

AGENT'S AUTHORITY: My agent is authorized to make all health care decisions for me, including decisions to provide, withhold, or withdraw artificial nutrition and hydration and all other forms of health care to keep me alive, except as I state here (*add additional sheets if needed*):

WHEN AGENT'S AUTHORITY BECOMES EFFECTIVE: My agent's authority becomes effective when my primary physician determines that I am unable to make my own health care decisions unless I mark the following box:

If I *initial* this box [   ], my agent's authority to make health care decisions for me takes effect immediately.

AGENT'S OBLIGATION: My agent shall make health care decisions for me in accordance with this power of attorney for health care, any instructions I give in this form, and my other wishes to the extent known to my agent. To the extent my wishes are unknown, my agent shall make health care decisions for me in accordance with what my agent determines to be in my best interest. In determining my best interest, my agent shall consider my personal values to the extent known to my agent.

NOMINATION OF GUARDIAN: If a guardian of my person needs to be appointed for me by a court, I nominate the agent designated in this form.

Durable Power of Attorney for Financial Affairs

I, _____ , grant a durable power of attorney for financial affairs to _____ (name), of _____
_____ (address), to act as my attorney-in-fact. This power of attorney shall become effective upon my disability, as certified by my primary physician or, if my primary physician is not available, by any other attending physician. This power of attorney grants no power or authority regarding health care decisions to my designated attorney-in-fact.

I give my attorney-in-fact the maximum power under law to perform the following specific acts on my behalf: all acts relating to any and all of my financial and/or business affairs, including all banking and financial institution transactions, all real estate transactions, all insurance and annuity transactions, all claims and litigation, and all business transactions. My attorney-in-fact is granted full power to act on my behalf in the same manner as if I were personally present.

My attorney-in-fact accepts this appointment and agrees to act in my best interest as he or she considers advisable. This power of attorney may be revoked by me at any time and is automatically revoked on my death. This power of attorney shall not be affected by my present or future disability or incapacity. My attorney-in-fact shall not be compensated for his or her services nor shall my attorney-in-fact be liable to me, my estate, heirs, successors, or assigns for acting or refraining from acting under this document, except for willful misconduct or gross negligence. Any third party who receives a signed copy of this document may act under it. Revocation of this document is not effective unless a third party has actual knowledge of such revocation.

Designation of Primary Physician

I designate the following physician as my primary physician: _____ (name), of _____ (address).

Organ Donation

In the event of my death, I have placed my initials next to the following part(s) of my body that I wish donated for the purposes that I have *initialed* below:

[   ] any organs or parts **OR**

[   ] eyes   [   ] bone and connective tissue   [   ] skin

[   ] heart   [   ] kidney(s)   [   ] liver

[   ] lung(s)   [   ] pancreas   [   ] other _____

for the purposes of:

[   ] any purpose authorized by law **OR**

[   ] transplantation   [   ] research   [   ] therapy

[   ] medical education   [   ] other limitations _____

Signature

I sign this Advance Health Care Directive, consisting of the following sections, which I have *initialed* below and have elected to adopt:

[   ] Living Will (Instructions for Health Care)

[   ] Selection of Health Care Agent (Power of Attorney for Health Care)

[   ] Durable Power of Attorney for Financial Affairs

[   ] Designation of Primary Physician

[   ] Organ Donation

BY SIGNING HERE I INDICATE THAT I UNDERSTAND THE PURPOSE AND EF-FECT OF THIS DOCUMENT.

Signature _____   Date _____

City, County, and State of Residence _____

Notary Acknowledgment

State of _____

County of _____

On _____ , _____ came before me personally and, under oath, stated that he or she is the person described in the above document and he or she signed the above document in my presence. I declare under penalty of perjury that the person whose name is subscribed to this instrument appears to be of sound mind and under no duress, fraud, or undue influence.

_____

Notary Public

My commission expires _____

Witness Acknowledgment

The declarant is personally known to me and I believe him or her to be of sound mind and under no duress, fraud, or undue influence. I did not sign the declarant's signature above for or at the direction of the declarant and I am not appointed as the health care agent or attorney-in-fact herein. I am at least eighteen (18) years of age and I am not related to the declarant by blood, adoption, or marriage, entitled to any portion of the estate of the declarant according to the laws of intestate succession or under any will of declarant or codicil thereto, or directly financially responsible for declarant's medical care. I am not a health care provider of the declarant or an employee of the health facility in which the declarant is a patient.

Witness Signature _____ Date _____

Printed Name of Witness _____

Witness Signature _____ Date _____

Printed Name of Witness _____

Acceptance of Health Care Agent and Financial Attorney-in-Fact

I accept my appointment as Health Care Agent:

Signature _____ Date _____

I accept my appointment as Attorney-in-Fact for Financial Affairs:

Signature _____ Date _____

Maryland Advance Health Care Directive

On this date of _____ , I, _____ , do hereby sign, execute, and adopt the following as my Advance Health Care Directive. I direct any and all persons or entities involved with my health care in any manner that these decisions are my wishes and were adopted without duress or force and of my own free will. I have placed my *initials* next to the sections of this Directive that I have adopted:

[   ] Living Will
[   ] Selection of Health Care Agent
[   ] Durable Power of Attorney for Financial Affairs
[   ] Designation of Primary Physician
[   ] Organ Donation

Living Will

If I am not able to make an informed decision regarding my health care, I direct my health care providers to follow my instructions as set forth below (*initial those statements you wish to be included in the document and cross through those statements which do not apply*):

(1) If my death from a terminal condition is imminent and even if life-sustaining procedures are used there is no reasonable expectation of my recovery (*initial one*):

[   ] I direct that my life NOT be extended by life-sustaining procedures, including the administration of nutrition and hydration artificially.

[   ] I direct that my life NOT be extended by life-sustaining procedures, except that, if I am unable to take food by mouth, I wish to receive nutrition and hydration artificially.

[   ] I direct that, even in a terminal condition, I be given all available medical treatment in accordance with accepted health care standards.

(2) If I am in a persistent vegetative state, that is, if I am not conscious and am not aware of my environment or able to interact with others, and there is no reasonable expectation of my recovery within a medically-appropriate period (*initial one*):

[   ] I direct that my life NOT be extended by life-sustaining procedures, including the administration of nutrition and hydration artificially.

[   ] I direct that my life NOT be extended by life-sustaining procedures, except that if I am unable to take in food by mouth, I wish to receive nutrition and hydration artificially.

[   ] I direct that I be given all available medical treatment in accordance with accepted health care standards.

(3) If I am pregnant my agent shall follow these specific instructions (*list instructions*):

Selection of Health Care Agent

(Cross through if you do not want to appoint a health care agent to make health care decisions for you. If you do want to appoint an agent, cross through any items in the form that you do not want to apply.)

I, _____ , appoint the following individual as my agent to make health care decisions for me _____ (name), of _____ _____ (address).

My agent has full power and authority to make health care decisions for me, including the power to:

(1) Request, receive, and review any information, oral or written, regarding my physical or mental health, including, but not limited to, medical and hospital records, and consent to disclosure of this information,

(2) Employ and discharge my health care providers,

(3) Authorize my admission to or discharge from (including transfer to another facility) any hospital, hospice, nursing home, adult home, or other medical care facility, and

(4) Consent to the provision, withholding, or withdrawal of health care, including, in appropriate circumstances, life-sustaining procedures.

The authority of my agent is subject to the following provisions and limitations (*insert any provisions and limitations*):

My agent's authority becomes operative (*initial the option that applies*):
[   ]   When my attending physician and a second physician determine that I am incapable of making an informed decision regarding my health care; **OR**
[   ]   When this document is signed.

My agent is to make health care decisions for me based on the health care instructions I give in this document and on my wishes as otherwise known to my agent. If my wishes are unknown or unclear, my agent is to make health care decisions for me in accordance with my best interest, to be determined by my agent after considering the benefits, burdens, and risks that might result from a given treatment or course of treatment, or from the withholding or withdrawal of a treatment or course of treatment. My agent shall not be liable for the costs of care based solely on this authorization.

Durable Power of Attorney for Financial Affairs

I, _____ , grant a durable power of attorney for financial affairs to _____ (name), of _____
_____ (address), to act as my attorney-in-fact. This power of attorney shall become effective upon my disability, as certified by my primary physician or, if my primary physician is not available, by any other attending physician. This power of attorney grants no power or authority regarding health care decisions to my designated attorney-in-fact.

I give my attorney-in-fact the maximum power under law to perform the following specific acts on my behalf: all acts relating to any and all of my financial and/or business affairs, including all banking and financial institution transactions, all real estate transactions, all insurance and annuity transactions, all claims and litigation, and all business transactions. My attorney-in-fact is granted full power to act on my behalf in the same manner as if I were personally present.

My attorney-in-fact accepts this appointment and agrees to act in my best interest as he or she considers advisable. This power of attorney may be revoked by me at any time and is automatically revoked on my death. This power of attorney shall not be affected by my present or future disability or incapacity. My attorney-in-fact shall not be compensated for his or her services nor shall my attorney-in-fact be liable to me, my estate, heirs, successors, or assigns for acting or refraining from acting under this document, except for willful misconduct or gross negligence. Any third party who receives a signed copy of this document may act under it. Revocation of this document is not effective unless a third party has actual knowledge of such revocation.

Designation of Primary Physician

I designate the following physician as my primary physician: _____
(name), of _____ (address).

Organ Donation

In the event of my death, I have placed my initials next to the following part(s) of my body that I wish donated for the purposes that I have *initialed* below:

[   ] any organs or parts **OR**

[   ] eyes   [   ] bone and connective tissue   [   ] skin

[   ] heart   [   ] kidney(s)   [   ] liver

[   ] lung(s)   [   ] pancreas   [   ] other _____

for the purposes of:

[   ] any purpose authorized by law **OR**

[   ] transplantation   [   ] research   [   ] therapy

[   ] medical education   [   ] other limitations _____

Signature

I sign this Advance Health Care Directive, consisting of the following sections, which I have *initialed* below and have elected to adopt:

[   ]   Living Will

[   ]   Selection of Health Care Agent

[   ]   Durable Power of Attorney for Financial Affairs

[   ]   Designation of Primary Physician

[   ]   Organ Donation

BY SIGNING HERE I INDICATE THAT I UNDERSTAND THE PURPOSE AND EFFECT OF THIS DOCUMENT.

Signature _____ Date _____

City, County, and State of Residence _____

Notary Acknowledgment

State of _____

County of _____

On _____ , _____ came before me personally and, under oath, stated that he or she is the person described in the above document and he or she signed the above document in my presence. I declare under penalty of perjury that the person whose name is subscribed to this instrument appears to be of sound mind and under no duress, fraud, or undue influence.

_____

Notary Public

My commission expires _____

Witness Acknowledgment

The declarant is personally known to me and I believe him or her to be of sound mind and under no duress, fraud, or undue influence. I did not sign the declarant's signature above for or at the direction of the declarant and I am not appointed as the health care agent or attorney-in-fact herein. I am at least eighteen (18) years of age and I am not related to the declarant by blood, adoption, or marriage, entitled to any portion of the estate of the declarant according to the laws of intestate succession or under any will of declarant or codicil thereto, or directly financially responsible for declarant's medical care. I am not a health care provider of the declarant or an employee of the health facility in which the declarant is a patient.

Witness Signature _____ Date _____

Printed Name of Witness _____

Witness Signature _____ Date _____

Printed Name of Witness _____

Acceptance of Health Care Agent and Financial Attorney-in-Fact

I accept my appointment as Health Care Agent:

Signature _____ Date _____

I accept my appointment as Attorney-in-Fact for Financial Affairs:

Signature _____ Date _____

Massachusetts Advance Health Care Directive

On this date of _____ , I, _____ , do hereby sign, execute, and adopt the following as my Advance Health Care Directive. I direct any and all persons or entities involved with my health care in any manner that these decisions are my wishes and were adopted without duress or force and of my own free will. I have placed my *initials* next to the sections of this Directive that I have adopted:

[   ] Living Will (Declaration and Directive to Physicians)
[   ] Selection of Health Care Agent
[   ] Durable Power of Attorney for Financial Affairs
[   ] Designation of Primary Physician
[   ] Organ Donation

Living Will (Declaration and Directive to Physicians)

I, _____ , willfully and voluntarily make known my desire that my life not be artificially prolonged under the circumstances set forth below, and, pursuant to any and all applicable laws in the State of Massachusetts, I declare that:

If at any time I should have an incurable injury, disease, or illness which has been certified as a terminal condition by my attending physician and one (1) additional physician, both of whom have personally examined me, and such physicians have determined that there can be no recovery from such condition and my death is imminent, and where the application of life-prolonging procedures would serve only to artificially prolong the dying process, I direct that such procedures be withheld or withdrawn, and that I be permitted to die naturally with only the administration of medication, the administration of nutrition, or the performance of any medical procedure deemed necessary to provide me with comfort, care, or to alleviate pain.

If at any time I should have been diagnosed as being in a persistent vegetative state which has been certified as incurable by my attending physician and one (1) additional physician, both of whom have personally examined me, and such physicians have determined that there can be no recovery from such condition, and where the application of life-prolonging procedures would serve only to artificially prolong the dying process, I direct that such procedures be withheld or withdrawn, and that I be permitted to die naturally with only the administration of medication, the administration of nutrition, or the performance of any medical procedure deemed necessary to provide me with comfort, care, or to alleviate pain.

In the absence of my ability to give directions regarding my treatment in the above situations, including directions regarding the use of such life-prolonging procedures, it is my intention that this declaration shall be honored by my family, my physician, and any court of law, as the final expression of my legal right to refuse medical and surgical treatment. I declare that I fully accept the consequences for such refusal. If I am diagnosed as pregnant, this document shall have no force and effect during my pregnancy.

I understand the full importance of this declaration and I am emotionally and mentally competent to make this declaration and Living Will. No person shall be in any way responsible for the making or placing into effect of this declaration and Living Will or for carrying out my express directions. I also understand that I may revoke this document at any time.

Selection of Health Care Agent

I, _____ , hereby appoint _____

(name), of _____ (address), as my health care agent to make any and all health care decisions for me, except to the extent that I state otherwise below. This Health Care Proxy shall take effect in the event I become unable to make or communicate my own health care decisions.

I direct my agent to make health care decisions in accord with my wishes and limitations as may be stated below, or as he or she otherwise knows. If my wishes are unknown, I direct my agent to make health care decisions in accord with what he or she determines to be my best interests.

Other directions (*optional, add additional pages if necessary*):

Durable Power of Attorney for Financial Affairs

I, _____ , grant a durable power of attorney for financial affairs to _____ (name), of _____ _____ (address), to act as my attorney-in-fact. This power of attorney shall become effective upon my disability, as certified by my primary physician or, if my primary physician is not available, by any other attending physician. This power of attorney grants no power or authority regarding health care decisions to my designated attorney-in-fact.

I give my attorney-in-fact the maximum power under law to perform the following specific acts on my behalf: all acts relating to any and all of my financial and/or business affairs, including all banking and financial institution transactions, all real estate transactions, all insurance and annuity transactions, all claims and litigation, and all business transactions. My attorney-in-fact is granted full power to act on my behalf in the same manner as if I were personally present.

My attorney-in-fact accepts this appointment and agrees to act in my best interest as he or she considers advisable. This power of attorney may be revoked by me at any time and is automatically revoked on my death. This power of attorney shall not be affected by my present or future disability or incapacity. My attorney-in-fact shall not be compensated for his or her services nor shall my attorney-in-fact be liable to me, my estate, heirs, successors, or assigns for acting or refraining from acting under this document, except for willful misconduct or gross negligence. Any third party who receives a signed copy of this document may act under it. Revocation of this document is not effective unless a third party has actual knowledge of such revocation.

Designation of Primary Physician

I designate the following physician as my primary physician: _____ (name), of _____._____ (address).

Organ Donation

In the event of my death, I have placed my initials next to the following part(s) of my body that I wish donated for the purposes that I have *initialed* below:

[   ] any organs or parts **OR**

[   ] eyes   [   ] bone and connective tissue   [   ] skin

[   ] heart   [   ] kidney(s)   [   ] liver

[   ] lung(s)   [   ] pancreas   [   ] other _____

for the purposes of:

[   ] any purpose authorized by law **OR**

[   ] transplantation   [   ] research   [   ] therapy

[   ] medical education   [   ] other limitations _____

Signature

I sign this Advance Health Care Directive, consisting of the following sections, which I have *initialed* below and have elected to adopt:

[   ] Living Will (Declaration and Directive to Physicians)

[   ] Selection of Health Care Agent

[   ] Durable Power of Attorney for Financial Affairs

[   ] Designation of Primary Physician

[   ] Organ Donation

BY SIGNING HERE I INDICATE THAT I UNDERSTAND THE PURPOSE AND EFFECT OF THIS DOCUMENT.

Signature _____ Date _____

City, County, and State of Residence _____

Notary Acknowledgment

State of _____

County of _____

On _____ , _____ came before me personally and, under oath, stated that he or she is the person described in the above document and he or she signed the above document in my presence. I declare under penalty of perjury that the person whose name is subscribed to this instrument appears to be of sound mind and under no duress, fraud, or undue influence.

_____

Notary Public
My commission expires _____

Witness Acknowledgment

(1) The Declarant is personally known to me and, to the best of my knowledge, the Declarant signed this instrument freely, under no constraint or undue influence, and is of sound mind and memory and legal age, and fully aware of the possible consequences of this action.

(2) I am at least nineteen (19) years of age and I am not related to the Declarant in any manner by blood, marriage, or adoption.

(3) I am not the Declarant's attending physician, or a patient or employee of the Declarant's attending physician, or a patient, physician, or employee of the health care facility in which the Declarant is a patient, unless such person is required or allowed to witness the execution of this document by the laws of the state in which this document is executed.

(4) I am not entitled to any portion of the Declarant's estate on the Declarant's death under the laws of intestate succession of any state or country, nor under the Last Will and Testament of the Declarant or any Codicil to such Last Will and Testament.

(5) I have no claim against any portion of the Declarant's estate on the Declarant's death.

(6) I am not directly financially responsible for the Declarant's medical care.

(7) I did not sign the Declarant's signature for the Declarant or on the direction of the Declarant, nor have I been paid any fee for acting as a witness to the execution of this document.

Witness Signature _____   Date _____

Printed Name of Witness _____

Witness Signature _____   Date _____

Printed Name of Witness _____

Acceptance of Health Care Agent and Financial Attorney-in-Fact

I accept my appointment as Health Care Agent:

Signature _____   Date _____

I accept my appointment as Attorney-in-Fact for Financial Affairs:

Signature _____   Date _____

Michigan Advance Health Care Directive

On this date of _____ , I, _____ , do hereby sign, execute, and adopt the following as my Advance Health Care Directive. I direct any and all persons or entities involved with my health care in any manner that these decisions are my wishes and were adopted without duress or force and of my own free will. I have placed my *initials* next to the sections of this Directive that I have adopted:

[   ]   Living Will (Declaration and Directive to Physicians)
[   ]   Selection of Health Care Agent (Designation of Patient Advocate for Health Care)
[   ]   Durable Power of Attorney for Financial Matters
[   ]   Designation of Primary Physician
[   ]   Organ Donation

Living Will (Declaration and Directive to Physicians)

I, _____ , willfully and voluntarily make known my desire that my life not be artificially prolonged under the circumstances set forth below, and, pursuant to any and all applicable laws in the State of Michigan, I declare that:

If at any time I should have an incurable injury, disease, or illness which has been certified as a terminal condition by my attending physician and one (1) additional physician, both of whom have personally examined me, and such physicians have determined that there can be no recovery from such condition and my death is imminent, and where the application of life-prolonging procedures would serve only to artificially prolong the dying process, I direct that such procedures be withheld or withdrawn, and that I be permitted to die naturally with only the administration of medication, the administration of nutrition, or the performance of any medical procedure deemed necessary to provide me with comfort, care, or to alleviate pain.

If at any time I should have been diagnosed as being in a persistent vegetative state which has been certified as incurable by my attending physician and one (1) additional physician, both of whom have personally examined me, and such physicians have determined that there can be no recovery from such condition, and where the application of life-prolonging procedures would serve only to artificially prolong the dying process, I direct that such procedures be withheld or withdrawn, and that I be permitted to die naturally with only the administration of medication, the administration of nutrition, or the performance of any medical procedure deemed necessary to provide me with comfort, care, or to alleviate pain.

In the absence of my ability to give directions regarding my treatment in the above situations, including directions regarding the use of such life-prolonging procedures, it is my intention that this Declaration shall be honored by my family, my physician, and any court of law, as the final expression of my legal right to refuse medical and surgical treatment. I declare that I fully accept the consequences for such refusal. If I am diagnosed as pregnant, this document shall have no force and effect during my pregnancy.

I understand the full importance of this Declaration and I am emotionally and mentally competent to make this Declaration and Living Will. No person shall be in any way responsible for the making or placing into effect of this Declaration and Living Will or for carrying out my express directions. I also understand that I may revoke this document at any time.

Selection of Health Care Agent
(Designation of Patient Advocate for Health Care)

I, _____ , am of sound mind, and I voluntarily make this designation. I designate _____ (name), of _____ _____ (address), as my patient advocate to make care, custody, or medical treatment decisions for me only when I become unable to participate in medical treatment decisions. The determination of when I am unable to participate in medical treatment decisions shall be made by my attending physician and another physician or licensed psychologist.

I authorize my patient advocate to decide to withhold or withdraw medical treatment which could or would allow me to die. I am fully aware that such a decision could or would lead to my death. In making decisions for me, my patient advocate shall be guided by my wishes, whether expressed orally, in a living will, or in this designation. If my wishes as to a particular situation have not been expressed, my patient advocate shall be guided by his or her best judgment of my probable decision, given the benefits, burdens, and consequences of the decision, even if my death, or the chance of my death, is one consequence.

My patient advocate shall have the same authority to make care, custody, and medical treatment decisions as I would if I had the capacity to make them EXCEPT (*here list the limitations, if any, you wish to place on your patient advocate's authority*):

This designation of patient advocate shall not be affected by my disability or incapacity. This designation of patient advocate is governed by Michigan law, although I request that it be honored in any state in which I may be found. I reserve the power to revoke this designation at any time by communicating my intent to revoke it in any manner in which I am able to communicate. Photostatic copies of this document, after it is signed and witnessed, shall have the same legal force as the original document. I voluntarily sign this designation of patient advocate after careful consideration. I accept its meaning and I accept its consequences.

Durable Power of Attorney for Financial Affairs

I, _____ , grant a durable power of attorney for financial affairs to _____ (name), of _____ _____ (address), to act as my attorney-in-fact. This power of attorney shall become effective upon my disability, as certified by my primary physician or, if my primary physician is not available, by any other attending physician. This power of attorney grants no power or authority regarding health care decisions to my designated attorney-in-fact.

I give my attorney-in-fact the maximum power under law to perform the following specific acts on my behalf: all acts relating to any and all of my financial and/or business affairs, including all banking and financial institution transactions, all real estate transactions, all insurance and annuity transactions, all claims and litigation, and all business transactions. My attorney-in-fact is granted full power to act on my behalf in the same manner as if I were personally present.

My attorney-in-fact accepts this appointment and agrees to act in my best interest as he or she considers advisable. This power of attorney may be revoked by me at any time and is automatically revoked on my death. This power of attorney shall not be affected by my present or future disability or incapacity. My attorney-in-fact shall not be compensated for his or her services nor shall my attorney-in-fact be liable to me, my estate, heirs, successors, or assigns for acting or refraining from acting under this document, except for willful misconduct or gross negligence. Any third party who receives a signed copy of this document may act under it. Revocation of this document is not effective unless a third party has actual knowledge of such revocation.

Designation of Primary Physician

I designate the following physician as my primary physician: _____ (name), of _____ (address).

Organ Donation

In the event of my death, I have placed my initials next to the following part(s) of my body that I wish donated for the purposes that I have *initialed* below:

[   ] any organs or parts **OR**

[   ] eyes   [   ] bone and connective tissue   [   ] skin

[   ] heart   [   ] kidney(s)   [   ] liver

[   ] lung(s)   [   ] pancreas   [   ] other _____

for the purposes of:

[   ] any purpose authorized by law **OR**

[   ] transplantation   [   ] research   [   ] therapy

[   ] medical education   [   ] other limitations _____

Signature

I sign this Advance Health Care Directive, consisting of the following sections, which I have *initialed* below and have elected to adopt:

[   ] Living Will (Declaration and Directive to Physicians)

[   ] Selection of Health Care Agent (Designation of Patient Advocate for Health Care)

[   ] Durable Power of Attorney for Financial Affairs

[   ] Designation of Primary Physician

[   ] Organ Donation

BY SIGNING HERE I INDICATE THAT I UNDERSTAND THE PURPOSE AND EFFECT OF THIS DOCUMENT.

Signature _____ Date _____

City, County, and State of Residence _____

Notary Acknowledgment

State of _____

County of _____

On _____ , _____ came before me personally and, under oath, stated that he or she is the person described in the above document and he or she signed the above document in my presence. I declare under penalty of perjury that the person whose name is subscribed to this instrument appears to be of sound mind and under no duress, fraud, or undue influence.

_____

Notary Public

My commission expires _____

Witness Acknowledgment

On _____ , in the presence of all of us, the above-named Declarant published and signed this Living Will and Directive to Physicians, and then at the Declarant's request, and in the Declarant's presence, and in each other's presence, we all signed below as witnesses, and we each declare, under penalty of perjury, that, to the best of our knowledge:

(1) The Declarant is personally known to me and, to the best of my knowledge, the Declarant signed this instrument freely, under no constraint or undue influence, and is of sound mind and memory and legal age, and fully aware of the possible consequences of this action.

(2) I am at least nineteen (19) years of age and I am not related to the Declarant in any manner by blood, marriage, or adoption.

(3) I am not the Declarant's attending physician, or a patient or employee of the Declarant's attending physician, or a patient, physician, or employee of the health care facility in which the Declarant is a patient, unless such person is required or allowed to witness the execution of this document by the laws of the state in which this document is executed.

(4) I am not entitled to any portion of the Declarant's estate on the Declarant's death under the laws of intestate succession of any state or country, nor under the Last Will and Testament of the Declarant or any Codicil to such Last Will and Testament.

(5) I have no claim against any portion of the Declarant's estate on the Declarant's death.

(6) I am not directly financially responsible for the Declarant's medical care.

(7) I did not sign the Declarant's signature for the Declarant or on the direction of the Declarant, nor have I been paid any fee for acting as a witness to the execution of this document.

Witness Signature _____   Date _____

Printed Name of Witness _____

Witness Signature _____   Date _____

Printed Name of Witness _____

Acceptance of Health Care Agent and Financial Attorney-in-Fact

I accept my appointment as Health Care Agent:

Signature _____   Date _____

I accept my appointment as Attorney-in-Fact for Financial Affairs:

Signature _____   Date _____

Minnesota Advance Health Care Directive

On this date of _____ , I, _____ , do hereby sign, execute, and adopt the following as my Advance Health Care Directive. I direct any and all persons or entities involved with my health care in any manner that these decisions are my wishes and were adopted without duress or force and of my own free will. I have placed my *initials* next to the sections of this Directive that I have adopted:

[   ] Living Will (Health Care Instructions)
[   ] Selection of Health Care Agent
[   ] Durable Power of Attorney for Financial Affairs
[   ] Designation of Primary Physician
[   ] Organ Donation

Part 1: Living Will (Health Care Instructions)

NOTE: Complete this Part if you wish to give health care instructions. If you appoint an agent in Part 2, completing this Part is optional but would be very helpful to your agent. However, if you choose not to appoint an agent in Part I, you MUST complete some or all of this Part if you wish to make a valid health care directive.

I, _____ , being an adult of sound mind, willfully and voluntarily make this statement as a directive to be followed if I am in a terminal condition and become unable to participate in decisions regarding my health care. I understand that my health care providers are legally bound to act consistently with my wishes, within the limits of reasonable medical practice and other applicable law. I also understand that I have the right to make medical and health care decisions for myself as long as I am able to do so and to revoke this living will at any time.

The following are my feelings and wishes regarding my health care (*you may state the circumstances under which this living will applies*):

I particularly DO want to have all appropriate health care that will help in the following ways (*you may give instructions for care you do want*):

I particularly do NOT want the following (*you may list specific treatment you do not want in certain circumstances*):

I particularly DO want to have the following kinds of life-sustaining treatment if I am diagnosed to have a terminal condition (*you may list the specific types of life-sustaining treatment that you do want if you have a terminal condition*):

I particularly do NOT want the following kinds of life-sustaining treatment if I am diagnosed to have a terminal condition (*you may list the specific types of life-sustaining treatment that you do not want if you have a terminal condition*):

I recognize that if I reject artificially-administered sustenance, then I may die of dehydration or malnutrition rather than from my illness or injury. The following are my feelings and wishes regarding artificially-administered sustenance should I have a terminal condition (*you may *indicate whether you wish to receive food and fluids given to you in some other way than by mouth if you have a terminal condition):*

Thoughts I feel are relevant to my instructions (*you may, but need not, give your religious beliefs, philosophy, or other personal values that you feel are important. You may also state preferences concerning the location of your care):*

Part 2: Selection of Health Care Agent

THIS IS WHO I WANT TO MAKE HEALTH CARE DECISIONS FOR ME IF I AM UNABLE TO DECIDE OR SPEAK FOR MYSELF. (*I know I can change my agent at any time and I know I do not have to appoint an agent.*)

When I am unable to decide or speak for myself, I trust and appoint _____

_____ (name), _____ (address).

THIS IS WHAT I WANT MY HEALTH CARE AGENT TO BE ABLE TO DO IF I AM UNABLE TO DECIDE OR SPEAK FOR MYSELF. (*I know I can change these choices.*)

My health care agent is automatically given the powers listed below in paragraphs (1) through (6). My health care agent must follow my health care instructions in this document or any other instructions I have given to my agent. If I have not given health care instructions, then my agent must act in my best interest. Whenever I am unable to decide or speak for myself, my health care agent has the power to:

(1) Make any health care decision for me. This includes the power to give, refuse, or withdraw consent to any care, treatment, service, or procedures. This includes deciding whether to stop or not start health care that is keeping me or might keep me alive, and deciding about intrusive mental health treatment,

(2) Choose my health care providers,

(3) Choose where I live and receive care and support when those choices relate to my health care needs, and

(4) Review my medical records and have the same rights that I would have to give my medical records to other people.

If I do NOT want my health care agent to have a power listed above in paragraphs (1) through (4), **OR** if I want to LIMIT any power in paragraphs (1) through (4), I MUST say that here (*insert comments and attach additional pages if needed*):

My health care agent is NOT automatically given the powers listed below in paragraphs (5) and (6). If I WANT my agent to have any of the powers in paragraphs (5) and (6), I must *initial* the line in front of the power; then my agent WILL HAVE that power.

[   ] (5) To decide whether to donate any parts of my body, including organs, tissues, and eyes, when I die.

[   ] (6) To decide what will happen with my body when I die (burial, cremation, etc.).

If I want to say anything more about my health care agent's powers or limits on the powers, I can say it here (*insert comments and attach additional pages if needed*):

Durable Power of Attorney for Financial Affairs

I, _____ , grant a durable power of attorney for financial affairs to _____ (name), of _____
_____ (address), to act as my attorney-in-fact. This power of attorney shall become effective upon my disability, as certified by my primary physician or, if my primary physician is not available, by any other attending physician. This power of attorney grants no power or authority regarding health care decisions to my designated attorney-in-fact.

I give my attorney-in-fact the maximum power under law to perform the following specific acts on my behalf: all acts relating to any and all of my financial and/or business affairs, including all banking and financial institution transactions, all real estate transactions, all insurance

and annuity transactions, all claims and litigation, and all business transactions. My attorney-in-fact is granted full power to act on my behalf in the same manner as if I were personally present.

My attorney-in-fact accepts this appointment and agrees to act in my best interest as he or she considers advisable. This power of attorney may be revoked by me at any time and is automatically revoked on my death. This power of attorney shall not be affected by my present or future disability or incapacity. My attorney-in-fact shall not be compensated for his or her services nor shall my attorney-in-fact be liable to me, my estate, heirs, successors, or assigns for acting or refraining from acting under this document, except for willful misconduct or gross negligence. Any third party who receives a signed copy of this document may act under it. Revocation of this document is not effective unless a third party has actual knowledge of such revocation.

Designation of Primary Physician

I designate the following physician as my primary physician: _____
(name), of _____ (address).

Organ Donation

In the event of my death, I have placed my initials next to the following part(s) of my body that I wish donated for the purposes that I have *initialed* below:
[   ] any organs or parts **OR**
[   ] eyes   [   ] bone and connective tissue   [   ] skin
[   ] heart   [   ] kidney(s)   [   ] liver
[   ] lung(s)   [   ] pancreas   [   ] other _____
for the purposes of:
[   ] any purpose authorized by law **OR**
[   ] transplantation   [   ] research   [   ] therapy
[   ] medical education   [   ] other limitations _____

Signature

I sign this Advance Health Care Directive, consisting of the following sections, which I have *initialed* below and have elected to adopt:
[   ]   Living Will (Health Care Instructions)
[   ]   Selection of Health Care Agent
[   ]   Durable Power of Attorney for Financial Affairs
[   ]   Designation of Primary Physician
[   ]   Organ Donation
BY SIGNING HERE I INDICATE THAT I UNDERSTAND THE PURPOSE AND EFFECT OF THIS DOCUMENT.

Signature _____   Date _____

City, County, and State of Residence _____

Notary Acknowledgment

State of _____

County of _____

On _____ , _____ came before me personally and, under oath, stated that he or she is the person described in the above document and he or she signed the above document in my presence. I declare under penalty of perjury that the person whose name is subscribed to this instrument appears to be of sound mind and under no duress, fraud, or undue influence.

_____
Notary Public
My commission expires _____

Witness Acknowledgment

The declarant is personally known to me and I believe him or her to be of sound mind and under no duress, fraud, or undue influence. I did not sign the declarant's signature above for or at the direction of the declarant and I am not appointed as the health care agent or attorney-in-fact herein. I am at least eighteen (18) years of age and I am not related to the declarant by blood, adoption, or marriage, entitled to any portion of the estate of the declarant according to the laws of intestate succession or under any will of declarant or codicil thereto, or directly financially responsible for declarant's medical care. I am not a health care provider of the declarant or an employee of the health facility in which the declarant is a patient.

Witness Signature _____   Date _____

Printed Name of Witness _____

Witness Signature _____   Date _____

Printed Name of Witness _____

Acceptance of Health Care Agent and Financial Attorney-in-Fact

I accept my appointment as Health Care Agent:

Signature _____   Date _____

I accept my appointment as Attorney-in-Fact for Financial Affairs:

Signature _____   Date _____

Mississippi Advance Health Care Directive

On this date of _____ , I, _____ , do hereby sign, execute, and adopt the following as my Advance Health Care Directive. I direct any and all persons or entities involved with my health care in any manner that these decisions are my wishes and were adopted without duress or force and of my own free will. I have placed my *initials* next to the sections of this Directive that I have adopted:

[   ] Living Will (Advance Health Care Instructions)

[   ] Selection of Health Care Agent (Power of Attorney for Health Care)

[   ] Durable Power of Attorney for Financial Affairs

[   ] Designation of Primary Physician

[   ] Organ Donation

PART 1 of this form lets you give specific instructions about any aspect of your health care. Choices are provided for you to express your wishes regarding the provision, withholding, or withdrawal of treatment to keep you alive, including the provision of artificial nutrition and hydration, as well as the provision of pain relief. Space is provided for you to add to the choices you have made or for you to write out any additional wishes.

You have the right to give instructions about your own health care. You also have the right to name someone else to make health care decisions for you. This form lets you do either or both of these things. It also lets you express your wishes regarding the designation of your primary physician. If you use this form, you may complete or modify all or any part of it. You are free to use a different form.

PART 2 of this form is a Power of Attorney for Health Care. Part 2 lets you name another individual as agent to make health care decisions for you if you become incapable of making your own decisions or if you want someone else to make those decisions for you now even though you are still capable. Unless related to you, your agent may not be an owner, operator, or employee of a residential long-term health care institution at which you are receiving care. Unless the form you sign limits the authority of your agent, your agent may make all health care decisions for you. This form has a place for you to limit the authority of your agent. You need not limit the authority of your agent if you wish to rely on your agent for all health care decisions that may have to be made. If you choose not to limit the authority of your agent, your agent will have the right to:

(1) Consent or refuse consent to any care, treatment, service, or procedure to maintain, diagnose, or otherwise affect a physical or mental condition,

(2) Select or discharge health care providers and institutions,

(3) Approve or disapprove diagnostic tests, surgical procedures, programs of medication, and orders not to resuscitate, and

(4) Direct the provision, withholding, or withdrawal of artificial nutrition and hydration and all other forms of health care.

PART 3 of this form lets you designate a person you choose to handle your financial matters while you are unable to do so.

PART 4 of this form lets you designate a physician to have primary responsibility for your health care.

PART 5 of this form allows you to specify your desires concerning organ donation after death.

After completing this form, sign and date the form at the end in front of two (2) witnesses and a notary public. Give a copy of the signed and completed form to your physician, any other health care providers you may have, any health care institution at which you are receiving care, and any health care agents you have named. You should talk to the person you have named as agent to make sure that he or she understands your wishes and is willing to take the responsibility. You have the right to revoke this advance health care directive or replace this form at any time.

Part 1: Living Will (Advance Health Care Instructions)

END-OF-LIFE DECISIONS: I direct that my health care providers and others involved in my care provide, withhold, or withdraw treatment in accordance with the choice I have *initialed* below:

[   ] (1) Choice NOT To Prolong Life: I do NOT want my life to be prolonged if:

(a) I have an incurable and irreversible condition that will result in my death within a relatively short time;

(b) I become unconscious and, to a reasonable degree of medical certainty, I will not regain consciousness; **OR**

(c) the likely risks and burdens of treatment would outweigh the expected benefits.

OR

[   ] (2) Choice TO Prolong Life: I DO want my life to be prolonged as long as possible within the limits of generally-accepted health care standards.

ARTIFICIAL NUTRITION AND HYDRATION: Artificial nutrition and hydration must be provided, withheld, or withdrawn in accordance with the choice I have made above unless I *initial* the following box:

If I *initial* this box [   ], artificial nutrition and hydration must be provided regardless of my condition and regardless of the choice I have made above.

RELIEF FROM PAIN: Except as I state in the following space, I direct that treatment for alleviation of pain or discomfort be provided at all times, even if it hastens my death (*list exceptions*):

OTHER WISHES: (*If you do not agree with any of the optional choices above and wish to write your own, or if you wish to add to the instructions you have given above, you may do so here.*) I direct that (*add additional sheets if needed*):

Part 2: Selection of Health Care Agent (Power of Attorney for Health Care)

DESIGNATION OF AGENT: I designate the following individual as my agent to make health care decisions for me _____ (name), of _____
_____ (address).

AGENT'S AUTHORITY: My agent is authorized to make all health care decisions for me, including decisions to provide, withhold, or withdraw artificial nutrition and hydration, and all other forms of health care to keep me alive, except as I state here (*add additional sheets if needed*):

WHEN AGENT'S AUTHORITY BECOMES EFFECTIVE: My agent's authority becomes effective when my primary physician determines that I am unable to make my own health care decisions unless I mark the following box:

If I *initial* this box [   ], my agent's authority to make health care decisions for me takes effect immediately.

AGENT'S OBLIGATION: My agent shall make health care decisions for me in accordance with this power of attorney for health care, any instructions I give in Part 2 of this form, and my other wishes to the extent known to my agent. To the extent my wishes are unknown, my agent shall make health care decisions for me in accordance with what my agent determines to be in my best interest. In determining my best interest, my agent shall consider my personal values to the extent known to my agent.

NOMINATION OF GUARDIAN: If a guardian of my person needs to be appointed for me by a court, I nominate the agent designated in this form.

Part 3: Durable Power of Attorney for Financial Affairs

I, _____ , grant a durable power of attorney for financial affairs to _____ (name), of _____
_____ (address), to act as my attorney-in-fact. This power of attorney shall become effective upon my disability, as certified by my primary physician or, if my primary physician is not available, by any other attending physician. This power of attorney grants no power or authority regarding health care decisions to my designated attorney-in-fact.

I give my attorney-in-fact the maximum power under law to perform the following specific acts on my behalf: all acts relating to any and all of my financial and/or business affairs, including all banking and financial institution transactions, all real estate transactions, all insurance and annuity transactions, all claims and litigation, and all business transactions. My attorney-in-fact is granted full power to act on my behalf in the same manner as if I were personally present.

My attorney-in-fact accepts this appointment and agrees to act in my best interest as he or she considers advisable. This power of attorney may be revoked by me at any time and is automatically revoked on my death. This power of attorney shall not be affected by my present or future disability or incapacity. My attorney-in-fact shall not be compensated for his or her services nor shall my attorney-in-fact be liable to me, my estate, heirs, successors, or assigns for acting or refraining from acting under this document, except for willful misconduct or gross negligence. Any third party who receives a signed copy of this document may act under it. Revocation of this document is not effective unless a third party has actual knowledge of such revocation.

Part 4: Designation of Primary Physician

I designate the following physician as my primary physician: _____
(name), of _____ (address).

Part 5: Organ Donation

In the event of my death, I have placed my initials next to the following part(s) of my body that I wish donated for the purposes that I have *initialed* below:

[   ] any organs or parts **OR**

[   ] eyes   [   ] bone and connective tissue   [   ] skin

[   ] heart   [   ] kidney(s)   [   ] liver

[   ] lung(s)   [   ] pancreas   [   ] other _____

for the purposes of:

[   ] any purpose authorized by law **OR**

[   ] transplantation   [   ] research   [   ] therapy

[   ] medical education   [   ] other limitations _____

Signature

I sign this Advance Health Care Directive, consisting of the following sections, which I have *initialed* below and have elected to adopt:

[   ] Living Will (Advance Health Care Instructions)

[   ] Selection of Health Care Agent (Power of Attorney for Health Care)

[   ] Durable Power of Attorney for Financial Affairs

[   ] Designation of Primary Physician

[   ] Organ Donation

BY SIGNING HERE I INDICATE THAT I UNDERSTAND THE PURPOSE AND EFFECT OF THIS DOCUMENT.

Signature _____ Date _____

City, County, and State of Residence _____

Notary Acknowledgment

State of _____

County of _____

On _____ , _____ came before me personally and, under oath, stated that he or she is the person described in the above document and he or she signed the above document in my presence. I declare under penalty of perjury that the person whose name is subscribed to this instrument appears to be of sound mind and under no duress, fraud, or undue influence.

_____

Notary Public

My commission expires _____

Witness Acknowledgment

WITNESS #1

I declare under penalty of perjury pursuant to Section 97-9-61, Mississippi Code of 1972, that the principal is personally known to me, that the principal signed or acknowledged this power of attorney in my presence, that the principal appears to be of sound mind and under no duress, fraud, or undue influence, that I am not the person appointed as agent by this document, and that I am not a health care provider, or an employee of a health care provider or facility. I am at least eighteen (18) years of age and I am not related to the principal by blood, marriage, or adoption, and to the best of my knowledge, I am not entitled to any part of the estate of the principal upon the death of the principal under a will now existing or by operation of law.

Witness #1 Signature _____ Date _____

Printed Name of Witness _____

WITNESS #2

I declare under penalty of perjury pursuant to Section 97-9-61, Mississippi Code of 1972, that the principal is personally known to me, that the principal signed or acknowledged this power of attorney in my presence, that the principal appears to be of sound mind and under no duress, fraud, or undue influence, that I am not the person appointed as agent by this document, and that I am at least eighteen (18) years of age and I am not a health care provider, or an employee of a health care provider or facility.

Witness #2 Signature _____ Date _____

Printed Name of Witness _____

Acceptance of Health Care Agent and Financial Attorney-in-Fact

I accept my appointment as Health Care Agent:

Signature _____ Date _____

I accept my appointment as Attorney-in-Fact for Financial Affairs:

Signature _____ Date _____

Missouri Advance Health Care Directive

On this date of _____ , I, _____ , do hereby sign, execute, and adopt the following as my Advance Health Care Directive. I direct any and all persons or entities involved with my health care in any manner that these decisions are my wishes and were adopted without duress or force and of my own free will. I have placed my *initials* next to the sections of this Directive that I have adopted:

[   ] Living Will

[   ] Selection of Health Care Agent (Durable Power of Attorney for Health Care)

[   ] Durable Power of Attorney for Financial Affairs

[   ] Designation of Primary Physician

[   ] Organ Donation

Living Will Declaration

I have the primary right to make my own decisions concerning treatment that might unduly prolong the dying process. By this declaration I express to my physician, family, and friends my intent. If I should have a terminal condition it is my desire that my dying not be prolonged by administration of death-prolonging procedures. If my condition is terminal and I am unable to participate in decisions regarding my medical treatment, I direct my attending physician to withhold or withdraw medical procedures that merely prolong the dying process and are not necessary to my comfort or to alleviate pain. It is not my intent to authorize affirmative or deliberate acts or omissions to shorten my life, rather, only to permit the natural process of dying.

Selection of Health Care Agent
(Durable Power of Attorney for Health Care)

I, _____ , hereby designate _____
(name), of _____ (address), as my attorney-in-fact.

This is a durable power of attorney and the authority of my attorney-in-fact shall not terminate if I become disabled or incapacitated.

This power of attorney becomes effective upon certification by two (2) licensed physicians that I am incapacitated and can no longer make my own medical decisions. The powers and duties of my attorney-in-fact shall cease upon certification that I am no longer incapacitated. This determination of incapacity shall be periodically reviewed by my attending physician and my attorney-in-fact. I authorize my attorney-in-fact to make any and all health care decisions for me, including decisions to withhold or withdraw any form of life support. I expressly authorize my attorney-in-fact to make all decisions regarding artificially-supplied nutrition and hydration in all medical circumstances.

Durable Power of Attorney for Financial Affairs

I, _____ , grant a durable power of attorney for financial affairs to _____ (name), of _____
_____ (address), to act as my attorney-in-fact. This power of attorney shall become effective upon my disability, as certified by my primary physician or, if my primary physician is not available, by any other attending physician. This power of attorney grants no power or authority regarding health care decisions to my designated attorney-in-fact.

I give my attorney-in-fact the maximum power under law to perform the following specific acts on my behalf: all acts relating to any and all of my financial and/or business affairs, including all banking and financial institution transactions, all real estate transactions, all insurance and annuity transactions, all claims and litigation, and all business transactions. My attorney-in-fact is granted full power to act on my behalf in the same manner as if I were personally present.

My attorney-in-fact accepts this appointment and agrees to act in my best interest as he or she considers advisable. This power of attorney may be revoked by me at any time and is automatically revoked on my death. This power of attorney shall not be affected by my present or future disability or incapacity. My attorney-in-fact shall not be compensated for his or her services nor shall my attorney-in-fact be liable to me, my estate, heirs, successors, or assigns for acting or refraining from acting under this document, except for willful misconduct or gross negligence. Any third party who receives a signed copy of this document may act under it. Revocation of this document is not effective unless a third party has actual knowledge of such revocation.

Designation of Primary Physician

I designate the following physician as my primary physician: _____
(name), of _____ (address).

Organ Donation

In the event of my death, I have placed my initials next to the following part(s) of my body that I wish donated for the purposes that I have *initialed* below:
[   ] any organs or parts **OR**
[   ] eyes   [   ] bone and connective tissue   [   ] skin
[   ] heart   [   ] kidney(s)   [   ] liver
[   ] lung(s)   [   ] pancreas   [   ] other _____
for the purposes of:
[   ] any purpose authorized by law **OR**
[   ] transplantation   [   ] research   [   ] therapy
[   ] medical education   [   ] other limitations _____

Signature

I sign this Advance Health Care Directive, consisting of the following sections, which I have *initialed* below and have elected to adopt:

[   ] Living Will
[   ] Selection of Health Care Agent (Durable Power of Attorney for Health Care)
[   ] Durable Power of Attorney for Financial Affairs
[   ] Designation of Primary Physician
[   ] Organ Donation

BY SIGNING HERE I INDICATE THAT I UNDERSTAND THE PURPOSE AND EFFECT OF THIS DOCUMENT.

Signature _____ Date _____

City, County, and State of Residence _____

Notary Acknowledgment

State of _____
County of _____

On _____ , _____ came before me personally and, under oath, stated that he or she is the person described in the above document and he or she signed the above document in my presence. I declare under penalty of perjury that the person whose name is subscribed to this instrument appears to be of sound mind and under no duress, fraud, or undue influence.

_____
Notary Public
My commission expires _____

Witness Acknowledgment

The declarant is personally known to me and I believe him or her to be of sound mind and under no duress, fraud, or undue influence. I did not sign the declarant's signature above for or at the direction of the declarant and I am not appointed as the health care agent or attorney-in-fact herein. I am at least eighteen (18) years of age and I am not related to the declarant by blood, adoption, or marriage, entitled to any portion of the estate of the declarant according to the laws of intestate succession or under any will of declarant or codicil thereto, or directly financially responsible for declarant's medical care. I am not a health care provider of the declarant or an employee of the health facility in which the declarant is a patient.

Witness Signature _____ Date _____

Printed Name of Witness _____

Witness Signature _____ Date _____

Printed Name of Witness _____

Acceptance of Health Care Agent and Financial Attorney-in-Fact

I accept my appointment as Health Care Agent:

Signature _____ Date _____

I accept my appointment as Attorney-in-Fact for Financial Affairs:

Signature _____ Date _____

Montana Advance Health Care Directive

On this date of _____ , I, _____ , do hereby sign, execute, and adopt the following as my Advance Health Care Directive. I direct any and all persons or entities involved with my health care in any manner that these decisions are my wishes and were adopted without duress or force and of my own free will. I have placed my *initials* next to the sections of this Directive that I have adopted:

[   ] Living Will
[   ] Selection of Health Care Agent
[   ] Durable Power of Attorney for Financial Affairs
[   ] Designation of Primary Physician
[   ] Organ Donation

Living Will Declaration

If I should have an incurable or irreversible condition that, without the administration of life-sustaining treatment, will, in the opinion of my attending physician, cause my death within a relatively short time and I am no longer able to make decisions regarding my medical treatment, I direct my attending physician, pursuant to the Montana Rights of the Terminally Ill Act, to withhold or withdraw treatment that only prolongs the process of dying and is not necessary to my comfort or to alleviate pain.

Selection of Health Care Agent

If I should have an incurable and irreversible condition that, without the administration of life-sustaining treatment, will, in the opinion of my attending physician, cause my death within a relatively short time and I am no longer able to make decisions regarding my medical treatment, I appoint _____ (name), of _____ _____(address), to make decisions on my behalf regarding withholding or withdrawal of treatment that only prolongs the process of dying and is not necessary for my comfort or to alleviate pain, pursuant to the Montana Rights of the Terminally Ill Act. If the individual I have appointed is not reasonably available or is unwilling to serve, I direct my attending physician, pursuant to the Montana Rights of the Terminally Ill Act, to withhold or withdraw treatment that only prolongs the process of dying and is not necessary for my comfort or to alleviate pain.

Durable Power of Attorney for Financial Affairs

I, _____ , grant a durable power of attorney for financial affairs to _____ (name), of _____ _____ (address), to act as my attorney-in-fact. This power of attorney shall become effective upon my disability, as certified by my primary physician or, if my primary physician is not available, by any other attending physician. This power of attorney grants no power or authority regarding health care decisions to my designated attorney-in-fact.

I give my attorney-in-fact the maximum power under law to perform the following specific acts on my behalf: all acts relating to any and all of my financial and/or business affairs, including all banking and financial institution transactions, all real estate transactions, all insurance and annuity transactions, all claims and litigation, and all business transactions. My attorney-in-fact is granted full power to act on my behalf in the same manner as if I were personally present.

My attorney-in-fact accepts this appointment and agrees to act in my best interest as he or she considers advisable. This power of attorney may be revoked by me at any time and is automatically revoked on my death. This power of attorney shall not be affected by my present or future disability or incapacity. My attorney-in-fact shall not be compensated for his or her services nor shall my attorney-in-fact be liable to me, my estate, heirs, successors, or assigns for acting or refraining from acting under this document, except for willful misconduct or gross negligence. Any third party who receives a signed copy of this document may act under it. Revocation of this document is not effective unless a third party has actual knowledge of such revocation.

Designation of Primary Physician

I designate the following physician as my primary physician: _____ (name), of _____ (address).

Organ Donation

In the event of my death, I have placed my initials next to the following part(s) of my body that I wish donated for the purposes that I have *initialed* below:

[   ] any organs or parts **OR**

[ ] eyes	[ ] bone and connective tissue	[ ] skin
[ ] heart	[ ] kidney(s)	[ ] liver
[ ] lung(s)	[ ] pancreas	[ ] other _____

for the purposes of:

[   ] any purpose authorized by law **OR**

[ ] transplantation	[ ] research	[ ] therapy
[ ] medical education	[ ] other limitations _____	

Signature

I sign this Advance Health Care Directive, consisting of the following sections, which I have *initialed* below and have elected to adopt:

[   ] Living Will
[   ] Selection of Health Care Agent
[   ] Durable Power of Attorney for Financial Affairs
[   ] Designation of Primary Physician
[   ] Organ Donation
BY SIGNING HERE I INDICATE THAT I UNDERSTAND THE PURPOSE AND EFFECT OF THIS DOCUMENT.

Signature _____ Date _____

City, County, and State of Residence _____

Notary Acknowledgment

State of _____
County of _____

On _____ , _____ came before me personally and, under oath, stated that he or she is the person described in the above document and he or she signed the above document in my presence. I declare under penalty of perjury that the person whose name is subscribed to this instrument appears to be of sound mind and under no duress, fraud, or undue influence.

_____
Notary Public
My commission expires _____

Witness Acknowledgment

The declarant is personally known to me and I believe him or her to be of sound mind and under no duress, fraud, or undue influence. I did not sign the declarant's signature above for or at the direction of the declarant and I am not appointed as the health care agent or attorney-in-fact herein. I am at least eighteen (18) years of age and I am not related to the declarant by blood, adoption, or marriage, entitled to any portion of the estate of the declarant according to the laws of intestate succession or under any will of declarant or codicil thereto, or directly financially responsible for declarant's medical care. I am not a health care provider of the declarant or an employee of the health facility in which the declarant is a patient.

Witness Signature _____ Date _____

Printed Name of Witness _____

Witness Signature _____ Date _____

Printed Name of Witness _____

Acceptance of Health Care Agent and Financial Attorney-in-Fact

I accept my appointment as Health Care Agent:

Signature _____ Date _____

I accept my appointment as Attorney-in-Fact for Financial Affairs:

Signature _____ Date _____

Nebraska Advance Health Care Directive

On this date of _____ , I, _____ , do hereby sign, execute, and adopt the following as my Advance Health Care Directive. I direct any and all persons or entities involved with my health care in any manner that these decisions are my wishes and were adopted without duress or force and of my own free will. I have placed my *initials* next to the sections of this Directive that I have adopted:

[   ] Living Will
[   ] Selection of Health Care Agent (Power of Attorney for Health Care)
[   ] Durable Power of Attorney for Financial Affairs
[   ] Designation of Primary Physician
[   ] Organ Donation

Living Will Declaration

If I should lapse into a persistent vegetative state or have an incurable and irreversible condition that, without the administration of life-sustaining treatment, will, in the opinion of my attending physician, cause my death within a relatively short time and I am no longer able to make decisions regarding my medical treatment, I direct my attending physician, pursuant to the Rights of the Terminally Ill Act, to withhold or withdraw life sustaining treatment that is not necessary for my comfort or to alleviate pain.

Selection of Health Care Agent (Power of Attorney for Health Care)

I appoint _____ (name), of _____
_____ (address), as my attorney-in-fact for health care. I authorize my attorney-in-fact appointed by this document to make health care decisions for me when I am determined to be incapable of making my own health care decisions. I have read the warning which accompanies this document and understand the consequences of executing a power of attorney for health care. I direct that my attorney-in-fact comply with the following instructions or limitations on the following page:

I direct that my attorney-in-fact comply with the following instructions on life-sustaining treatment (*optional*):

I direct that my attorney-in-fact comply with the following instructions on artificially-administered nutrition and hydration (*optional*):

I have read this power of attorney for health care. I understand that it allows another person to make life and death decisions for me if I am incapable of making such decisions. I also understand that I can revoke this power of attorney for health care at any time by notifying my attorney-in-fact, my physician, or the facility in which I am a patient or resident. I also understand that I can require in this power of attorney for health care that the fact of my incapacity in the future be confirmed by a second physician.

Durable Power of Attorney for Financial Affairs

I, _____ , grant a durable power of attorney for financial affairs to _____ (name), of _____ _____ (address), to act as my attorney-in-fact. This power of attorney shall become effective upon my disability, as certified by my primary physician or, if my primary physician is not available, by any other attending physician. This power of attorney grants no power or authority regarding health care decisions to my designated attorney-in-fact.

I give my attorney-in-fact the maximum power under law to perform the following specific acts on my behalf: all acts relating to any and all of my financial and/or business affairs, including all banking and financial institution transactions, all real estate transactions, all insurance and annuity transactions, all claims and litigation, and all business transactions. My attorney-in-fact is granted full power to act on my behalf in the same manner as if I were personally present.

My attorney-in-fact accepts this appointment and agrees to act in my best interest as he or she considers advisable. This power of attorney may be revoked by me at any time and is automatically revoked on my death. This power of attorney shall not be affected by my present or future disability or incapacity. My attorney-in-fact shall not be compensated for his or her services nor shall my attorney-in-fact be liable to me, my estate, heirs, successors, or assigns for acting or refraining from acting under this document, except for willful misconduct or gross negligence. Any third party who receives a signed copy of this document may act under it. Revocation of this document is not effective unless a third party has actual knowledge of such revocation.

Designation of Primary Physician

I designate the following physician as my primary physician: _____
(name), of _____ (address).

Organ Donation

In the event of my death, I have placed my initials next to the following part(s) of my body that I wish donated for the purposes that I have *initialed* below:

[   ] any organs or parts **OR**

[   ] eyes   [   ] bone and connective tissue   [   ] skin

[   ] heart   [   ] kidney(s)   [   ] liver

[   ] lung(s)   [   ] pancreas   [   ] other _____

for the purposes of:

[   ] any purpose authorized by law **OR**

[   ] transplantation   [   ] research   [   ] therapy

[   ] medical education   [   ] other limitations _____

Signature

I sign this Advance Health Care Directive, consisting of the following sections, which I have *initialed* below and have elected to adopt:

[   ] Living Will

[   ] Selection of Health Care Agent (Power of Attorney for Health Care)

[   ] Durable Power of Attorney for Financial Affairs

[   ] Designation of Primary Physician

[   ] Organ Donation

BY SIGNING HERE I INDICATE THAT I UNDERSTAND THE PURPOSE AND EFFECT OF THIS DOCUMENT.

Signature _____ Date _____

City, County, and State of Residence _____

Notary Acknowledgment

State of _____

County of _____

On _____ , _____ came before me personally and, under oath, stated that he or she is the person described in the above document and he or she signed the above document in my presence. I declare under penalty of perjury that the person whose name is subscribed to this instrument appears to be of sound mind and under no duress, fraud, or undue influence.

_____

Notary Public

My commission expires _____

Witness Acknowledgment

The declarant is personally known to me and I believe him or her to be of sound mind and under no duress, fraud, or undue influence. I did not sign the declarant's signature above for or at the direction of the declarant and I am not appointed as the health care agent or attorney-in-fact herein. I am at least eighteen (18) years of age and I am not related to the declarant by blood, adoption, or marriage, entitled to any portion of the estate of the declarant according to the laws of intestate succession or under any will of declarant or codicil thereto, or directly financially responsible for declarant's medical care. I am not a health care provider of the declarant or an employee of the health facility in which the declarant is a patient.

Witness Signature _____   Date _____

Printed Name of Witness _____

Witness Signature _____   Date _____

Printed Name of Witness _____

Acceptance of Health Care Agent and Financial Attorney-in-Fact

I accept my appointment as Health Care Agent:

Signature _____   Date _____

I accept my appointment as Attorney-in-Fact for Financial Affairs:

Signature _____   Date _____

Nevada Advance Health Care Directive

On this date of _____ , I, _____ , do hereby sign, execute, and adopt the following as my Advance Health Care Directive. I direct any and all persons or entities involved with my health care in any manner that these decisions are my wishes and were adopted without duress or force and of my own free will. I have placed my *initials* next to the sections of this Directive that I have adopted:

[   ]   Living Will
[   ]   Selection of Health Care Agent (Durable Power of Attorney for Health Care Decisions)
[   ]   Durable Power of Attorney for Financial Affairs
[   ]   Designation of Primary Physician
[   ]   Organ Donation

Living Will Declaration

If I should have an incurable and irreversible condition that, without the administration of life-sustaining treatment, will, in the opinion of my attending physician, cause my death within a relatively short time, and I am no longer able to make decisions regarding my medical treatment, I direct my attending physician, pursuant to NRS 449.535 to 449.690, inclusive, to withhold or withdraw treatment that only prolongs the process of dying and is not necessary for my comfort or to alleviate pain.

If you wish to include this statement in this declaration, you must *initial* the statement in the box provided:
[   ] Withholding or withdrawal of artificial nutrition and hydration may result in death by starvation or dehydration. *Initial* this box if you want to receive or continue receiving artificial nutrition and hydration by way of the gastro-intestinal tract after all other treatment is withheld pursuant to this declaration.

Selection of Health Care Agent
(Durable Power of Attorney for Health Care Decisions)

If I should have an incurable and irreversible condition that, without the administration of life-sustaining treatment, will, in the opinion of my attending physician, cause my death within a relatively short time, and I am no longer able to make decisions regarding my medical treatment, I appoint _____ (name), of _____ _____ (address), to act as my attorney-in-fact for all health care decisions and to make all decisions on my behalf regarding withholding or withdrawal of treatment that only prolongs the process of dying and is not necessary for my comfort or to alleviate pain, pursuant to NRS 449.535 to 449.690, inclusive. (If the person I have so appointed is not reasonably available or is unwilling to serve, I direct my attending physician, pursuant to those sections, to withhold or withdraw treatment that only prolongs the process of dying and is not necessary for my comfort or to alleviate pain.) [*Strike language in parentheses if you do not desire it.*]

If you wish to include this statement in this declaration, you must *initial* the statement in the box provided:

[   ] Withholding or withdrawal of artificial nutrition and hydration may result in death by starvation or dehydration. *Initial* this box if you want to receive or continue receiving artificial nutrition and hydration by way of the gastro-intestinal tract after all other treatment is withheld pursuant to this declaration.

I understand the consequences of executing a power of attorney for health care. I have read this power of attorney for health care. I understand that it allows another person to make life and death decisions for me if I am incapable of making such decisions. I also understand that I can revoke this power of attorney for health care at any time by notifying my attorney-in-fact, my physician, or the facility in which I am a patient or resident. I also understand that I can require in this power of attorney for health care that the fact of my incapacity in the future be confirmed by a second physician.

Durable Power of Attorney for Financial Affairs

I, _____ , grant a durable power of attorney for financial affairs to _____ (name), of _____
_____ (address), to act as my attorney-in-fact. This power of attorney shall become effective upon my disability, as certified by my primary physician or, if my primary physician is not available, by any other attending physician. This power of attorney grants no power or authority regarding health care decisions to my designated attorney-in-fact.

I give my attorney-in-fact the maximum power under law to perform the following specific acts on my behalf: all acts relating to any and all of my financial and/or business affairs, including all banking and financial institution transactions, all real estate transactions, all insurance and annuity transactions, all claims and litigation, and all business transactions. My attorney-in-fact is granted full power to act on my behalf in the same manner as if I were personally present.

My attorney-in-fact accepts this appointment and agrees to act in my best interest as he or she considers advisable. This power of attorney may be revoked by me at any time and is automatically revoked on my death. This power of attorney shall not be affected by my present or future disability or incapacity. My attorney-in-fact shall not be compensated for his or her services nor shall my attorney-in-fact be liable to me, my estate, heirs, successors, or assigns for acting or refraining from acting under this document, except for willful misconduct or gross negligence. Any third party who receives a signed copy of this document may act under it. Revocation of this document is not effective unless a third party has actual knowledge of such revocation.

Designation of Primary Physician

I designate the following physician as my primary physician: _____ (name), of _____ (address).

Organ Donation

In the event of my death, I have placed my initials next to the following part(s) of my body that I wish donated for the purposes that I have *initialed* below:

[   ] any organs or parts **OR**

[   ] eyes   [   ] bone and connective tissue   [   ] skin

[   ] heart   [   ] kidney(s)   [   ] liver

[   ] lung(s)   [   ] pancreas   [   ] other _____

for the purposes of:

[   ] any purpose authorized by law **OR**

[   ] transplantation   [   ] research   [   ] therapy

[   ] medical education   [   ] other limitations _____

Signature

I sign this Advance Health Care Directive, consisting of the following sections, which I have *initialed* below and have elected to adopt:

[   ]   Living Will

[   ]   Selection of Health Care Agent (Durable Power of Attorney for Health Care Decisions)

[   ]   Durable Power of Attorney for Financial Affairs

[   ]   Designation of Primary Physician

[   ]   Organ Donation

BY SIGNING HERE I INDICATE THAT I UNDERSTAND THE PURPOSE AND EFFECT OF THIS DOCUMENT.

Signature _____ Date _____

City, County, and State of Residence _____

Notary Acknowledgment

State of _____

County of _____

On _____ , _____ came before me personally and, under oath, stated that he or she is the person described in the above document and he or she signed the above document in my presence. I declare under penalty of perjury that the person whose name is subscribed to this instrument appears to be of sound mind and under no duress, fraud, or undue influence.

_____
Notary Public
My commission expires _____

Witness Acknowledgment

The declarant is personally known to me and I believe him or her to be of sound mind and under no duress, fraud, or undue influence. I did not sign the declarant's signature above for or at the direction of the declarant and I am not appointed as the health care agent or attorney-in-fact herein. I am at least eighteen (18) years of age and I am not related to the declarant by blood, adoption, or marriage, entitled to any portion of the estate of the declarant according to the laws of intestate succession or under any will of declarant or codicil thereto, or directly financially responsible for declarant's medical care. I am not a health care provider of the declarant or an employee of the health facility in which the declarant is a patient.

Witness Signature _____   Date _____

Printed Name of Witness _____

Witness Signature _____   Date _____

Printed Name of Witness _____

Acceptance of Health Care Agent and Financial Attorney-in-Fact

I accept my appointment as Health Care Agent:

Signature _____   Date _____

I accept my appointment as Attorney-in-Fact for Financial Affairs:

Signature _____   Date _____

New Hampshire Advance Health Care Directive

On this date of _____ , I, _____ , do hereby sign, execute, and adopt the following as my Advance Health Care Directive. I direct any and all persons or entities involved with my health care in any manner that these decisions are my wishes and were adopted without duress or force and of my own free will. I have placed my *initials* next to the sections of this Directive that I have adopted:

[   ] Living Will
[   ] Selection of Health Care Agent (Durable Power of Attorney for Health Care)
[   ] Durable Power of Attorney for Financial Affairs
[   ] Designation of Primary Physician
[   ] Organ Donation

Living Will Declaration

I, _____ , being of sound mind, willfully and voluntarily make known my desire that my dying shall not be artificially prolonged under the circumstances set forth below, and do hereby declare:

If at any time I should have an incurable injury, disease, or illness certified to be a terminal condition or a permanently-unconscious condition by two (2) physicians who have personally examined me, one of whom shall be my attending physician, and the physicians have determined that my death will occur whether or not life-sustaining procedures are utilized or that I will remain in a permanently-unconscious condition and where the application of life-sustaining procedures would serve only to artificially prolong the dying process, I direct that such procedures be withheld or withdrawn, and that I be permitted to die naturally with only the administration of medication, sustenance, or the performance of any medical procedure deemed necessary to provide me with comfort care. I realize that situations could arise in which the only way to allow me to die would be to discontinue artificial nutrition and hydration.

In carrying out any instruction I have given under this section, I authorize that (*initial your choice*):

[   ] Artificial nutrition and hydration should NOT be started or, if started, be discontinued.

[   ] Artificial nutrition and hydration SHOULD be provided and not be removed.

In the absence of my ability to give directions regarding the use of such life-sustaining procedures, it is my intention that this declaration shall be honored by my family and physicians as the final expression of my right to refuse medical or surgical treatment and to accept the consequences of such refusal. I understand the full import of this declaration and I am emotionally and mentally competent to make this declaration.

Selection of Health Care Agent
(Durable Power of Attorney for Health Care)

I, _____ , hereby appoint _____
(name), of _____ (address),
as my agent to make any and all health care decisions for me, except to the extent I state
otherwise in this document or as prohibited by law. This durable power of attorney for health
care shall take effect in the event I become unable to make my own health care decisions.

STATEMENT OF DESIRES, SPECIAL PROVISIONS, AND LIMITATIONS REGARD-
ING HEALTH CARE DECISIONS.

For your convenience in expressing your wishes, some general statements concerning the withholding or removal of life-sustaining treatment are set forth below. (Life-
sustaining treatment is defined as procedures without which a person would die,
such as, but not limited to the following: cardiopulmonary resuscitation, mechanical
respiration, kidney dialysis or the use of other external mechanical and technological devices, drugs to maintain blood pressure, blood transfusions, and antibiotics.)
There is also a section which allows you to set forth specific directions for these or
other matters. If you wish, you may indicate your agreement or disagreement with
any of the following statements and give your agent power to act in those specific
circumstances.

(*Initial your choices*):

[   ]   If I become permanently incompetent to make health care decisions, and if I am also
suffering from a terminal illness, I authorize my agent to direct that life-sustaining treatment
be discontinued.

[   ]   Whether terminally ill or not, if I become permanently unconscious, I authorize my
agent to direct that life-sustaining treatment be discontinued.

[   ]   I realize that situations could arise in which the only way to allow me to die would be
to discontinue artificial feeding (artificial nutrition and hydration). In carrying out any instruction I have given under this section, I authorize that (*initial your choice*):

>   (*If you fail to complete this section, your agent will not have the power to direct the
>   withdrawal of artificial nutrition and hydration*):

>   [   ]   Artificial nutrition and hydration should NOT be started or, if started, be dis-
>   continued.

>   [   ]   Artificial nutrition and hydration SHOULD be provided and not be removed.

Here you may include any specific desires or limitations you deem appropriate, such as when or what life-sustaining treatment you would want used or withheld, or instructions about refusing any specific types of treatment that are inconsistent with your religious beliefs or unacceptable to you for any other reason. You may leave this question blank if you desire (*attach additional pages as necessary*):

I hereby acknowledge that I have been provided with a disclosure statement explaining the effect of this document. I have read and understand the information contained in the disclosure statement.

Durable Power of Attorney for Financial Affairs

I, _____ , grant a durable power of attorney for financial affairs to _____ (name), of _____ _____ (address), to act as my attorney-in-fact. This power of attorney shall become effective upon my disability, as certified by my primary physician or, if my primary physician is not available, by any other attending physician. This power of attorney grants no power or authority regarding health care decisions to my designated attorney-in-fact.

I give my attorney-in-fact the maximum power under law to perform the following specific acts on my behalf: all acts relating to any and all of my financial and/or business affairs, including all banking and financial institution transactions, all real estate transactions, all insurance and annuity transactions, all claims and litigation, and all business transactions. My attorney-in-fact is granted full power to act on my behalf in the same manner as if I were personally present.

My attorney-in-fact accepts this appointment and agrees to act in my best interest as he or she considers advisable. This power of attorney may be revoked by me at any time and is automatically revoked on my death. This power of attorney shall not be affected by my present or future disability or incapacity. My attorney-in-fact shall not be compensated for his or her services nor shall my attorney-in-fact be liable to me, my estate, heirs, successors, or assigns for acting or refraining from acting under this document, except for willful misconduct or gross negligence. Any third party who receives a signed copy of this document may act under it. Revocation of this document is not effective unless a third party has actual knowledge of such revocation.

Designation of Primary Physician

I designate the following physician as my primary physician: _____
(name), of _____ (address).

Organ Donation

In the event of my death, I have placed my initials next to the following part(s) of my body that I wish donated for the purposes that I have *initialed* below:

[   ] any organs or parts **OR**

[   ] eyes   [   ] bone and connective tissue   [   ] skin

[   ] heart   [   ] kidney(s)   [   ] liver

[   ] lung(s)   [   ] pancreas   [   ] other _____

for the purposes of:

[   ] any purpose authorized by law **OR**

[   ] transplantation   [   ] research   [   ] therapy

[   ] medical education   [   ] other limitations _____

Signature

I sign this Advance Health Care Directive, consisting of the following sections, which I have *initialed* below and have elected to adopt:

[   ] Living Will

[   ] Selection of Health Care Agent (Durable Power of Attorney for Health Care)

[   ] Durable Power of Attorney for Financial Affairs

[   ] Designation of Primary Physician

[   ] Organ Donation

BY SIGNING HERE I INDICATE THAT I UNDERSTAND THE PURPOSE AND EFFECT OF THIS DOCUMENT.

Signature _____ Date _____

City, County, and State of Residence _____

Notary Acknowledgment

State of _____

County of _____

On _____ , _____ came before me personally and, under oath, stated that he or she is the person described in the above document and he or she signed the above document in my presence. I declare under penalty of perjury that the person whose name is subscribed to this instrument appears to be of sound mind and under no duress, fraud, or undue influence.

_____
Notary Public
My commission expires _____

Witness Acknowledgment

The declarant is personally known to me and I believe him or her to be of sound mind and under no duress, fraud, or undue influence. I did not sign the declarant's signature above for or at the direction of the declarant and I am not appointed as the health care agent or attorney-in-fact herein. I am at least eighteen (18) years of age and I am not related to the declarant by blood, adoption, or marriage, entitled to any portion of the estate of the declarant according to the laws of intestate succession or under any will of declarant or codicil thereto, or directly financially responsible for declarant's medical care. I am not a health care provider of the declarant or an employee of the health facility in which the declarant is a patient.

Witness Signature _____ Date _____

Printed Name of Witness _____

Witness Signature _____ Date _____

Printed Name of Witness _____

Acceptance of Health Care Agent and Financial Attorney-in-Fact

I accept my appointment as Health Care Agent:

Signature _____ Date _____

I accept my appointment as Attorney-in-Fact for Financial Affairs:

Signature _____ Date _____

New Jersey Advance Health Care Directive

On this date of _____ , I, _____ , do hereby sign, execute, and adopt the following as my Advance Health Care Directive. I direct any and all persons or entities involved with my health care in any manner that these decisions are my wishes and were adopted without duress or force and of my own free will. I have placed my *initials* next to the sections of this Directive that I have adopted:

[   ] Living Will

[   ] Selection of Health Care Agent

[   ] Durable Power of Attorney for Financial Affairs

[   ] Designation of Primary Physician

[   ] Organ Donation

Living Will

If I am incapable of making an informed decision regarding my health care, I direct my loved ones and health care providers to follow my instructions as set forth below:

If I am diagnosed as having an incurable and irreversible illness, disease, or condition and if my attending physician and at least one (1) additional physician who has personally examined me determine that my condition is terminal (*initial all those that apply*):

[   ] I direct that life-sustaining treatment which would serve only to artificially prolong my dying be withheld or ended. I also direct that I be given all medically-appropriate treatment and care necessary to make me comfortable and to relieve pain.

[   ] I direct that life-sustaining treatment be continued, if medically appropriate.

If there should come a time when I become permanently unconscious, and it is determined by my attending physician and at least one (1) additional physician with appropriate expertise who has personally examined me, that I have totally and irreversibly lost consciousness and my ability to interact with other people and my surroundings (*initial all those that apply*):

[   ] I direct that life-sustaining treatment be withheld or discontinued. I understand that I will not experience pain or discomfort in this condition, and I direct that I be given all medically-appropriate treatment and care necessary to provide for my personal hygiene and dignity.

[   ] I direct that life-sustaining treatment be continued, if medically appropriate.

If there comes a time when I am diagnosed as having an incurable and irreversible illness, disease, or condition which may not be terminal, but causes me to experience severe and worsening physical or mental deterioration, and I will never regain the ability to make decisions and express my wishes (*initial all those that apply*):

[   ] I direct that life-sustaining measures be withheld or discontinued and that I be given all medically-appropriate care necessary to make me comfortable and to relieve pain.

[   ] I direct that life-sustaining treatment be continued, if medically appropriate.

If I am receiving life-sustaining treatment that is experimental and not a proven therapy, or is likely to be ineffective or futile in prolonging life (*initial all those that apply*):

[   ] I direct that such life-sustaining treatment be withheld or withdrawn. I also direct that I be given all medically-appropriate care necessary to make me comfortable and to relieve pain.

[   ] I direct that life-sustaining treatment be continued, if medically appropriate.

If I am in the condition(s) described above, I feel especially strongly about the following forms of treatment (*initial all those that apply*):

[   ] I do NOT want cardiopulmonary resuscitation (CPR).

[   ] I do NOT want mechanical respiration.

[   ] I do NOT want tube feeding.

[   ] I do NOT want antibiotics.

[   ] I DO want maximum pain relief, even if it may hasten my death.

PREGNANCY: If I am pregnant at the time that I am diagnosed as having any of the conditions described above, I direct that my health care provider comply with following instructions (*optional*):

The State of New Jersey has determined that an individual may be declared legally dead when there has been an irreversible cessation of all functions of the entire brain, including the brain stem (also known as whole-brain death). However, individuals who do not accept this definition of brain death because of their personal religious beliefs may request that it not be applied in determining their death. *Initial* the following statement only if it applies to you:

[   ] To declare my death on the basis of the whole-brain death standard would violate my personal religious beliefs. I therefore wish my death to be declared only when my heartbeat and breathing have irreversibly stopped.

FURTHER INSTRUCTIONS: By writing this advance directive, I inform those who may become responsible for my health care of my wishes and intend to ease the burdens of decision-making which this responsibility may impose. I have discussed the terms of this designation with my health care representative and my representative has willingly agreed to accept the responsibility for acting on my behalf in accordance with this directive and my wishes. I understand the purpose and effect of this document and sign it knowingly, voluntarily, and after careful deliberation.

Selection of Health Care Agent

I, _____ , hereby appoint _____
(name), of _____ (address),
to be my health care representative to make any and all health care decisions for me, including decisions to accept or to refuse any treatment, service, or procedure used to diagnose or treat my physical or mental condition, and decisions to provide, withhold, or withdraw life-sustaining treatment. I direct my health care representative to make decisions on my behalf in accordance with my wishes as stated in this document, or as otherwise known to him or her. In the event my wishes are not clear, or if a situation arises that I did not anticipate, my health care representative is authorized to make decisions in my best interests. I direct that my health care representative comply with the following instructions and/or limitations (*optional*):

I direct that my health care representative comply with the following instructions in the event that I am pregnant when this Directive becomes effective (*optional*):

By writing this advance directive, I inform those who may become responsible for my health care of my wishes and intend to ease the burdens of decisionmaking which this responsibility may impose. I have discussed the terms of this designation with my health care representative and my representative has willingly agreed to accept the responsibility for acting on my behalf in accordance with this directive and my wishes. I understand the purpose and effect of this document and sign it knowingly, voluntarily, and after careful deliberation.

Durable Power of Attorney for Financial Affairs

I, _____ , grant a durable power of attorney for financial affairs
to _____ (name), of _____
_____ (address), to act as my attorney-in-fact. This power of attorney
shall become effective upon my disability, as certified by my primary physician or, if my primary
physician is not available, by any other attending physician. This power of attorney grants no
power or authority regarding health care decisions to my designated attorney-in-fact.

I give my attorney-in-fact the maximum power under law to perform the following specific
acts on my behalf: all acts relating to any and all of my financial and/or business affairs,
including all banking and financial institution transactions, all real estate transactions, all insurance and annuity transactions, all claims and litigation, and all business transactions. My
attorney-in-fact is granted full power to act on my behalf in the same manner as if I were
personally present.

My attorney-in-fact accepts this appointment and agrees to act in my best interest as he or she
considers advisable. This power of attorney may be revoked by me at any time and is automatically revoked on my death. This power of attorney shall not be affected by my present or
future disability or incapacity. My attorney-in-fact shall not be compensated for his or her
services nor shall my attorney-in-fact be liable to me, my estate, heirs, successors, or assigns
for acting or refraining from acting under this document, except for willful misconduct or
gross negligence. Any third party who receives a signed copy of this document may act under
it. Revocation of this document is not effective unless a third party has actual knowledge of
such revocation.

Designation of Primary Physician

I designate the following physician as my primary physician: _____
(name), of _____ (address).

Organ Donation

In the event of my death, I have placed my initials next to the following part(s) of my body that
I wish donated for the purposes that I have *initialed* below:
[   ] any organs or parts **OR**
[   ] eyes   [   ] bone and connective tissue   [   ] skin
[   ] heart   [   ] kidney(s)   [   ] liver
[   ] lung(s)   [   ] pancreas   [   ] other _____
for the purposes of:
[   ] any purpose authorized by law **OR**
[   ] transplantation   [   ] research   [   ] therapy
[   ] medical education   [   ] other limitations _____

Signature

I sign this Advance Health Care Directive, consisting of the following sections, which I have *initialed* below and have elected to adopt:

[   ]   Living Will
[   ]   Selection of Health Care Agent
[   ]   Durable Power of Attorney for Financial Affairs
[   ]   Designation of Primary Physician
[   ]   Organ Donation

BY SIGNING HERE I INDICATE THAT I UNDERSTAND THE PURPOSE AND EF-FECT OF THIS DOCUMENT.

Signature _____   Date _____

City, County, and State of Residence _____

Notary Acknowledgment

State of _____
County of _____

On _____ , _____ came before me per-sonally and, under oath, stated that he or she is the person described in the above document and he or she signed the above document in my presence. I declare under penalty of perjury that the person whose name is subscribed to this instrument appears to be of sound mind and under no duress, fraud, or undue influence.

_____
Notary Public
My commission expires _____

Witness Acknowledgment

The declarant is personally known to me and I believe him or her to be of sound mind and under no duress, fraud, or undue influence. I did not sign the declarant's signature above for or at the direction of the declarant and I am not appointed as the health care agent or attorney-in-fact herein. I am at least eighteen (18) years of age and I am not related to the declarant by blood, adoption, or marriage, entitled to any portion of the estate of the declarant according to the laws of intestate succession or under any will of declarant or codicil thereto, or directly financially responsible for declarant's medical care. I am not a health care provider of the declarant or an employee of the health facility in which the declarant is a patient.

Witness Signature _____   Date _____

Printed Name of Witness _____

Witness Signature _____   Date _____

Printed Name of Witness _____

Acceptance of Health Care Agent and Financial Attorney-in-Fact

I accept my appointment as Health Care Agent:

Signature _____   Date _____

I accept my appointment as Attorney-in-Fact for Financial Affairs:

Signature _____   Date _____

New Mexico Advance Health Care Directive

On this date of _____ , I, _____ , do hereby sign, execute, and adopt the following as my Advance Health Care Directive. I direct any and all persons or entities involved with my health care in any manner that these decisions are my wishes and were adopted without duress or force and of my own free will. I have placed my *initials* next to the sections of this Directive that I have adopted:

[   ] Living Will

[   ] Selection of Health Care Agent (Power of Attorney for Health Care)

[   ] Durable Power of Attorney for Financial Affairs

[   ] Designation of Primary Physician

[   ] Organ Donation

Living Will

If you are satisfied to allow your health care agent to determine what is best for you in making end-of-life decisions, you need not fill out this part of the form. If you do fill out this part of the form, you may cross out any wording you do not want.

If I am unable to make or communicate decisions regarding my health care, and if:

(1) I have an incurable or irreversible condition that will result in my death within a relatively short time, **OR**

(2) I become unconscious and, to a reasonable degree of medical certainty, I will not regain consciousness, **OR**

(3) the likely risks and burdens of treatment would outweigh the expected benefits,

THEN I direct that my health care providers and others involved in my care provide, withhold, or withdraw treatment in accordance with the choice I have *initialed* below in one of the following three (3) boxes that:

[   ] I Choose NOT To Prolong Life. I do not want my life to be prolonged.

[   ] I CHOOSE To Prolong Life. I want my life to be prolonged as long as possible within the limits of generally-accepted health care standards.

[   ] I CHOOSE To Let My Agent Decide. My agent under my power of attorney for health care may make life-sustaining treatment decisions for me.

If I have chosen above NOT to prolong life, I also specify by marking my *initials* below that:

[   ] I do NOT want artificial nutrition, **OR**

[   ] I DO want artificial nutrition.

[   ] I do NOT want artificial hydration unless required for my comfort, **OR**

[   ] I DO want artificial hydration.

Regardless of the choices I have made in this form and except as I state in the following space, I direct that the best medical care possible to keep me clean, comfortable, and free of pain or discomfort be provided at all times so that my dignity is maintained, even if this care hastens my death. I direct that (*if you wish to write your own instructions, or if you wish to add to the instructions you have given above, you may do so here. Add additional sheets if needed*):

A copy of this form has the same effect as the original. I understand that I may revoke this Advance Health Care Directive at any time, and that if I revoke it, I should promptly notify my supervising health care provider and any health care institution where I am receiving care and any others to whom I have given copies of this power of attorney. I understand that I may revoke the designation of an agent either by a signed writing or by personally informing the supervising health care provider.

Selection of Health Care Agent (Power of Attorney for Health Care)

I designate the following individual as my agent to make health care decisions for me _____ _____ (name), of _____ _____ (address). My agent is authorized to obtain and review medical records, reports, and information about me and to make all health care decisions for me, including decisions to provide, withhold, or withdraw artificial nutrition, hydration, and all other forms of health care to keep me alive, except as I state here (*add additional sheets if needed*):

My agent's authority becomes effective when my primary physician and one other qualified health care professional determine that I am unable to make my own health care decisions. If I *initial* this box [   ], my agent's authority to make health care decisions for me takes effect immediately.

My agent shall make health care decisions for me in accordance with this power of attorney for health care, any instructions I give in this Advance Health Care Directive, and my other wishes to the extent known to my agent. To the extent my wishes are unknown, my agent shall make health care decisions for me in accordance with what my agent determines to be in my best interest. In determining my best interest, my agent shall consider my personal values to the extent known to my agent.

If a guardian of my person needs to be appointed for me by a court, I nominate the agent designated in this form.

Durable Power of Attorney for Financial Affairs

I, _____ , grant a durable power of attorney for financial affairs to _____ (name), of _____
_____ (address), to act as my attorney-in-fact. This power of attorney shall become effective upon my disability, as certified by my primary physician or, if my primary physician is not available, by any other attending physician. This power of attorney grants no power or authority regarding health care decisions to my designated attorney-in-fact.

I give my attorney-in-fact the maximum power under law to perform the following specific acts on my behalf: all acts relating to any and all of my financial and/or business affairs, including all banking and financial institution transactions, all real estate transactions, all insurance and annuity transactions, all claims and litigation, and all business transactions. My attorney-in-fact is granted full power to act on my behalf in the same manner as if I were personally present.

My attorney-in-fact accepts this appointment and agrees to act in my best interest as he or she considers advisable. This power of attorney may be revoked by me at any time and is automatically revoked on my death. This power of attorney shall not be affected by my present or future disability or incapacity. My attorney-in-fact shall not be compensated for his or her services nor shall my attorney-in-fact be liable to me, my estate, heirs, successors, or assigns for acting or refraining from acting under this document, except for willful misconduct or gross negligence. Any third party who receives a signed copy of this document may act under it. Revocation of this document is not effective unless a third party has actual knowledge of such revocation.

Designation of Primary Physician

I designate the following physician as my primary physician: _____
(name), of _____ (address).

Organ Donation

In the event of my death, I have placed my initials next to the following part(s) of my body that I wish donated for the purposes that I have *initialed* below:

[   ] any organs or parts **OR**

[   ] eyes   [   ] bone and connective tissue   [   ] skin

[   ] heart   [   ] kidney(s)   [   ] liver

[   ] lung(s)   [   ] pancreas   [   ] other _____

for the purposes of:

[   ] any purpose authorized by law **OR**

[   ] transplantation   [   ] research   [   ] therapy

[   ] medical education   [   ] other limitations _____

Signature

I sign this Advance Health Care Directive, consisting of the following sections, which I have *initialed* below and have elected to adopt:

[   ] Living Will

[   ] Selection of Health Care Agent (Power of Attorney for Health Care)

[   ] Durable Power of Attorney for Financial Affairs

[   ] Designation of Primary Physician

[   ] Organ Donation

BY SIGNING HERE I INDICATE THAT I UNDERSTAND THE PURPOSE AND EFFECT OF THIS DOCUMENT.

Signature _____ Date _____

City, County, and State of Residence _____

Notary Acknowledgment

State of _____

County of _____

On _____ , _____ came before me personally and, under oath, stated that he or she is the person described in the above document and he or she signed the above document in my presence. I declare under penalty of perjury that the person whose name is subscribed to this instrument appears to be of sound mind and under no duress, fraud, or undue influence.

_____

Notary Public

My commission expires _____

Witness Acknowledgment

The declarant is personally known to me and I believe him or her to be of sound mind and under no duress, fraud, or undue influence. I did not sign the declarant's signature above for or at the direction of the declarant and I am not appointed as the health care agent or attorney-in-fact herein. I am at least eighteen (18) years of age and I am not related to the declarant by blood, adoption, or marriage, entitled to any portion of the estate of the declarant according to the laws of intestate succession or under any will of declarant or codicil thereto, or directly financially responsible for declarant's medical care. I am not a health care provider of the declarant or an employee of the health facility in which the declarant is a patient.

Witness Signature _____   Date _____

Printed Name of Witness _____

Witness Signature _____   Date _____

Printed Name of Witness _____

Acceptance of Health Care Agent and Financial Attorney-in-Fact

I accept my appointment as Health Care Agent:

Signature _____   Date _____

I accept my appointment as Attorney-in-Fact for Financial Affairs:

Signature _____   Date _____

New York Advance Health Care Directive

On this date of _____ , I, _____ , do hereby sign, execute, and adopt the following as my Advance Health Care Directive. I direct any and all persons or entities involved with my health care in any manner that these decisions are my wishes and were adopted without duress or force and of my own free will. I have placed my *initials* next to the sections of this Directive that I have adopted:

[   ] Living Will
[   ] Selection of Health Care Agent
[   ] Durable Power of Attorney for Financial Affairs
[   ] Designation of Primary Physician
[   ] Organ Donation

Living Will

I, _____ , being of sound mind, make this statement as a directive to be followed if I become permanently unable to participate in decisions regarding my medical care. These instructions reflect my firm and settled commitment to decline medical treatment under the circumstances indicated below. I direct my attending physician to withhold or withdraw treatment that merely prolongs my dying, if I should be in an incurable or irreversible mental or physical condition with no reasonable expectation of recovery, including but not limited to:

(1) a terminal condition,

(2) a permanently-unconscious condition, **OR**

(3) a minimally-conscious condition in which I am permanently unable to make decisions or express my wishes.

I direct that my treatment be limited to measures to keep me comfortable and to relieve pain, including any pain that might occur by withholding or withdrawing treatment. While I understand that I am not legally required to be specific about future treatments if I am in the condition(s) described above, I feel especially strongly about the following forms of treatment (*initial those that you choose*):

[   ] I do NOT want cardiac resuscitation.
[   ] I do NOT want mechanical respiration.
[   ] I do NOT want artificial nutrition and hydration.
[   ] I do NOT want antibiotics.
[   ] However, I DO want maximum pain relief, even if it may hasten my death.

Other directions (*add instructions and additional pages as needed*):

These directions express my legal right to refuse treatment, under the law of New York. I intend my instructions to be carried out, unless I have rescinded them in a new writing or by clearly indicating that I have changed my mind.

Selection of Health Care Agent

I, _____ , hereby appoint _____ (name), of _____ (address), as my health care agent to make any and all health care decisions for me, except to the extent I state otherwise. This health care proxy shall take effect in the event I become unable to make my own health care decisions. (*NOTE: Although not necessary, and neither encouraged nor discouraged, you may wish to state instructions or wishes, and limit your agent's authority. Unless your agent knows your wishes about artificial nutrition and hydration, he or she will not have the authority to decide about artificial nutrition and hydration. If you choose to state instructions, wishes, or limits, please do so below. Attach additional pages if needed*):

I direct my agent to make health care decisions in accordance with my wishes and instructions as stated above or as otherwise known to him or her. I also direct my agent to abide by any limitations on his or her authority as stated above or as otherwise known to him or her. I understand that, unless I revoke it, this proxy will remain in effect indefinitely.

Durable Power of Attorney for Financial Affairs

I, _____ , grant a durable power of attorney for financial affairs to _____ (name), of _____ _____ (address), to act as my attorney-in-fact. This power of attorney shall become effective upon my disability, as certified by my primary physician or, if my primary physician is not available, by any other attending physician. This power of attorney grants no power or authority regarding health care decisions to my designated attorney-in-fact.

I give my attorney-in-fact the maximum power under law to perform the following specific acts on my behalf: all acts relating to any and all of my financial and/or business affairs, including all banking and financial institution transactions, all real estate transactions, all insurance

and annuity transactions, all claims and litigation, and all business transactions. My attorney-in-fact is granted full power to act on my behalf in the same manner as if I were personally present.

My attorney-in-fact accepts this appointment and agrees to act in my best interest as he or she considers advisable. This power of attorney may be revoked by me at any time and is automatically revoked on my death. This power of attorney shall not be affected by my present or future disability or incapacity. My attorney-in-fact shall not be compensated for his or her services nor shall my attorney-in-fact be liable to me, my estate, heirs, successors, or assigns for acting or refraining from acting under this document, except for willful misconduct or gross negligence. Any third party who receives a signed copy of this document may act under it. Revocation of this document is not effective unless a third party has actual knowledge of such revocation.

Designation of Primary Physician

I designate the following physician as my primary physician: _____
(name), of _____ (address).

Organ Donation

In the event of my death, I have placed my initials next to the following part(s) of my body that I wish donated for the purposes that I have *initialed* below:

[   ] any organs or parts **OR**

[ ] eyes	[ ] bone and connective tissue	[ ] skin
[ ] heart	[ ] kidney(s)	[ ] liver
[ ] lung(s)	[ ] pancreas	[ ] other _____

for the purposes of:

[   ] any purpose authorized by law **OR**

[ ] transplantation	[ ] research	[ ] therapy
[ ] medical education	[ ] other limitations _____	

Signature

I sign this Advance Health Care Directive, consisting of the following sections, which I have *initialed* below and have elected to adopt:

[   ] Living Will
[   ] Selection of Health Care Agent
[   ] Durable Power of Attorney for Financial Affairs
[   ] Designation of Primary Physician
[   ] Organ Donation

BY SIGNING HERE I INDICATE THAT I UNDERSTAND THE PURPOSE AND EFFECT OF THIS DOCUMENT.

Signature _____   Date _____

City, County, and State of Residence _____

Notary Acknowledgment

State of _____

County of _____

On _____ , _____ came before me personally and, under oath, stated that he or she is the person described in the above document and he or she signed the above document in my presence. I declare under penalty of perjury that the person whose name is subscribed to this instrument appears to be of sound mind and under no duress, fraud, or undue influence.

_____

Notary Public
My commission expires _____

Witness Acknowledgment

The declarant is personally known to me and I believe him or her to be of sound mind and under no duress, fraud, or undue influence. I did not sign the declarant's signature above for or at the direction of the declarant and I am not appointed as the health care agent or attorney-in-fact herein. I am at least eighteen (18) years of age and I am not related to the declarant by blood, adoption, or marriage, entitled to any portion of the estate of the declarant according to the laws of intestate succession or under any will of declarant or codicil thereto, or directly financially responsible for declarant's medical care. I am not a health care provider of the declarant or an employee of the health facility in which the declarant is a patient.

Witness Signature _____ Date _____

Printed Name of Witness _____

Witness Signature _____ Date _____

Printed Name of Witness _____

Acceptance of Health Care Agent and Financial Attorney-in-Fact

I accept my appointment as Health Care Agent:

Signature _____ Date _____

I accept my appointment as Attorney-in-Fact for Financial Affairs:

Signature _____ Date _____

North Carolina Advance Health Care Directive

On this date of _____ , I, _____ , do hereby sign, execute, and adopt the following as my Advance Health Care Directive. I direct any and all persons or entities involved with my health care in any manner that these decisions are my wishes and were adopted without duress or force and of my own free will. I have placed my *initials* next to the sections of this Directive that I have adopted:

[   ] Living Will
[   ] Selection of Health Care Agent (Health Care Power of Attorney)
[   ] Durable Power of Attorney for Financial Affairs
[   ] Designation of Primary Physician
[   ] Organ Donation

Living Will

I, _____ , being of sound mind, desire that, as specified below, my life not be prolonged by extraordinary means or by artificial nutrition or hydration if my condition is determined to be terminal and incurable or if I am diagnosed as being in a persistent vegetative state. I am aware and understand that this writing authorizes a physician to withhold or discontinue extraordinary means or artificial nutrition or hydration, in accordance with my specifications set forth below (*initial any of the following, as desired*):

[   ] If my condition is determined to be terminal and incurable, I authorize the following:

    [   ] My physician may withhold or discontinue extraordinary means only.

    [   ] In addition to withholding or discontinuing extraordinary means if such means are necessary, my physician may withhold or discontinue either artificial nutrition or hydration, or both.

[   ] If my physician determines that I am in a persistent vegetative state, I authorize the following:

    [   ] My physician may withhold or discontinue extraordinary means only.

    [   ] In addition to withholding or discontinuing extraordinary means if such means are necessary, my physician may withhold or discontinue either artificial nutrition or hydration, or both.

Selection of Health Care Agent (Health Care Power of Attorney)

NOTICE: This document gives the person you designate as your health care agent broad powers to make health care decisions, including mental health treatment decisions for you. Except to the extent that you express specific limitations or restrictions on the authority of your health care agent, this power includes the power to consent to your doctor not giving treatment or stopping treatment necessary to keep you alive, admit you to a facility, and administer certain treatments and medications. This power exists only as to those health care decisions for which you are unable to give informed consent. This form does not impose a duty on your health care agent to exercise granted powers, but when a power is exercised, your health care agent will have to use due care to act in your best interests and in accordance with this document. For mental health treatment decisions, your health care agent will act according to how the health agent believes you would act if you were making the decision. This health care power of attorney may be revoked by you at any time in any manner by which you are able to communicate your intent to revoke to your health care agent and your attending physician. Because the powers granted by this document are broad and sweeping, you should discuss your wishes concerning life-sustaining procedures, mental health treatment, and other health care decisions with your health care agent. Use of this form in the creation of a health care power of attorney is lawful and is authorized pursuant to North Carolina law. However, use of this form is an optional and nonexclusive method for creating a health care power of attorney and North Carolina law does not bar the use of any other or different form of power of attorney for health care that meets the statutory requirements.

I, _____ , being of sound mind, hereby appoint _____ _____ (name), of _____ _____ (address), as my health care attorney-in-fact (herein referred to as my "health care agent") to act for me and in my name (in any way I could act in person) to make health care decisions for me as authorized in this document.

Absent revocation, the authority granted in this document shall become effective when and if the physician or physicians designated below determine that I lack sufficient understanding or capacity to make or communicate decisions relating to my health care and will continue in effect during my incapacity, until my death. This determination shall be made by the following physician or physicians (*you may include here a designation of your choice, including your attending physician or eligible psychologist, or any other physician or eligible psychologist. You may also name two or more physicians or eligible psychologists, if desired, both of whom must make this determination before the authority granted to the health care agent becomes effective. Attach additional sheets if needed*):

_____ (name), of _____
_____(address)

_____ (name), of _____
_____(address)

_____ (name), of _____
_____(address)

For decisions related to mental health treatment, this determination shall be made by the following physician or eligible psychologist (*include here a designation of your choice*):

_____ (name), of _____
_____(address)

Except as indicated below, I hereby grant to my health care agent named above full power and authority to make health care decisions, including mental health treatment decisions, on my behalf, including, but not limited to, the following (*initial your choices*):

[　　] (1) To request, review, and receive any information, verbal or written, regarding my physical or mental health, including, but not limited to medical and hospital records, and to consent to the disclosure of this information,

[　　] (2) To employ or discharge my health care providers,

[　　] (3) To consent to and authorize my admission to and discharge from a hospital, nursing or convalescent home, or other institution,

[　　] (4) To consent to and authorize my admission to and retention in a facility for the care or treatment of mental illness,

[　　] (5) To consent to and authorize the administration of medications for mental health treatment and electroconvulsive treatment (ECT), commonly referred to as "shock treatment,"

[　　] (6) To give consent for, withdraw consent for, or withhold consent for x-ray, anesthesia, medication, surgery, and all other diagnostic and treatment procedures ordered by or under the authorization of a licensed physician, dentist, or podiatrist. This authorization specifically includes the power to consent to measures for relief of pain,

[　　] (7) To authorize the withholding or withdrawal of life-sustaining procedures when and if my physician determines that I am terminally ill, am permanently in a coma, suffer severe dementia, or am in a persistent vegetative state. I desire that my life NOT be prolonged by life-sustaining procedures if I am terminally ill, am permanently in a coma, suffer severe dementia, or am in a persistent vegetative state. (*Life-sustaining procedures are those forms of medical care that only serve to artificially prolong the dying process and may include mechanical ventilation, dialysis, antibiotics, artificial nutrition and hydration, and other forms of medical treatment which sustain, restore, or supplant vital bodily functions. Life-sustaining procedures do not include care necessary to provide comfort or alleviate pain.*)

[　　] (8) To exercise any right I may have to make a disposition of any part or all of my body for medical purposes, donate my organs, authorize an autopsy, and direct the disposition of my remains,

[　　] (9) To take any lawful actions that may be necessary to carry out these decisions, including the granting of releases of liability to medical providers.

NOTICE: The grant of power on the previous page is intended to be as broad as possible so that your health care agent will have authority to make any decisions you could make to obtain or terminate any type of health care. If you wish to limit the scope of your health care agent's powers, you may do so in this section.

In exercising the authority to make health care decisions on my behalf, the authority of my health care agent is subject to the following special provisions and limitations (*here you may include any specific limitations you deem appropriate such as: your own definition of when life-sustaining treatment should be withheld or discontinued, or instructions to refuse any specific types of treatment that are inconsistent with your religious beliefs or unacceptable to you for any other reason. Attach additional pages if needed):*

In exercising the authority to make mental health decisions on my behalf, the authority of my health care agent is subject to the following special provisions and limitations (*here you may include any specific limitations you deem appropriate such as: limiting the grant of authority to make only mental health treatment decisions, your own instructions regarding the administration or withholding of psychotropic medications and electroconvulsive treatment (ECT), instructions regarding your admission to and retention in a health care facility for mental health treatment, or instructions to refuse any specific types of treatment that are unacceptable to you. Attach additional pages as needed):*

NOTICE: This health care power of attorney may incorporate or be combined with an advance instruction for mental health treatment, executed in accordance with Part 2 of Article 3 of Chapter 122C of the North Carolina General Statutes, which you may use to state your instructions regarding mental health treatment in the event you lack sufficient understanding or capacity to make or communicate mental health treatment decisions. Because your health care agent's decisions must be consistent with any statements you have expressed in an advance instruction, you should indicate here whether you have executed an advance instruction for mental health treatment (*indicate your actions and attach additional pages if needed*):

If it becomes necessary for a court to appoint a guardian of my person, I nominate my health care agent acting under this document to be the guardian of my person and to serve without bond or security. The guardian shall act consistently with N.C.G.S. 35A-1201(a)(5).

No person who relies in good faith upon the authority of or any representations by my health care agent shall be liable to me or my estate, heirs, successors, assigns, or personal representatives, for actions or omissions by my health care agent. The powers conferred on my health care agent by this document may be exercised by my health care agent alone, and my health care agent's signature or act under the authority granted in this document may be accepted by persons as fully authorized by me and with the same force and effect as if I were personally present, competent, and acting on my own behalf. All acts performed in good faith by my health care agent pursuant to this power of attorney are done with my consent and shall have the same validity and effect as if I were present and exercised the powers myself, and shall inure to the benefit of and bind me or my estate, heirs, successors, assigns, and personal representatives. The authority of my health care agent pursuant to this power of attorney shall be superior to and binding upon my family, relatives, friends, and others.

I revoke any prior health care power of attorney. My health care agent shall be entitled to sign, execute, deliver, and acknowledge any contract or other document that may be necessary, desirable, convenient, or proper in order to exercise and carry out any of the powers described in this document and incur reasonable costs on my behalf, incident to the exercise of these powers; provided, however, that except as shall be necessary in order to exercise the powers described in this document relating to my health care, my health care agent shall not have any authority over my property or financial affairs. My health care agent and his or her estate, heirs, successors, and assigns are hereby released and forever discharged by me or my estate, heirs, successors, assigns, and personal representatives from all liability and claims or demands of all kinds arising out of the acts or omissions of my health care agent pursuant to this document, except for willful misconduct or gross negligence. No act or omission of my health care agent, any other person, institution, or facility acting in good faith in reliance on the authority of my health care agent pursuant to this health care power of attorney shall be considered suicide, nor the cause of my death for any civil or criminal purposes, nor shall it be considered unprofessional conduct or as lack of professional competence. Any person, institution, or facility against whom criminal or civil liability is asserted because of conduct authorized by this health care power of attorney may interpose this document as a defense.

Durable Power of Attorney for Financial Affairs

I, _____ , grant a durable power of attorney for financial affairs to _____ (name), of _____ _____ (address), to act as my attorney-in-fact. This power of attorney shall become effective upon my disability, as certified by my primary physician or, if my primary physician is not available, by any other attending physician. This power of attorney grants no power or authority regarding health care decisions to my designated attorney-in-fact.

I give my attorney-in-fact the maximum power under law to perform the following specific acts on my behalf: all acts relating to any and all of my financial and/or business affairs, including all banking and financial institution transactions, all real estate transactions, all insurance and annuity transactions, all claims and litigation, and all business transactions. My attorney-in-fact is granted full power to act on my behalf in the same manner as if I were personally present.

My attorney-in-fact accepts this appointment and agrees to act in my best interest as he or she considers advisable. This power of attorney may be revoked by me at any time and is automatically revoked on my death. This power of attorney shall not be affected by my present or future disability or incapacity. My attorney-in-fact shall not be compensated for his or her services nor shall my attorney-in-fact be liable to me, my estate, heirs, successors, or assigns for acting or refraining from acting under this document, except for willful misconduct or gross negligence. Any third party who receives a signed copy of this document may act under it. Revocation of this document is not effective unless a third party has actual knowledge of such revocation.

Designation of Primary Physician

I designate the following physician as my primary physician: _____
(name), of _____ (address).

Organ Donation

In the event of my death, I have placed my initials next to the following part(s) of my body that I wish donated for the purposes that I have *initialed* below:

[   ] any organs or parts **OR**

[   ] eyes   [   ] bone and connective tissue   [   ] skin

[   ] heart   [   ] kidney(s)   [   ] liver

[   ] lung(s)   [   ] pancreas   [   ] other _____

for the purposes of:

[   ] any purpose authorized by law **OR**

[   ] transplantation   [   ] research   [   ] therapy

[   ] medical education   [   ] other limitations _____

Signature

I sign this Advance Health Care Directive, consisting of the following sections, which I have *initialed* below and have elected to adopt:

[   ] Living Will

[   ] Selection of Health Care Agent (Health Care Power of Attorney)

[   ] Durable Power of Attorney for Financial Affairs

[   ] Designation of Primary Physician

[   ] Organ Donation

BY SIGNING HERE I INDICATE THAT I UNDERSTAND THE PURPOSE AND EFFECT OF THIS DOCUMENT.

Signature _____   Date _____

City, County, and State of Residence _____

Notary Acknowledgment

State of _____

County of _____

On _____ , _____ came before me personally and, under oath, stated that he or she is the person described in the above document and he or she signed the above document in my presence. I declare under penalty of perjury that the person whose name is subscribed to this instrument appears to be of sound mind and under no duress, fraud, or undue influence.

_____
Notary Public
My commission expires _____

Witness Acknowledgment

The declarant is personally known to me and I believe him or her to be of sound mind and under no duress, fraud, or undue influence. I did not sign the declarant's signature above for or at the direction of the declarant and I am not appointed as the health care agent or attorney-in-fact herein. I am at least eighteen (18) years of age and I am not related to the declarant by blood, adoption, or marriage, entitled to any portion of the estate of the declarant according to the laws of intestate succession or under any will of declarant or codicil thereto, or directly financially responsible for declarant's medical care. I am not a health care provider of the declarant or an employee of the health facility in which the declarant is a patient.

Witness Signature _____   Date _____

Printed Name of Witness _____

Witness Signature _____   Date _____

Printed Name of Witness _____

Acceptance of Health Care Agent and Financial Attorney-in-Fact

I accept my appointment as Health Care Agent:

Signature _____   Date _____

I accept my appointment as Attorney-in-Fact for Financial Affairs:

Signature _____   Date _____

North Dakota Advance Health Care Directive

On this date of _____ , I, _____ , do hereby sign, execute, and adopt the following as my Advance Health Care Directive. I direct any and all persons or entities involved with my health care in any manner that these decisions are my wishes and were adopted without duress or force and of my own free will. I have placed my *initials* next to the sections of this Directive that I have adopted:

[   ] Living Will
[   ] Selection of Health Care Agent
[   ] Durable Power of Attorney for Financial Affairs
[   ] Designation of Primary Physician
[   ] Organ Donation

Living Will Declaration

I, _____ , declare that I have made the following decisions concerning the following:

(1) LIFE-PROLONGING TREATMENT (*initial [a], [b], or [c]*):

[   ] (a) I direct that life-prolonging treatment be withheld or withdrawn and that I be permitted to die naturally if two (2) physicians certify that I am in a terminal condition that is an incurable or irreversible condition which, without the administration of life-prolonging treatment, will result in my imminent death; and the application of life-prolonging treatment would serve only to artificially prolong the process of my dying; and that I am not pregnant. It is my intention that this declaration be honored by my family and physicians as the final expression of my legal right to refuse medical or surgical treatment and that they accept the consequences of that refusal, which is death.

[   ] (b) I direct that life-prolonging treatment, which could extend my life, be used if two (2) physicians certify that I am in a terminal condition that is an incurable or irreversible condition which, without the administration of life-prolonging treatment, will result in my imminent death. It is my intention that this declaration be honored by my family and physicians as the final expression of my legal right to direct that medical or surgical treatment be provided.

[   ] (c) I make no statement concerning life-prolonging treatment.

(2) ADMINISTRATION OF NUTRITION WHEN MY DEATH IS IMMINENT (*initial [a], [b], [c], or [d]*):

[   ] (a) I DO wish to receive nutrition.

[   ] (b) I DO wish to receive nutrition UNLESS I cannot physically assimilate nutrition, nutrition would be physically harmful, cause unreasonable physical pain, or would only prolong the process of my dying.

[   ] (c) I do NOT wish to receive nutrition.

[   ] (d) I make no statement concerning the administration of nutrition.

(3)   ADMINISTRATION OF HYDRATION WHEN MY DEATH IS IMMINENT (*initial [a], [b], [c], or [d]*):

[   ] (a) I DO wish to receive hydration.

[   ] (b) I DO wish to receive hydration UNLESS I cannot physically assimilate hydration, hydration would be physically harmful, cause unreasonable physical pain, or would only prolong the process of my dying.

[   ] (c) I do NOT wish to receive hydration.

[   ] (d) I make no statement concerning the administration of hydration.

Concerning the administration of nutrition and hydration, I understand that if I make no statement about nutrition or hydration, my attending physician may withhold or withdraw nutrition or hydration if he or she determines that I cannot physically assimilate nutrition or hydration or that nutrition or hydration would be physically harmful or cause unreasonable physical pain. If I have been diagnosed as pregnant and that diagnosis is known to my physician, this declaration is not effective during the course of my pregnancy. I understand the importance of this declaration, am voluntarily signing this declaration, am at least eighteen (18) years of age, and am emotionally and mentally competent to make this declaration. I understand that I may revoke this declaration at any time.

Selection of Health Care Agent

NOTE: None of the following may be designated as your agent: your treating health care provider, a non-relative employee of your treating health care provider, an operator of a long-term care facility, or a non-relative employee of an operator of a long-term care facility. For the purposes of this document, "health care decision" means consent, refusal of consent, or withdrawal of consent to any care, treatment, service, or procedure to maintain, diagnose, or treat an individual's physical or mental condition. If you want to limit the authority of your agent to make health care decisions for you, you can state the limitations on the following page. You can indicate your desires by including a statement of your desires in the same paragraph. Your agent must make health care decisions that are consistent with your known desires. You can, but are not required to state your desires in the following provided space. You should consider whether you want to include a statement of your desires concerning life-prolonging care, treatment, services, and procedures. You can also include a statement of your desires concerning other matters relating to your health care. You can also make your desires known to your agent by discussing your desires with him or her or by some other means. If there are any types of treatment that you do not want to be used, you should state them in the following space. If you want to limit in any other way the authority given your agent by this document, you should state the limits in the following space. If you do not state any limits, your agent will have broad powers to make health care decisions for you, except to the extent that there are limits provided by law. You may attach additional pages if you need more space to complete your statement. If you attach additional pages, you must date and sign EACH of the additional pages at the same time you date and sign this document.

I, _____ , do hereby designate and appoint _____

_____ (name), of _____

_____ (address), as my attorney-in-fact for health care.

By this document I intend to create a durable power of attorney for health care. Subject to any special provisions or limitations in this document, I hereby grant to my agent full power and authority to make health care decisions for me to the same extent that I could make such decisions for myself if I had the capacity to do so. In exercising this authority, my agent shall make health care decisions that are consistent with my desires as stated in this document or otherwise made known to my agent, including my desires concerning obtaining, refusing, or withdrawing life-prolonging care, treatment, services, and procedures.

STATEMENT OF DESIRES CONCERNING LIFE-PROLONGING CARE, TREATMENT, SERVICES, AND PROCEDURES (*insert statement if desired*):

ADDITIONAL STATEMENT OF DESIRES, SPECIAL PROVISIONS, AND LIMITATIONS REGARDING HEALTH CARE DECISIONS (*insert statement if desired*):

Subject to any limitations in this document, my agent has the power and authority to do all of the following (*initial your choices*):

[   ] (1) Request, review, and receive any information, verbal or written, regarding my physical or mental health, including medical and hospital records.

[   ] (2) Execute on my behalf any releases or other documents that may be required in order to obtain this information.

[   ] (3) Consent to the disclosure of this information (*if you want to limit the authority of your agent to receive and disclose information relating to your health, you must state the limitations on the previous page*).

Where necessary to implement the health care decisions that my agent is authorized by this document to make, my agent has the power and authority to execute on my behalf all of the following (*initial your choices*):

[   ] (1) Documents titled or purporting to be a "Refusal to Permit Treatment" and "Leaving Hospital Against Medical Advice."

[   ] (2) Any necessary waiver or release from liability required by a hospital or physician.

I revoke any prior durable power of attorney for health care.

Durable Power of Attorney for Financial Affairs

I, _____ , grant a durable power of attorney for financial affairs to _____ (name), of _____ _____ (address), to act as my attorney-in-fact. This power of attorney shall become effective upon my disability, as certified by my primary physician or, if my primary physician is not available, by any other attending physician. This power of attorney grants no power or authority regarding health care decisions to my designated attorney-in-fact.

I give my attorney-in-fact the maximum power under law to perform the following specific acts on my behalf: all acts relating to any and all of my financial and/or business affairs, including all banking and financial institution transactions, all real estate transactions, all insurance and annuity transactions, all claims and litigation, and all business transactions. My attorney-in-fact is granted full power to act on my behalf in the same manner as if I were personally present.

My attorney-in-fact accepts this appointment and agrees to act in my best interest as he or she considers advisable. This power of attorney may be revoked by me at any time and is automatically revoked on my death. This power of attorney shall not be affected by my present or future disability or incapacity. My attorney-in-fact shall not be compensated for his or her services nor shall my attorney-in-fact be liable to me, my estate, heirs, successors, or assigns for acting or refraining from acting under this document, except for willful misconduct or gross negligence. Any third party who receives a signed copy of this document may act under it. Revocation of this document is not effective unless a third party has actual knowledge of such revocation.

Designation of Primary Physician

I designate the following physician as my primary physician: _____ (name), of _____ (address).

Organ Donation

In the event of my death, I have placed my initials next to the following part(s) of my body that I wish donated for the purposes that I have *initialed* below:

[   ] any organs or parts **OR**

[   ] eyes   [   ] bone and connective tissue   [   ] skin

[   ] heart   [   ] kidney(s)   [   ] liver

[   ] lung(s)   [   ] pancreas   [   ] other _____

for the purposes of:

[   ] any purpose authorized by law **OR**

[   ] transplantation   [   ] research   [   ] therapy

[   ] medical education   [   ] other limitations _____

Signature

I sign this Advance Health Care Directive, consisting of the following sections, which I have *initialed* below and have elected to adopt:

[   ]   Living Will

[   ]   Selection of Health Care Agent

[   ]   Durable Power of Attorney for Financial Affairs

[   ]   Designation of Primary Physician

[   ]   Organ Donation

BY SIGNING HERE I INDICATE THAT I UNDERSTAND THE PURPOSE AND EF-FECT OF THIS DOCUMENT.

Signature _____   Date _____

City, County, and State of Residence _____

Notary Acknowledgment

State of _____

County of _____

On _____ , _____ came before me personally and, under oath, stated that he or she is the person described in the above document and he or she signed the above document in my presence. I declare under penalty of perjury that the person whose name is subscribed to this instrument appears to be of sound mind and under no duress, fraud, or undue influence.

_____

Notary Public

My commission expires _____

Witness Acknowledgment

The declarant is personally known to me and I believe him or her to be of sound mind and under no duress, fraud, or undue influence. I did not sign the declarant's signature above for or at the direction of the declarant and I am not appointed as the health care agent or attorney-in-fact herein. I am at least eighteen (18) years of age and I am not related to the declarant by blood, adoption, or marriage, entitled to any portion of the estate of the declarant according to the laws of intestate succession or under any will of declarant or codicil thereto, or directly financially responsible for declarant's medical care. I am not a health care provider of the declarant or an employee of the health facility in which the declarant is a patient.

Witness Signature _____ Date _____

Printed Name of Witness _____

Witness Signature _____ Date _____

Printed Name of Witness _____

Acceptance of Health Care Agent and Financial Attorney-in-Fact

I accept my appointment as Health Care Agent:

Signature _____ Date _____

I accept my appointment as Attorney-in-Fact for Financial Affairs:

Signature _____ Date _____

Ohio Advance Health Care Directive

On this date of _____ , I, _____ , do hereby sign, execute, and adopt the following as my Advance Health Care Directive. I direct any and all persons or entities involved with my health care in any manner that these decisions are my wishes and were adopted without duress or force and of my own free will. I have placed my *initials* next to the sections of this Directive that I have adopted:

[   ]   Living Will
[   ]   Selection of Health Care Agent (Durable Power of Attorney for Health Care)
[   ]   Durable Power of Attorney for Financial Affairs
[   ]   Designation of Primary Physician
[   ]   Organ Donation

Living Will Declaration

NOTICE: This form of a Living Will Declaration is designed to serve as evidence of an individual's desire that life-sustaining medical treatment, including artificially- or technologically-supplied nutrition and hydration, be withheld or withdrawn if the individual is unable to communicate and is in a terminal condition or a permanently-unconscious state. If you would choose not to withhold or withdraw any or all forms of life-sustaining treatment, you have the legal right to so choose and you might want to state your medical treatment preferences in writing in another form of Declaration. Under Ohio law, a Living Will Declaration may be relied on only for individuals in a terminal condition or a permanently-unconscious state. If you wish to direct your medical treatment in other circumstances, you should consider preparing a Durable Power of Attorney for Health Care.

I, _____ , being of sound mind and not subject to duress, fraud, or undue influence, intending to create a Living Will Declaration under Chapter 2133 of the Ohio Revised Code, do voluntarily make known my desire that my dying shall not be artificially-prolonged. If I am unable to give directions regarding the use of life-sustaining treatment when I am in a terminal condition or a permanently-unconscious state, it is my intention that this Living Will Declaration shall be honored by my family and physicians as the final expression of my legal right to refuse medical or surgical treatment. I am a competent adult who understands and accepts the consequences of such refusal and the purpose and effect of this document (*initial all the following that you choose*):

In the event I am in a terminal condition, I declare and direct that my attending physician shall (*initial all that you choose*):

[   ] Administer NO life-sustaining treatment, including cardiopulmonary resuscitation;

[   ] Withdraw life-sustaining treatment, including cardiopulmonary resuscitation, if such treatment has commenced, and in the case of cardiopulmonary resuscitation, issue a do-not-resuscitate order;

[   ] Permit me to die naturally and provide me with only the care necessary to make me comfortable and to relieve my pain but not to postpone my death.

In the event I am in a permanently-unconscious state, I declare and direct that my attending physician shall (*initial all that you choose*):

[   ] Administer NO life-sustaining treatment, including cardiopulmonary resuscitation, except for the provision of artificially- or technologically-supplied nutrition or hydration unless, in the following paragraph, I have authorized its withholding or withdrawal;

[   ] Withdraw such treatment, including cardiopulmonary resuscitation, if such treatment has commenced, and, in the case of cardiopulmonary resuscitation, issue a do-not-resuscitate order;

[   ] Permit me to die naturally and provide me with only that care necessary to make me comfortable and to relieve my pain but not to postpone my death.

[   ] In addition, if I have *initialed* the foregoing box, I authorize my attending physician to withhold, or in the event that treatment has already commenced, to withdraw the provision of artificially- or technologically-supplied nutrition and hydration, if I am in a permanently-unconscious state and if my attending physician and at least one other physician who has examined me determine, to a reasonable degree of medical certainty and in accordance with reasonable medical standards, that such nutrition or hydration will not or will no longer serve to provide comfort to me or alleviate my pain.

OTHER DIRECTIONS: In the event my attending physician determines that life-sustaining treatment should be withheld or withdrawn, he or she shall make a good faith effort and use reasonable diligence to notify one (1) of the persons named below in the following order of priority:

(1) _____ (name), _____ (relationship), of _____ (address).

(2) _____ (name), _____ (relationship), of _____ (address).

[   ] I have a durable power of attorney for health care (*initial if true*).

For purposes of this Living Will Declaration:
(1) "Life-Sustaining Treatment" means any medical procedure, treatment, intervention, or other measure including artificially- or technologically-supplied nutrition and hydration that, when administered, will serve principally to prolong the process of dying.
(2) "Terminal Condition" means an irreversible, incurable, and untreatable condition caused by disease, illness, or injury from which, to a reasonable degree of medical certainty as deter-

mined in accordance with reasonable medical standards by my attending physician and one (1) other physician who has examined me, both of the following apply:

(a) There can be no recovery; and

(b) Death is likely to occur within a relatively short time if life-sustaining treatment is not administered.

(3) "Permanently-Unconscious State" means a state of permanent unconsciousness that, to a reasonable degree of medical certainty as determined in accordance with reasonable medical standards by my attending physician and one (1) other physician who has examined me, is characterized by both of the following:

(a) I am irreversibly unaware of myself and my environment, and

(b) There is a total loss of cerebral cortical functioning, resulting in my having no capacity to experience pain or suffering.

Selection of Health Care Agent
(Durable Power of Attorney for Health Care)

NOTICE: This is an important legal document. Before executing this document, you should know these facts: This document gives the person you designate (the attorney-in-fact) the power to make MOST health care decisions for you if you lose the capacity to make informed health care decisions for yourself. This power is effective only when your attending physician determines that you have lost the capacity to make informed health care decisions for yourself and, notwithstanding this document, as long as you have the capacity to make informed health care decisions for yourself, you retain the right to make all medical and other health care decisions for yourself. You may include specific limitations in this document on the authority of the attorney-in-fact to make health care decisions for you. Subject to any specific limitations you include in this document, if your attending physician determines that you have lost the capacity to make an informed decision on a health care matter, the attorney-in-fact GENERALLY will be authorized by this document to make health care decisions for you to the same extent as you could make those decisions yourself, if you had the capacity to do so. The authority of the attorney-in-fact to make health care decisions for you GENERALLY will include the authority to give informed consent, refuse to give informed consent, or withdraw informed consent to any care, treatment, service, or procedure to maintain, diagnose, or treat a physical or mental condition. HOWEVER, even if the attorney-in-fact has general authority to make health care decisions for you under this document, the attorney-in-fact NEVER will be authorized to do any of the following:

(1) Refuse or withdraw informed consent to life-sustaining treatment (unless your attending physician and one (1) other physician who examines you determine, to a reasonable degree of medical certainty and in accordance with reasonable medical standards, that either of the following applies:

(a) You are suffering from an irreversible, incurable, and untreatable condition caused by disease, illness, or injury from which:

(i) there can be no recovery, and

(ii) your death is likely to occur within a relatively short time if life-sustaining treatment is not administered, and your attending physician additionally determines, to a reasonable degree of medical certainty and in accordance with reasonable medical standards, that there is no reasonable possibility that you will regain the capacity to make informed health care decisions for yourself, OR

(b) You are in a state of permanent unconsciousness that is characterized by you being irreversibly unaware of yourself and your environment and by a total loss of cerebral cortical functioning, resulting in you having no capacity to experience pain or suffering, and your attending physician additionally determines, to a reasonable degree of medical certainty and in accordance with reasonable medical standards, that there is no reasonable possibility that you will regain the capacity to make informed health care decisions for yourself);

(2) Refuse or withdraw informed consent to health care necessary to provide you with comfort care (except that, if the attorney-in-fact is not prohibited from doing so under paragraph [4] below, the attorney-in-fact could refuse or withdraw informed consent to the provision of nutrition or hydration to you as described under paragraph [4] below). (You should understand that "comfort care" is defined in Ohio law to mean artificially- or technologically-administered sustenance [nutrition] or fluids [hydration] when administered to diminish your pain or discomfort, not to postpone your death, and any other medical or nursing procedure, treatment, intervention, or other measure that would be taken to diminish your pain or discomfort, not to postpone your death. Consequently, if your attending physician were to determine that a previously-described medical or nursing procedure, treatment, intervention, or other measure will not or will no longer serve to provide comfort to you or alleviate your pain, then, subject to paragraph [4] below, your attorney-in-fact would be authorized to refuse or withdraw informed consent to the procedure, treatment, intervention, or other measure.);

(3) Refuse or withdraw informed consent to health care for you if you are pregnant and if the refusal or withdrawal would terminate the pregnancy (unless the pregnancy or health care would pose a substantial risk to your life, or unless your attending physician and at least one (1) other physician who examines you determine, to a reasonable degree of medical certainty and in accordance with reasonable medical standards, that the fetus would not be born alive);

(4) Refuse or withdraw informed consent to the provision of artificially- or technologically-administered sustenance (nutrition) or fluids (hydration) to you, unless:

(a) You are in a terminal condition or in a permanently-unconscious state,

(b) Your attending physician and at least one (1) other physician who has examined you determine, to a reasonable degree of medical certainty and in accordance with reasonable medical standards, that nutrition or hydration will not or will no longer serve to provide comfort to you or alleviate your pain,

(c) If, but only if, you are in a permanently-unconscious state, you authorize the attorney-in-fact to refuse or withdraw informed consent to the provision of nutrition or hydration to you by doing both of the following in this document:

(i) including a statement in capital letters or other conspicuous type, including, but not limited to, a different font, bigger type, or boldface type that the attorney-in-fact may refuse or withdraw informed consent to the provision of nutrition or hydration to you if you are in a permanently-unconscious state and if the determination that nutrition or hydration will not or will no longer serve to provide comfort to you or alleviate your pain is made, or checking or otherwise marking a box or line (if any) that is adjacent to a similar statement on this document;

(ii) placing your initials or signature underneath or adjacent to the statement, check, or other mark previously described.

(d) Your attending physician determines, in good faith, that you authorized the attorney-in-fact to refuse or withdraw informed consent to the provision of nutrition or hydration to you if you are in a permanently-unconscious state by complying with the requirements of paragraphs (4)(c)(i) and (4)(c)(ii) above.

(5) Withdraw informed consent to any health care to which you previously consented, unless a change in your physical condition has significantly decreased the benefit of that health care to you, or unless the health care is not, or is no longer significantly effective in achieving the purposes for which you consented to its use.

Additionally, when exercising authority to make health care decisions for you, the attorney-in-fact will have to act consistently with your desires or, if your desires are unknown, to act in your best interest. You may express your desires to the attorney-in-fact by including them in this document or by making them known to the attorney-in-fact in another manner. When acting pursuant to this document, the attorney-in-fact GENERALLY will have the same rights that you have to receive information about proposed health care, review health care records, and consent to the disclosure of health care records. You can limit that right in this document if you so choose. Generally, you may designate any competent adult as the attorney-in-fact under this document. However, you CANNOT designate your attending physician or the administrator of any nursing home in which you are receiving care as the attorney-in-fact under this document. Additionally, you CANNOT designate an employee or agent of your attending physician or an employee or agent of a health care facility at which you are being treated as the attorney-in-fact under this document, unless either type of employee or agent is a competent adult and related to you by blood, marriage, or adoption, or unless either type of employee or agent is a competent adult and you and the employee or agent are members of the same religious order. This document has no expiration date under Ohio law, but you may choose to specify a date upon which your Durable Power of Attorney for Health Care generally will expire. However, if you specify an expiration date and then lack the capacity to make informed health care decisions for yourself on that date, the document and the power it grants to your attorney-in-fact will continue in effect until you regain the capacity to make informed health care decisions for yourself. You have the right to revoke the designation of the attorney-in-fact and the right to revoke this entire document at any time and in any manner. Any such revocation generally will be effective when you express your intention to make the revocation. However, if you made your attending physician aware of this document, any such revocation will be effective only when you communicate it to your attending physician, or when a witness to the revocation or other health care personnel to whom the revocation is communicated by such a witness communicates it to your attending physician. If you execute this document and create a valid Durable Power of Attorney for Health Care with it, it will revoke any prior valid durable power of attorney for health care that you created, unless you indicate otherwise in this document. This document is not valid as a Durable Power of Attorney for Health Care unless it is acknowledged before a notary public or is signed by at least two (2) adult witnesses who are present when you sign or acknowledge your signature. No person who is related to you by blood, marriage, or adoption may be a witness. The attorney-in-fact, your attending physician, and the administrator of any nursing home in which you are receiving care also are ineligible to be witnesses. If there is anything in this document that you do not understand, you should ask your lawyer to explain it to you.

I, _____ , intending to create a Durable Power of Attorney for Health Care under Chapter 1337 of the Ohio Revised Code, do hereby designate and appoint _____ (name), of _____ _____ (address), as my attorney-in-fact who shall act as my agent to make health care decisions for me as authorized in this document.

I hereby grant to my agent full power and authority to make all health care decisions for me to the same extent that I could make such decisions for myself if I had the capacity to do so, at any time during which I do not have the capacity to make or communicate informed health care decisions for myself. My agent shall have the authority to give, withdraw, or refuse to give informed consent to any medical or nursing procedure, treatment, intervention, or other measure used to maintain, diagnose, or treat my physical or mental condition. In exercising this authority, my agent shall make health care decisions that are consistent with my desires as stated in this document or otherwise made known to my agent by me or, if I have not made my desires known, that are, in the judgment of my agent, in my best interests.

Where necessary or desirable to implement the health care decisions that my agent is authorized to make pursuant to this document, my agent has the power and authority to do any and all of the following:
(1) If I am in a terminal condition, to give, withdraw, or refuse to give informed consent to life-sustaining treatment, including the provision of artificially- or technologically-supplied nutrition or hydration;
(2) If I am in a permanently-unconscious state, to give informed consent to life-sustaining treatment, withdraw, or refuse to give informed consent to life-sustaining treatment; provided, however, my agent is not authorized to refuse or direct the withdrawal of artificially- or technologically-supplied nutrition or hydration unless I have specifically authorized such refusal or withdrawal in this document;
(3) To request, review, and receive any information, verbal or written, regarding my physical or mental health, including, but not limited to, all of my medical and health care facility records;
(4) To execute on my behalf any releases or other documents that may be required in order to obtain this information;
(5) To consent to the further disclosure of this information if necessary;

(6) To select, employ, and discharge health care personnel, such as physicians, nurses, therapists, and other medical professionals, including individuals and services providing home health care, as my agent shall determine to be appropriate;

(7) To select and contract with any medical or health care facility on my behalf, including, but not limited to, hospitals, nursing homes, assisted-residence facilities, and the like; and

(8) To execute on my behalf any or all of the following:

(a) documents that are written consents to medical treatment or written requests that I be transferred to another facility,

(b) documents that are Do Not Resuscitate Orders, Discharge Orders, or other similar orders, and

(c) any other document necessary or desirable to implement health care decisions that my agent is authorized to make pursuant to this document.

WITHDRAWAL OF NUTRITION AND HYDRATION WHEN IN A PERMANENTLY-UNCONSCIOUS STATE.

[   ] If I have *initialed* the foregoing box, my agent may refuse, or in the event treatment has already commenced, withdraw informed consent to the provision of artificially- or technologically-supplied nutrition and hydration if I am in a permanently-unconscious state and if my attending physician and at least one (1) other physician who has examined me determines, to a reasonable degree of medical certainty and in accordance with reasonable medical standards, that such nutrition or hydration will not or will no longer serve to provide comfort to me or alleviate my pain.

This Durable Power of Attorney for Health Care shall not be affected by my disability or by lapse of time. This Durable Power of Attorney for Health Care shall have no expiration date. Any invalid or unenforceable power, authority, or provision of this instrument shall not affect any other power, authority, or provision or the appointment of my agent to make health care decisions. I hereby revoke any prior Durable Powers of Attorney for Health Care executed by me under Chapter 1337 of the Ohio Revised Code.

Durable Power of Attorney for Financial Affairs

I, _____ , grant a durable power of attorney for financial affairs to _____ (name), of _____ _____ (address), to act as my attorney-in-fact. This power of attorney shall become effective upon my disability, as certified by my primary physician or, if my primary physician is not available, by any other attending physician. This power of attorney grants no power or authority regarding health care decisions to my designated attorney-in-fact.

I give my attorney-in-fact the maximum power under law to perform the following specific acts on my behalf: all acts relating to any and all of my financial and/or business affairs, including all banking and financial institution transactions, all real estate transactions, all insurance and annuity transactions, all claims and litigation, and all business transactions. My attorney-in-fact is granted full power to act on my behalf in the same manner as if I were personally present.

My attorney-in-fact accepts this appointment and agrees to act in my best interest as he or she considers advisable. This power of attorney may be revoked by me at any time and is automatically revoked on my death. This power of attorney shall not be affected by my present or future disability or incapacity. My attorney-in-fact shall not be compensated for his or her services nor shall my attorney-in-fact be liable to me, my estate, heirs, successors, or assigns for acting or refraining from acting under this document, except for willful misconduct or gross negligence. Any third party who receives a signed copy of this document may act under it. Revocation of this document is not effective unless a third party has actual knowledge of such revocation.

Designation of Primary Physician

I designate the following physician as my primary physician: _____ (name), of _____ (address).

Organ Donation

In the event of my death, I have placed my initials next to the following part(s) of my body that I wish donated for the purposes that I have *initialed* below:

[   ] any organs or parts **OR**

[ ] eyes	[ ] bone and connective tissue	[ ] skin
[ ] heart	[ ] kidney(s)	[ ] liver
[ ] lung(s)	[ ] pancreas	[ ] other _____

for the purposes of:

[   ] any purpose authorized by law **OR**

[ ] transplantation	[ ] research	[ ] therapy
[ ] medical education	[ ] other limitations _____	

Signature

I sign this Advance Health Care Directive, consisting of the following sections, which I have *initialed* below and have elected to adopt:

[   ] Living Will

[   ] Selection of Health Care Agent (Durable Power of Attorney for Health Care)

[   ] Durable Power of Attorney for Financial Affairs

[   ] Designation of Primary Physician

[   ] Organ Donation

BY SIGNING HERE I INDICATE THAT I UNDERSTAND THE PURPOSE AND EFFECT OF THIS DOCUMENT.

Signature _____   Date _____

City, County, and State of Residence _____

Notary Acknowledgment

State of _____

County of _____

On _____ , _____ came before me personally and, under oath, stated that he or she is the person described in the above document and he or she signed the above document in my presence. I declare under penalty of perjury that the person whose name is subscribed to this instrument appears to be of sound mind and under no duress, fraud, or undue influence.

_____

Notary Public
My commission expires _____

Witness Acknowledgment

The declarant is personally known to me and I believe him or her to be of sound mind and under no duress, fraud, or undue influence. I did not sign the declarant's signature above for or at the direction of the declarant and I am not appointed as the health care agent or attorney-in-fact herein. I am at least eighteen (18) years of age and I am not related to the declarant by blood, adoption, or marriage, entitled to any portion of the estate of the declarant according to the laws of intestate succession or under any will of declarant or codicil thereto, or directly financially responsible for declarant's medical care. I am not a health care provider of the declarant or an employee of the health facility in which the declarant is a patient.

Witness Signature _____ Date _____

Printed Name of Witness _____

Witness Signature _____ Date _____

Printed Name of Witness _____

Acceptance of Health Care Agent and Financial Attorney-in-Fact

I accept my appointment as Health Care Agent:

Signature _____ Date _____

I accept my appointment as Attorney-in-Fact for Financial Affairs:

Signature _____ Date _____

Oklahoma Advance Health Care Directive

On this date of _____ , I, _____ , do hereby sign, execute, and adopt the following as my Advance Health Care Directive. I direct any and all persons or entities involved with my health care in any manner that these decisions are my wishes and were adopted without duress or force and of my own free will. I have placed my *initials* next to the sections of this Directive that I have adopted:

[   ]   Living Will
[   ]   Selection of Health Care Agent (Health Care Proxy)
[   ]   Durable Power of Attorney for Financial Affairs
[   ]   Designation of Primary Physician
[   ]   Organ Donation

Living Will

I, _____ , being of sound mind and eighteen (18) years of age or older, willfully and voluntarily make known my desire, by my instructions to others through my living will, or by my appointment of a health care proxy, or both, that my life shall not be artificially-prolonged under the circumstances set forth below. I thus do hereby declare:

If my attending physician and another physician determine that I am no longer able to make decisions regarding my medical treatment, I direct my attending physician and other health care providers, pursuant to the Oklahoma Rights of the Terminally Ill or Persistently Unconscious Act, to withhold or withdraw treatment from me under the circumstances I have indicated by my initials. I understand that I will be given treatment that is necessary for my comfort or to alleviate my pain (*initial your choices*):

If I have a terminal condition:

[   ]   I direct that life-sustaining treatment shall be withheld or withdrawn if such treatment would only prolong my process of dying, and if my attending physician and another physician determine that I have an incurable and irreversible condition that even with the administration of life-sustaining treatment will cause my death within six (6) months.

[   ]   I understand that the subject of the artificial administration of nutrition and hydration (food and water) that will only prolong the process of dying from an incurable and irreversible condition is of particular importance. I understand that if I do not sign this paragraph, artificially-administered nutrition and hydration will be administered to me. I further understand that if I sign this paragraph, I am authorizing the withholding or withdrawal of artificially-administered nutrition (food) and hydration (water).

[   ] I direct that (*add other medical directives, if any*):

If I am persistently unconscious:

[   ] I direct that life-sustaining treatment be withheld or withdrawn if such treatment will only serve to maintain me in an irreversible condition, as determined by my attending physician and another physician, in which thought and awareness of self and environment are absent.

[   ] I understand that the subject of the artificial administration of nutrition and hydration (food and water) for individuals who have become persistently unconscious is of particular importance. I understand that if I do not sign this paragraph, artificially-administered nutrition and hydration will be administered to me. I further understand that if I sign this paragraph, I am authorizing the withholding or withdrawal of artificially-administered nutrition (food) and hydration (water).

[   ] I direct that (*add other medical directives, if any*):

Selection of Health Care Agent (Health Care Proxy)

If my attending physician and another physician determine that I am no longer able to make decisions regarding my medical treatment, I direct my attending physician and other health care providers pursuant to the Oklahoma Rights of the Terminally Ill or Persistently Unconscious Act to follow the instructions of _____ (name), of _____ _____ (address), whom I appoint as my health care proxy. My health care proxy is authorized to make whatever medical treatment decisions I could make if I were able, except that decisions regarding life-sustaining treatment can be made by my health care proxy only as I indicate by my *initials* in the following sections:

If I have a terminal condition:

[   ] I authorize my health care proxy to direct that life-sustaining treatment be withheld or withdrawn if such treatment would only prolong my process of dying and if my attending physician and another physician determine that I have an incurable and irreversible condition that even with the administration of life-sustaining treatment will cause my death within six (6) months.

[   ] I understand that the subject of the artificial administration of nutrition and hydration (food and water) is of particular importance. I understand that if I do not sign this paragraph, artificially-administered nutrition (food) or hydration (water) will be administered to me. I further understand that if I sign this paragraph, I am authorizing the withholding or withdrawal of artificially-administered nutrition and hydration.

[   ] I authorize my health care proxy to (*add other medical directives, if any*):

If I am persistently unconscious:

[   ] I authorize my health care proxy to direct that life-sustaining treatment be withheld or withdrawn if such treatment will only serve to maintain me in an irreversible condition, as determined by my attending physician and another physician, in which thought and awareness of self and environment are absent.

[   ] I understand that the subject of the artificial administration of nutrition and hydration (food and water) is of particular importance. I understand that if I do not sign this paragraph, artificially-administered nutrition (food) and hydration (water) will be administered to me. I further understand that if I sign this paragraph, I am authorizing the withholding and withdrawal of artificially-administered nutrition and hydration

[   ] I authorize my health care proxy to (*add other medical directives, if any*):

I understand that if I have completed both a living will and have appointed a health care proxy, and if there is a conflict between my health care proxy's decision and my living will, my living will shall take precedence unless I indicate otherwise. I also understand that if I have been diagnosed as pregnant and that diagnosis is known to my attending physician, this advance directive shall have no force or effect during the course of my pregnancy. In the absence of my ability to give directions regarding the use of life-sustaining procedures, it is my intention that this advance directive shall be honored by my family and physicians as the final expression of my legal right to refuse medical or surgical treatment including, but not limited to, the administration of any life-sustaining procedures, and I accept the consequences of such refusal. This advance directive shall be in effect until it is revoked. I understand that I may revoke this advance directive at any time. I understand and agree that if I have any prior directives, and if I sign this advance directive, my prior directives are revoked. I understand the full importance of this advance directive and I am emotionally and mentally competent to make this advance directive.

NOTE: A physician or other health care provider who is furnished the original or a photocopy of the advance directive shall make it a part of the declarant's medical record and if unwilling to comply with the advance directive, shall promptly so advise the declarant. In the case of a qualified patient, the patient's health care proxy, in consultation with the attending physician, shall have the authority to make treatment decisions for the patient including the withholding or withdrawal of life-sustaining procedures if so indicated in the patient's advance directive. A person executing an advanced directive appointing a health care proxy who may not have an attending physician for reasons based on established religious beliefs or tenets may designate an individual other than the designated health care proxy, in lieu of an attending physician and other physician, to determine the lack of decisional capacity of the person. Such designation shall be specified and included as part of the advanced directive executed pursuant to the provisions of this section.

Durable Power of Attorney for Financial Affairs

I, _____ , grant a durable power of attorney for financial affairs to _____ (name), of _____ _____ (address), to act as my attorney-in-fact. This power of attorney shall become effective upon my disability, as certified by my primary physician or, if my primary physician is not available, by any other attending physician. This power of attorney grants no power or authority regarding health care decisions to my designated attorney-in-fact.

I give my attorney-in-fact the maximum power under law to perform the following specific acts on my behalf: all acts relating to any and all of my financial and/or business affairs, including all banking and financial institution transactions, all real estate transactions, all insurance and annuity transactions, all claims and litigation, and all business transactions. My attorney-in-fact is granted full power to act on my behalf in the same manner as if I were personally present.

My attorney-in-fact accepts this appointment and agrees to act in my best interest as he or she considers advisable. This power of attorney may be revoked by me at any time and is automatically revoked on my death. This power of attorney shall not be affected by my present or future disability or incapacity. My attorney-in-fact shall not be compensated for his or her services nor shall my attorney-in-fact be liable to me, my estate, heirs, successors, or assigns for acting or refraining from acting under this document, except for willful misconduct or gross negligence. Any third party who receives a signed copy of this document may act under it. Revocation of this document is not effective unless a third party has actual knowledge of such revocation.

Designation of Primary Physician

I designate the following physician as my primary physician: _____
(name), of _____ (address).

Organ Donation

In the event of my death, I have placed my initials next to the following part(s) of my body that I wish donated for the purposes that I have *initialed* below:
[   ] any organs or parts **OR**
[   ] eyes   [   ] bone and connective tissue   [   ] skin
[   ] heart   [   ] kidney(s)   [   ] liver
[   ] lung(s)   [   ] pancreas   [   ] other _____
for the purposes of:
[   ] any purpose authorized by law **OR**
[   ] transplantation   [   ] research   [   ] therapy
[   ] medical education   [   ] other limitations _____

Signature

I sign this Advance Health Care Directive, consisting of the following sections, which I have *initialed* below and have elected to adopt:
[   ] Living Will
[   ] Selection of Health Care Agent (Health Care Proxy)
[   ] Durable Power of Attorney for Financial Affairs
[   ] Designation of Primary Physician
[   ] Organ Donation
BY SIGNING HERE I INDICATE THAT I UNDERSTAND THE PURPOSE AND EFFECT OF THIS DOCUMENT.

Signature _____   Date _____

City, County, and State of Residence _____

Notary Acknowledgment

State of _____

County of _____

On _____ , _____ came before me personally and, under oath, stated that he or she is the person described in the above document and he or she signed the above document in my presence. I declare under penalty of perjury that the person whose name is subscribed to this instrument appears to be of sound mind and under no duress, fraud, or undue influence.

_____
Notary Public
My commission expires _____

Witness Acknowledgment

The declarant is personally known to me and I believe him or her to be of sound mind and under no duress, fraud, or undue influence. I did not sign the declarant's signature above for or at the direction of the declarant and I am not appointed as the health care agent or attorney-in-fact herein. I am at least eighteen (18) years of age and I am not related to the declarant by blood, adoption, or marriage, entitled to any portion of the estate of the declarant according to the laws of intestate succession or under any will of declarant or codicil thereto, or directly financially responsible for declarant's medical care. I am not a health care provider of the declarant or an employee of the health facility in which the declarant is a patient.

Witness Signature _____ Date _____

Printed Name of Witness _____

Witness Signature _____ Date _____

Printed Name of Witness _____

Acceptance of Health Care Agent and Financial Attorney-in-Fact

I accept my appointment as Health Care Agent:

Signature _____ Date _____

I accept my appointment as Attorney-in-Fact for Financial Affairs:

Signature _____ Date _____

Oregon Advance Health Care Directive

On this date of _____ , I, _____ , do hereby sign, execute, and adopt the following as my Advance Health Care Directive. I direct any and all persons or entities involved with my health care in any manner that these decisions are my wishes and were adopted without duress or force and of my own free will. I have placed my *initials* next to the sections of this Directive that I have adopted:

[   ] Living Will (Health Care Instructions)
[   ] Selection of Health Care Agent (Appointment of Health Care Representative)
[   ] Durable Power of Attorney for Financial Affairs
[   ] Designation of Primary Physician
[   ] Organ Donation

IMPORTANT INFORMATION ABOUT THIS ADVANCE DIRECTIVE
This is an important legal document. It can control critical decisions about your health care. Before signing, consider these important facts:
LIVING WILL (HEALTH CARE INSTRUCTIONS): You also have the right to give instructions for health care providers to follow if you become unable to direct your care.
APPOINTMENT OF HEALTH CARE REPRESENTATIVE: You have the right to name a person to direct your health care when you cannot do so. This person is called your health care representative. You can write in this document any restrictions you want on how your representative will make decisions for you. Your representative must follow your desires as stated in this document or otherwise made known. If your desires are unknown, your representative must try to act in your best interest. Your representative can resign at any time.
COMPLETING THIS FORM: This form is valid only if you sign it voluntarily and when you are of sound mind. If you do not want an advance directive, you do not have to sign this form. Unless you have limited the duration of this advance directive, it will not expire. If you have set an expiration date, and you become unable to direct your health care before that date, this advance directive will not expire until you are able to make those decisions again. You may revoke this document at any time. To do so, notify your representative and your health care provider of the revocation. Despite this document, you have the right to decide your own health care as long as you are able to do so. If there is anything in this document that you do not understand, ask a lawyer to explain it to you.

Unless revoked or suspended, this advance directive will continue for (*initial one*):
[   ] My entire life
[   ] Other period (_____ years)

Living Will (Health Care Instructions)

NOTE: In filling out these instructions, keep the following in mind: The term "as my physician recommends" means that you want your physician to try life support if your physician believes it could be helpful and then discontinue it if it is not helping your health condition or symptoms. Life support and tube feeding are defined below. If you refuse tube feeding, you should understand that malnutrition, dehydration, and death will probably result. You will get care for your comfort and cleanliness, no matter what choices you make. You may either give specific instructions by filling out paragraphs (1) to (4) below, or you may use the general instruction provided by paragraph (5).

Here are my desires about my health care if my doctor and another knowledgeable doctor confirm that I am in a medical condition described below:

(1) CLOSE TO DEATH. If I am close to death and life support would only postpone the moment of my death:

(a) (*initial one*):

[   ] I DO want to receive tube feeding.

[   ] I want tube feeding ONLY as my physician recommends.

[   ] I do NOT want tube feeding.

(b) (*initial one*):

[   ] I DO want any other life support that may apply.

[   ] I want life support ONLY as my physician recommends.

[   ] I want NO life support.

(2) PERMANENTLY UNCONSCIOUS. If I am unconscious and it is very unlikely that I will ever become conscious again:

(a) (*initial one*):

[   ] I DO want to receive tube feeding.

[   ] I want tube feeding ONLY as my physician recommends.

[   ] I do NOT want tube feeding.

(b) (*initial one*):

[   ] I DO want any other life support that may apply.

[   ] I want life support ONLY as my physician recommends.

[   ] I want NO life support.

(3) ADVANCED PROGRESSIVE ILLNESS. If I have a progressive illness that will be fatal and is in an advanced stage, and I am consistently and permanently unable to communicate by any means, swallow food and water safely, care for myself, and recognize my family and other people, and it is very unlikely that my condition will substantially improve:

(a) (*initial one*):

[   ] I DO want to receive tube feeding.

[   ] I want tube feeding ONLY as my physician recommends.

[   ] I do NOT want tube feeding.

(b) (*initial one*):

[   ] I DO want any other life support that may apply.

[   ] I want life support ONLY as my physician recommends.

[   ] I want NO life support.

(4) EXTRAORDINARY SUFFERING. If life support would not help my medical condition and would make me suffer permanent and severe pain:

(a) (*initial one*):

[   ] I DO want to receive tube feeding.

[   ] I want tube feeding ONLY as my physician recommends.

[   ] I do NOT want tube feeding.

(b) (*initial one*):

[   ] I DO want any other life support that may apply.

[   ] I want life support ONLY as my physician recommends.

[   ] I want NO life support.

(5) GENERAL INSTRUCTION (*initial if this applies*):

[   ] I do NOT want my life to be prolonged by life support. I also do NOT want tube feeding as life support. I want my doctors to allow me to die naturally if my doctor and another knowledgeable doctor confirm I am in any of the medical conditions listed in paragraphs (1) to (4) above.

(6) ADDITIONAL CONDITIONS OR INSTRUCTIONS (*insert description of what you want done*):

(7) OTHER DOCUMENTS. A health care power of attorney is any document you may have signed to appoint a representative to make health care decisions for you (*initial one*):

[   ] I HAVE previously signed a health care power of attorney. I want it to remain in effect unless I appointed a health care representative after signing the health care power of attorney.

[   ] I have a health care power of attorney, and I REVOKE it.

[   ] I do NOT have a health care power of attorney.

Selection of Health Care Agent
(Appointment of Health Care Representative)

I appoint _____ (name), of _____
_____ (address), as my health care representative. I authorize my representative to direct my health care when I cannot do so.

NOTE: You may not appoint your doctor, an employee of your doctor, or an owner, operator, or employee of your health care facility, unless that person is related to you by blood, marriage, or adoption, or that person was appointed before your admission into the health care facility.

(1) LIMITS. Special Conditions or Instructions (*insert any conditions or instructions*):

(*Initial if this applies*):
[   ] I have executed a Living Will Health Care Instruction or Directive to Physicians. My representative is to honor it.

(2) LIFE SUPPORT. Life support refers to any medical means for maintaining life, including procedures, devices, and medications. If you refuse life support, you will still get routine measures to keep you clean and comfortable (*initial if this applies*):
[   ] My representative MAY decide about life support for me. (If you don't initial this space, then your representative may NOT decide about life support.)

(3) TUBE FEEDING. One sort of life support is food and water supplied artificially by medical device, known as tube feeding (*initial if this applies*):
[   ] My representative MAY decide about tube feeding for me. (If you don't initial this space, then your representative may NOT decide about tube feeding.)

Durable Power of Attorney for Financial Affairs

I, _____ , grant a durable power of attorney for financial affairs to _____ (name), of _____ _____ (address), to act as my attorney-in-fact. This power of attorney shall become effective upon my disability, as certified by my primary physician or, if my primary physician is not available, by any other attending physician. This power of attorney grants no power or authority regarding health care decisions to my designated attorney-in-fact.

I give my attorney-in-fact the maximum power under law to perform the following specific acts on my behalf: all acts relating to any and all of my financial and/or business affairs, including all banking and financial institution transactions, all real estate transactions, all insurance and annuity transactions, all claims and litigation, and all business transactions. My attorney-in-fact is granted full power to act on my behalf in the same manner as if I were personally present.

My attorney-in-fact accepts this appointment and agrees to act in my best interest as he or she considers advisable. This power of attorney may be revoked by me at any time and is automatically revoked on my death. This power of attorney shall not be affected by my present or future disability or incapacity. My attorney-in-fact shall not be compensated for his or her services nor shall my attorney-in-fact be liable to me, my estate, heirs, successors, or assigns for acting or refraining from acting under this document, except for willful misconduct or gross negligence. Any third party who receives a signed copy of this document may act under it. Revocation of this document is not effective unless a third party has actual knowledge of such revocation.

Designation of Primary Physician

I designate the following physician as my primary physician: _____
(name), of _____ (address).

Organ Donation

In the event of my death, I have placed my initials next to the following part(s) of my body that I wish donated for the purposes that I have *initialed* below:
[   ] any organs or parts **OR**
[   ] eyes   [   ] bone and connective tissue   [   ] skin
[   ] heart   [   ] kidney(s)   [   ] liver
[   ] lung(s)   [   ] pancreas   [   ] other _____
for the purposes of:
[   ] any purpose authorized by law **OR**
[   ] transplantation   [   ] research   [   ] therapy
[   ] medical education   [   ] other limitations _____

Signature

I sign this Advance Health Care Directive, consisting of the following sections, which I have *initialed* below and have elected to adopt:
[   ] Living Will (Health Care Instructions)
[   ] Selection of Health Care Agent (Appointment of Health Care Representative)
[   ] Durable Power of Attorney for Financial Affairs
[   ] Designation of Primary Physician
[   ] Organ Donation
BY SIGNING HERE I INDICATE THAT I UNDERSTAND THE PURPOSE AND EFFECT OF THIS DOCUMENT.

Signature _____   Date _____

City, County, and State of Residence _____

Notary Acknowledgment

State of _____

County of _____

On _____ , _____ came before me personally and, under oath, stated that he or she is the person described in the above document and he or she signed the above document in my presence. I declare under penalty of perjury that the person whose name is subscribed to this instrument appears to be of sound mind and under no duress, fraud, or undue influence.

_____

Notary Public

My commission expires _____

Witness Acknowledgment

The declarant is personally known to me and I believe him or her to be of sound mind and under no duress, fraud, or undue influence. I did not sign the declarant's signature above for or at the direction of the declarant and I am not appointed as the health care agent or attorney-in-fact herein. I am at least eighteen (18) years of age and I am not related to the declarant by blood, adoption, or marriage, entitled to any portion of the estate of the declarant according to the laws of intestate succession or under any will of declarant or codicil thereto, or directly financially responsible for declarant's medical care. I am not a health care provider of the declarant or an employee of the health facility in which the declarant is a patient.

Witness Signature _____ Date _____

Printed Name of Witness _____

Witness Signature _____ Date _____

Printed Name of Witness _____

Acceptance of Health Care Agent and Financial Attorney-in-Fact

I accept my appointment as Health Care Agent:

Signature _____ Date _____

I accept my appointment as Attorney-in-Fact for Financial Affairs:

Signature _____ Date _____

Pennsylvania Advance Health Care Directive

On this date of _____ , I, _____ , do hereby sign, execute, and adopt the following as my Advance Health Care Directive. I direct any and all persons or entities involved with my health care in any manner that these decisions are my wishes and were adopted without duress or force and of my own free will. I have placed my *initials* next to the sections of this Directive that I have adopted:

[   ] Living Will
[   ] Selection of Health Care Agent (Health Care Surrogate)
[   ] Durable Power of Attorney for Financial Affairs
[   ] Designation of Primary Physician
[   ] Organ Donation

Living Will Declaration

I, _____ , being of sound mind, willfully and voluntarily make this declaration to be followed if I become incompetent. This declaration reflects my firm and settled commitment to refuse life-sustaining treatment under the circumstances indicated below.

I direct my attending physician to withhold or withdraw life-sustaining treatment that serves only to prolong the process of my dying, if I should be in a terminal condition or in a state of permanent unconsciousness.

I direct that treatment be limited to measures to keep me comfortable and to relieve pain, including any pain that might occur by withholding or withdrawing life-sustaining treatment. In addition, if I am in the condition described above, I feel especially strong about the following forms of treatment (*initial "I DO" or "I do NOT"*):

I [   ] DO **OR** [   ] do NOT want cardiac resuscitation.
I [   ] DO **OR** [   ] do NOT want mechanical respiration.
I [   ] DO **OR** [   ] do NOT want tube feeding or any other artificial or invasive form of nutrition (food) or hydration (water).
I [   ] DO **OR** [   ] do NOT want blood or blood products.
I [   ] DO **OR** [   ] do NOT want any form of surgery or invasive diagnostic tests.
I [   ] DO **OR** [   ] do NOT want kidney dialysis.
I [   ] DO **OR** [   ] do NOT want antibiotics.

I realize that if I do not specifically indicate my preference regarding any of the forms of treatment listed above, I may receive that form of treatment.

OTHER INSTRUCTIONS (*include any other instructions*):

Selection of Health Care Agent
(Appointment of Health Care Surrogate)

(*Initial "I DO" or "I do NOT"*):

I [   ] DO **OR** [   ] do NOT want to designate another person as my surrogate to make medical treatment decisions for me if I should be incompetent and in a terminal condition or in a state of permanent unconsciousness. (*List name and address of surrogate, if applicable*):

_____ (name), of _____
_____ (address)

Durable Power of Attorney for Financial Affairs

I, _____ , grant a durable power of attorney for financial affairs to _____ (name), of _____
_____ (address), to act as my attorney-in-fact. This power of attorney shall become effective upon my disability, as certified by my primary physician or, if my primary physician is not available, by any other attending physician. This power of attorney grants no power or authority regarding health care decisions to my designated attorney-in-fact.

I give my attorney-in-fact the maximum power under law to perform the following specific acts on my behalf: all acts relating to any and all of my financial and/or business affairs, including all banking and financial institution transactions, all real estate transactions, all insurance and annuity transactions, all claims and litigation, and all business transactions. My attorney-in-fact is granted full power to act on my behalf in the same manner as if I were personally present.

My attorney-in-fact accepts this appointment and agrees to act in my best interest as he or she considers advisable. This power of attorney may be revoked by me at any time and is automatically revoked on my death. This power of attorney shall not be affected by my present or future disability or incapacity. My attorney-in-fact shall not be compensated for his or her services nor shall my attorney-in-fact be liable to me, my estate, heirs, successors, or assigns for acting or refraining from acting under this document, except for willful misconduct or gross negligence. Any third party who receives a signed copy of this document may act under it. Revocation of this document is not effective unless a third party has actual knowledge of such revocation.

Designation of Primary Physician

I designate the following physician as my primary physician: _____ (name), of _____ (address).

Organ Donation

In the event of my death, I have placed my initials next to the following part(s) of my body that I wish donated for the purposes that I have *initialed* below:

[   ] any organs or parts **OR**

[   ] eyes   [   ] bone and connective tissue   [   ] skin

[   ] heart   [   ] kidney(s)   [   ] liver

[   ] lung(s)   [   ] pancreas   [   ] other _____

for the purposes of:

[   ] any purpose authorized by law **OR**

[   ] transplantation   [   ] research   [   ] therapy

[   ] medical education   [   ] other limitations _____

Signature

I sign this Advance Health Care Directive, consisting of the following sections, which I have *initialed* below and have elected to adopt:

[   ] Living Will

[   ] Selection of Health Care Agent (Health Care Surrogate)

[   ] Durable Power of Attorney for Financial Affairs

[   ] Designation of Primary Physician

[   ] Organ Donation

BY SIGNING HERE I INDICATE THAT I UNDERSTAND THE PURPOSE AND EFFECT OF THIS DOCUMENT.

Signature _____ Date _____

City, County, and State of Residence _____

Notary Acknowledgment

State of _____

County of _____

On _____ , _____ came before me per-sonally and, under oath, stated that he or she is the person described in the above document and he or she signed the above document in my presence. I declare under penalty of perjury that the person whose name is subscribed to this instrument appears to be of sound mind and under no duress, fraud, or undue influence.

_____

Notary Public

My commission expires _____

Witness Acknowledgment

The declarant is personally known to me and I believe him or her to be of sound mind and under no duress, fraud, or undue influence. I did not sign the declarant's signature above for or at the direction of the declarant and I am not appointed as the health care agent or attorney-in-fact herein. I am at least eighteen (18) years of age and I am not related to the declarant by blood, adoption, or marriage, entitled to any portion of the estate of the declarant according to the laws of intestate succession or under any will of declarant or codicil thereto, or directly financially responsible for declarant's medical care. I am not a health care provider of the declarant or an employee of the health facility in which the declarant is a patient.

Witness Signature _____   Date _____

Printed Name of Witness _____

Witness Signature _____   Date _____

Printed Name of Witness _____

Acceptance of Health Care Agent and Financial Attorney-in-Fact

I accept my appointment as Health Care Agent:

Signature _____   Date _____

I accept my appointment as Attorney-in-Fact for Financial Affairs:

Signature _____   Date _____

Rhode Island Advance Health Care Directive

On this date of _____ , I, _____ , do hereby sign, execute, and adopt the following as my Advance Health Care Directive. I direct any and all persons or entities involved with my health care in any manner that these decisions are my wishes and were adopted without duress or force and of my own free will. I have placed my *initials* next to the sections of this Directive that I have adopted:

[   ] Living Will
[   ] Selection of Health Care Agent (Durable Power of Attorney for Health Care)
[   ] Durable Power of Attorney for Financial Affairs
[   ] Designation of Primary Physician
[   ] Organ Donation

Living Will Declaration

I, _____ , being of sound mind, willfully and voluntarily make known my desire that my dying shall not be artificially-prolonged under the circumstances set forth below, and do hereby declare:

If I should have an incurable or irreversible condition that will cause my death, and if I am unable to make decisions regarding my medical treatment, I direct my attending physician to withhold or withdraw procedures that merely prolong the dying process and are not necessary to my comfort, or to alleviate pain.

OTHER DIRECTIONS (*include any other directions*):

This authorization DOES include [   ] or does NOT include [   ] the withholding or withdrawal of artificial feeding (*initial only one box above*).

Selection of Health Care Agent
(Durable Power of Attorney for Health Care)

WARNING TO PERSON EXECUTING THIS DOCUMENT: This is an important legal document which is authorized by the general laws of this state. Before executing this document, you should know these important facts: You must be at least eighteen (18) years of age and a resident of the state of Rhode Island for this document to be legally valid and binding. This document gives the person you designate as your agent (the attorney-in-fact) the power to make health care decisions for you. None of the following may be designated as your agent:

(1) your treating health care provider,

(2) a non-relative employee of your treating health care provider,

(3) an operator of a community care facility, OR

(4) a non-relative employee of an operator of a community care facility.

For the purposes of this document, "health care decision" means consent, refusal of consent, or withdrawal of consent to any care, treatment, service, or procedure to maintain, diagnose, or treat an individual's physical or mental condition.

Your agent must act consistently with your desires as stated in this document or otherwise made known. Except as you otherwise specify in this document, this document gives your agent the power to consent to your doctor not giving treatment or stopping treatment necessary to keep you alive. Notwithstanding this document, you have the right to make medical and other health care decisions for yourself so long as you can give informed consent with respect to the particular decision. In addition, no treatment may be given to you over your objection at the time, and health care necessary to keep you alive may not be stopped or withheld if you object at the time. This document gives your agent authority to consent, refuse to consent, or withdraw consent to any care, treatment, service, or procedure to maintain, diagnose, or treat a physical or mental condition. This power is subject to any statement of your desires and any limitation that you include in this document. You may state in this document any types of treatment that you do not desire. In addition, a court can take away the power of your agent to make health care decisions for you if your agent:

(1) authorizes anything that is illegal,

(2) acts contrary to your known desires, OR

(3) where your desires are not known, does anything that is clearly contrary to your best interests.

Unless you specify a specific period, this power will exist until you revoke it. Your agent's power and authority ceases upon your death except to inform your next of kin of your desire to be an organ and tissue donor.

You have the right to revoke the authority of your agent by notifying your agent or your treating doctor, hospital, or other health care provider orally or in writing of the revocation. Your agent has the right to examine your medical records and consent to their disclosure unless you limit this right in this document. This document revokes any prior durable power of attorney for health care. You should carefully read and follow the witnessing procedure described at the end of this form. This document will not be valid unless you comply with the witnessing procedure. If there is anything in this document that you do not understand, you should ask a lawyer to explain it to you. Your agent may need this document immediately in case of an emergency that requires a decision concerning your health care. Either keep this document where it is immediately available to your agent or give him or her an executed copy of this document. You may also want to give your doctor an executed copy of this document.

I, _____ , do hereby designate and appoint _____ _____ (name), of _____ _____ (address), as my attorney-in-fact (agent) to make health care decisions for me as authorized in this document. By this document I intend to create a durable power of attorney for health care. Subject to any limitations in this document, I hereby grant to my agent full power and authority to make health care decisions for me to the same extent that I could make such decisions for myself if I had the capacity to do so. In exercising this authority, my agent shall make health care decisions that are consistent with my desires as stated in this document or otherwise made known to my agent, including, but not limited to, my desires concerning obtaining, refusing, or withdrawing life-prolonging care, treatment, services, and procedures. (*If you want to limit the authority of your agent to make health care decisions for you, you can state the limitations below. You can indicate your desires by including a statement of your desires in the same paragraph. Your agent must make health care decisions that are consistent with your known desires. You can, but are not required to state your desires in the space provided below. You should consider whether you want to include a statement of your desires concerning life-prolonging care, treatment, services, and procedures. You can also include a statement of your desires concerning other matters relating to your health care. You can also make your desires known to your agent by discussing your desires with your agent or by some other means. If there are any types of treatment that you do not want to be used, you should state them in the space below. If you want to limit in any other way the authority given your agent by this document, you should state the limits in the space below. If you do not state any limits, your agent will have broad powers to make health care decisions for you, except to the extent that there are limits provided by law. You may attach additional pages if you need more space to complete your statement. If you attach additional pages, you must date and sign EACH of the additional pages at the same time you date and sign this document.*)

In exercising the authority under this durable power of attorney for health care, my agent shall act consistently with my desires as stated below and is subject to the special provisions and limitations stated below (*attach additional pages if necessary*):

Statement of desires concerning life-prolonging care, treatment, services, and procedures (*list desires and limits*):

Subject to any limitations in this document, my agent has the power and authority to do all of the following:

(1) Request, review, and receive any information, verbal or written, regarding my physical or mental health, including, but not limited to medical and hospital records.

(2) Execute on my behalf any releases or other documents that may be required in order to obtain this information.

(3) Consent to the disclosure of this information.

(*If you want to limit the authority of your agent to receive and disclose information relating to your health, you must state the limitations in the space above.*)

Where necessary to implement the health care decisions that my agent is authorized by this document to make, my agent has the power and authority to execute on my behalf all of the following:

(1) Documents titled or purporting to be a "Refusal to Permit Treatment" and "Leaving Hospital Against Medical Advice."

(2) Any necessary waiver or release from liability required by a hospital or physician.

I revoke any prior durable power of attorney for health care.

Durable Power of Attorney for Financial Affairs

I, _____ , grant a durable power of attorney for financial affairs to _____ (name), of _____ _____ (address), to act as my attorney-in-fact. This power of attorney shall become effective upon my disability, as certified by my primary physician or, if my primary physician is not available, by any other attending physician. This power of attorney grants no power or authority regarding health care decisions to my designated attorney-in-fact.

I give my attorney-in-fact the maximum power under law to perform the following specific acts on my behalf: all acts relating to any and all of my financial and/or business affairs, including all banking and financial institution transactions, all real estate transactions, all insurance and annuity transactions, all claims and litigation, and all business transactions. My attorney-in-fact is granted full power to act on my behalf in the same manner as if I were personally present.

My attorney-in-fact accepts this appointment and agrees to act in my best interest as he or she considers advisable. This power of attorney may be revoked by me at any time and is automatically revoked on my death. This power of attorney shall not be affected by my present or future disability or incapacity. My attorney-in-fact shall not be compensated for his or her services nor shall my attorney-in-fact be liable to me, my estate, heirs, successors, or assigns for acting or refraining from acting under this document, except for willful misconduct or gross negligence. Any third party who receives a signed copy of this document may act under it. Revocation of this document is not effective unless a third party has actual knowledge of such revocation.

Designation of Primary Physician

I designate the following physician as my primary physician: _____
(name), of _____ (address).

Organ Donation

In the event of my death, I have placed my initials next to the following part(s) of my body that I wish donated for the purposes that I have *initialed* below:

[   ] any organs or parts **OR**

[   ] eyes   [   ] bone and connective tissue   [   ] skin

[   ] heart   [   ] kidney(s)   [   ] liver

[   ] lung(s)   [   ] pancreas   [   ] other _____

for the purposes of:

[   ] any purpose authorized by law **OR**

[   ] transplantation   [   ] research   [   ] therapy

[   ] medical education   [   ] other limitations _____

Signature

I sign this Advance Health Care Directive, consisting of the following sections, which I have *initialed* below and have elected to adopt:

[   ] Living Will

[   ] Selection of Health Care Agent (Durable Power of Attorney for Health Care)

[   ] Durable Power of Attorney for Financial Affairs

[   ] Designation of Primary Physician

[   ] Organ Donation

BY SIGNING HERE I INDICATE THAT I UNDERSTAND THE PURPOSE AND EFFECT OF THIS DOCUMENT.

Signature _____   Date _____

City, County, and State of Residence _____

Notary Acknowledgment

State of _____

County of _____

On _____ , _____ came before me personally and, under oath, stated that he or she is the person described in the above document and he or she signed the above document in my presence. I declare under penalty of perjury that the person whose name is subscribed to this instrument appears to be of sound mind and under no duress, fraud, or undue influence.

_____

Notary Public

My commission expires _____

Witness Acknowledgment

The declarant is personally known to me and I believe him or her to be of sound mind and under no duress, fraud, or undue influence. I did not sign the declarant's signature above for or at the direction of the declarant and I am not appointed as the health care agent or attorney-in-fact herein. I am at least eighteen (18) years of age and I am not related to the declarant by blood, adoption, or marriage, entitled to any portion of the estate of the declarant according to the laws of intestate succession or under any will of declarant or codicil thereto, or directly financially responsible for declarant's medical care. I am not a health care provider of the declarant or an employee of the health facility in which the declarant is a patient.

Witness Signature _____ Date _____

Printed Name of Witness _____

Witness Signature _____ Date _____

Printed Name of Witness _____

Acceptance of Health Care Agent and Financial Attorney-in-Fact

I accept my appointment as Health Care Agent:

Signature _____ Date _____

I accept my appointment as Attorney-in-Fact for Financial Affairs:

Signature _____ Date _____

South Carolina Advance Health Care Directive

On this date of _____ , I, _____ , do hereby sign, execute, and adopt the following as my Advance Health Care Directive. I direct any and all persons or entities involved with my health care in any manner that these decisions are my wishes and were adopted without duress or force and of my own free will. I have placed my *initials* next to the sections of this Directive that I have adopted:

[   ] Living Will
[   ] Selection of Health Care Agent (Health Care Power of Attorney)
[   ] Durable Power of Attorney for Financial Affairs
[   ] Designation of Primary Physician
[   ] Organ Donation

Living Will

I willfully and voluntarily make known my desire that no life-sustaining procedures be used to prolong my dying if my condition is terminal or if I am in a state of permanent unconsciousness, and I declare:

If at any time I have a condition certified to be a terminal condition by two (2) physicians who have personally examined me, one (1) of whom is my attending physician, and the physicians have determined that my death could occur within a reasonably short period of time without the use of life-sustaining procedures or if the physicians certify that I am in a state of permanent unconsciousness and where the application of life-sustaining procedures would serve only to prolong the dying process, I direct that the procedures be withheld or withdrawn, and that I be permitted to die naturally with only the administration of medication or the performance of any medical procedure necessary to provide me with comfort care.

INSTRUCTIONS CONCERNING ARTIFICIAL NUTRITION AND HYDRATION: If my condition is terminal and could result in death within a reasonably short time (*initial one of the following statements*):

[   ] I direct that nutrition and hydration BE provided through any medically-indicated means, including medically- or surgically-implanted tubes.

[   ] I direct that nutrition and hydration NOT be provided through any medically-indicated means, including medically- or surgically-implanted tubes.

If I am in a persistent vegetative state or other condition of permanent unconsciousness (*initial one of the following statements*):

[   ] I direct that nutrition and hydration BE provided through any medically-indicated means, including medically- or surgically-implanted tubes.

[   ] I direct that nutrition and hydration NOT be provided through any medically-indicated means, including medically- or surgically-implanted tubes.

In the absence of my ability to give directions regarding the use of life-sustaining procedures, it is my intention that this Declaration be honored by my family and physicians and any health facility in which I may be a patient as the final expression of my legal right to refuse medical or surgical treatment, and I accept the consequences from the refusal. I am aware that this Declaration authorizes a physician to withhold or withdraw life-sustaining procedures. I am emotionally and mentally competent to make this Declaration.

APPOINTMENT OF AN AGENT FOR REVOCATION: You may give another person authority to revoke this declaration on your behalf. If you wish to do so, please enter that person's name in the space below (*optional*):

Name of Agent with Power to Revoke _____

Address _____

REVOCATION PROCEDURES: This declaration may be revoked by any one (1) of the following methods. However, a revocation is not effective until it is communicated to the attending physician:

(1) by being defaced, torn, obliterated, or otherwise destroyed, in expression of your intent to revoke, by you or by some person in your presence and by your direction. Revocation by destruction of one or more of multiple original declarations revokes all of the original declarations,

(2) by a written revocation signed and dated by you expressing your intent to revoke,

(3) by your oral expression of your intent to revoke the declaration. An oral revocation communicated to the attending physician by a person other than you is effective only if:

    (a) the person was present when the oral revocation was made;

    (b) the revocation was communicated to the physician within a reasonable time; OR

    (c) your physical or mental condition makes it impossible for the physician to confirm through subsequent conversation with you that the revocation has occurred. To be effective as a revocation, the oral expression clearly must indicate your desire that the declaration not be given effect or that life-sustaining procedures be administered.

(4) if you, in the space above, have authorized an agent to revoke the declaration, then the agent may revoke orally or by a written, signed, and dated instrument. An agent may revoke only if you are incompetent to do so. An agent may revoke the declaration permanently or temporarily,

(5) by your executing another declaration at a later time.

Selection of Health Care Agent (Health Care Power of Attorney)

INFORMATION ABOUT THIS DOCUMENT: This is an important legal document. Before signing this document, you should know these important facts:

(1) This document gives the person you name as your agent the power to make health care decisions for you if you cannot make the decision for yourself. This power includes the power to make decisions about life-sustaining treatment. Unless you state otherwise, your agent will have the same authority to make decisions about your health care as you would have.

(2) This power is subject to any limitations or statements of your desires that you include in this document. You may state in this document any treatment you do not desire or treatment you want to be sure you receive. Your agent will be obligated to follow your instructions when making decisions on your behalf. (*You may attach additional pages if you need more space to complete the statement.*)

(3) After you have signed this document, you have the right to make health care decisions for yourself if you are mentally competent to do so. After you have signed this document, no treatment may be given to you or stopped over your objection if you are mentally competent to make that decision.

(4) You have the right to revoke this document and terminate your agent's authority by informing either your agent or your health care provider orally or in writing.

(5) If there is anything in this document that you do not understand, you should ask a social worker, lawyer, or other person to explain it to you.

(6) This power of attorney will not be valid unless two (2) persons sign as witnesses. Each of these persons must witness either your signing of the power of attorney or your acknowledgment that the signature on the power of attorney is yours. If you are a patient in a health facility, no more than one (1) witness may be an employee of that facility. The following persons may not act as witnesses:

   (a) your spouse, children, grandchildren, and other lineal descendants, your parents, grandparents, and other lineal ancestors, your siblings and their lineal descendants, or a spouse of any of these persons;

   (b) a person who is directly financially responsible for your medical care;

   (c) a person who is named in your will, or, if you have no will, who would inherit your property by intestate succession;

   (d) a beneficiary of a life insurance policy on your life;

   (e) the person named in the health care power of attorney as your agent;

   (f) your physician or an employee of your physician;

   (g) any person who would have a claim against any portion of your estate (persons to whom you may owe money).

(7) Your agent must be a person who is eighteen (18) years old or older and of sound mind. It may not be your doctor or any other health care provider who is now providing you with treatment, an employee of your doctor or provider, or a spouse of the doctor, provider, or employee, unless the person is a relative of yours.

(8) You should inform the person that you want him or her to be your health care agent. You should discuss this document with your agent and your physician and give each a signed copy. If you are in a health care facility or a nursing care facility, a copy of this document should be included in your medical record.

I, _____ , hereby appoint: _____

(name), of _____(address), as my agent to make health care decisions for me as authorized in this document. By this document I intend to create a durable power of attorney effective upon, and only during, any period of mental incompetence. I grant to my agent full authority to make decisions for me regarding my health care. In exercising this authority, my agent shall follow my desires as stated in this document or otherwise expressed by me or known to my agent. In making any decision, my agent shall attempt to discuss the proposed decision with me to determine my desires if I am able to communicate in any way. If my agent cannot determine the choice I would want made, then my agent shall make a choice for me based upon what my agent believes to be in my best interests. My agent's authority to interpret my desires is intended to be as broad as possible, except for any limitations I may state below. Accordingly, unless specifically limited below, my agent is authorized as follows:

(1) To consent, refuse, or withdraw consent to any and all types of medical care, treatment, surgical procedures, diagnostic procedures, medication, and the use of mechanical or other procedures that affect any bodily function, including, but not limited to, artificial respiration, nutritional support and hydration, and cardiopulmonary resuscitation;

(2) To authorize, or refuse to authorize, any medication or procedure intended to relieve pain, even though such use may lead to physical damage, addiction, or hasten the moment of, but not intentionally cause, my death;

(3) To authorize my admission to or discharge from, even against medical advice, any hospital, nursing care facility, or similar facility or service;

(4) To take any other action necessary to making, documenting, and assuring implementation of decisions concerning my health care, including, but not limited to:

    (a) granting any waiver or release from liability required by any hospital, physician, nursing care provider, or other health care provider,

    (b) signing any documents relating to refusals of treatment or the leaving of a facility against medical advice,

    (c) pursuing any legal action in my name and, at the expense of my estate, to force compliance with my wishes as determined by my agent, **OR**

    (d) to seek actual or punitive damages for the failure to comply.

(5) The powers granted on the previous page do not include the following powers or are subject to the following rules or limitations (*add any rules or limitations*):

I understand that if I have a valid Declaration of a Desire for a Natural Death, the instructions contained in the Declaration will be given effect in any situation to which they are applicable. My agent will have authority to make decisions concerning my health care only in situations to which the Declaration does not apply.

WITH RESPECT TO ANY LIFE-SUSTAINING TREATMENT, I direct the following (*initial only one of the following four paragraphs*):

[   ] GRANT OF DISCRETION TO AGENT. I do NOT want my life to be prolonged nor do I want life-sustaining treatment to be provided or continued if my agent believes the burdens of the treatment outweigh the expected benefits. I want my agent to consider the relief of suffering, my personal beliefs, the expense involved, and the quality as well as the possible extension of my life in making decisions concerning life-sustaining treatment, **OR**

[   ] DIRECTIVE TO WITHHOLD OR WITHDRAW TREATMENT. I do NOT want my life to be prolonged and I do NOT want life-sustaining treatment if:

      (1) I have a condition that is incurable or irreversible and, without the administration of life-sustaining procedures, is expected to result in death within a relatively short period of time; **OR**

      (2) I am in a state of permanent unconsciousness.

OR

[   ] DIRECTIVE FOR MAXIMUM TREATMENT. I DO want my life to be prolonged to the greatest extent possible, within the standards of accepted medical practice, without regard to my condition, the chances I have for recovery, or the cost of the procedures, **OR**

[   ] DIRECTIVE IN MY OWN WORDS (*add other directives, if any*):

WITH RESPECT TO NUTRITION AND HYDRATION provided by means of a nasogastric tube or tube into the stomach, intestines, or veins, I wish to make clear that (*initial only one*):

[   ] I do NOT want to receive these forms of artificial nutrition and hydration, and they may be withheld or withdrawn under the conditions given above, **OR**

[   ] I DO want to receive these forms of artificial nutrition and hydration.

IF YOU DO NOT INITIAL EITHER OF THE ABOVE STATEMENTS, YOUR AGENT WILL NOT HAVE AUTHORITY TO DIRECT THAT NUTRITION AND HYDRATION NECESSARY FOR COMFORT CARE OR ALLEVIATION OF PAIN BE WITHDRAWN.

I revoke any prior Health Care Power of Attorney and any provisions relating to health care of any other prior power of attorney. This power of attorney is intended to be valid in any jurisdiction in which it is presented. If at any relevant time the Agent named herein is unable or unwilling to make decisions concerning my health care and those decisions are to be made by a guardian, the Probate Court, or a surrogate pursuant to the Adult Health Care Consent Act, it is my intention that the guardian, Probate Court, or surrogate make those decisions in accordance with my directions as stated in this document.

Durable Power of Attorney for Financial Affairs

I, _____ , grant a durable power of attorney for financial affairs to _____ (name), of _____ _____ (address), to act as my attorney-in-fact. This power of attorney shall become effective upon my disability, as certified by my primary physician or, if my primary physician is not available, by any other attending physician. This power of attorney grants no power or authority regarding health care decisions to my designated attorney-in-fact.

I give my attorney-in-fact the maximum power under law to perform the following specific acts on my behalf: all acts relating to any and all of my financial and/or business affairs, including all banking and financial institution transactions, all real estate transactions, all insurance and annuity transactions, all claims and litigation, and all business transactions. My attorney-in-fact is granted full power to act on my behalf in the same manner as if I were personally present.

My attorney-in-fact accepts this appointment and agrees to act in my best interest as he or she considers advisable. This power of attorney may be revoked by me at any time and is automatically revoked on my death. This power of attorney shall not be affected by my present or future disability or incapacity. My attorney-in-fact shall not be compensated for his or her services nor shall my attorney-in-fact be liable to me, my estate, heirs, successors, or assigns for acting or refraining from acting under this document, except for willful misconduct or gross negligence. Any third party who receives a signed copy of this document may act under it. Revocation of this document is not effective unless a third party has actual knowledge of such revocation.

Designation of Primary Physician

I designate the following physician as my primary physician: _____ (name), of _____ (address).

Organ Donation

In the event of my death, I have placed my initials next to the following part(s) of my body that I wish donated for the purposes that I have *initialed* below:

[   ] any organs or parts **OR**

[   ] eyes   [   ] bone and connective tissue   [   ] skin

[   ] heart   [   ] kidney(s)   [   ] liver

[   ] lung(s)   [   ] pancreas   [   ] other _____

for the purposes of:

[   ] any purpose authorized by law **OR**

[   ] transplantation   [   ] research   [   ] therapy

[   ] medical education   [   ] other limitations _____

Signature

I sign this Advance Health Care Directive, consisting of the following sections, which I have *initialed* below and have elected to adopt:

[   ] Living Will

[   ] Selection of Health Care Agent (Health Care Power of Attorney)

[   ] Durable Power of Attorney for Financial Affairs

[   ] Designation of Primary Physician

[   ] Organ Donation

BY SIGNING HERE I INDICATE THAT I UNDERSTAND THE PURPOSE AND EF-FECT OF THIS DOCUMENT.

Signature _____   Date _____

City, County, and State of Residence _____

Notary Acknowledgment

State of _____

County of _____

On _____ , _____ came before me per-sonally and, under oath, stated that he or she is the person described in the above document and he or she signed the above document in my presence. I declare under penalty of perjury that the person whose name is subscribed to this instrument appears to be of sound mind and under no duress, fraud, or undue influence.

_____

Notary Public

My commission expires _____

Witness Acknowledgment

The declarant is personally known to me and I believe him or her to be of sound mind and under no duress, fraud, or undue influence. I did not sign the declarant's signature above for or at the direction of the declarant and I am not appointed as the health care agent or attorney-in-fact herein. I am at least eighteen (18) years of age and I am not related to the declarant by blood, adoption, or marriage, entitled to any portion of the estate of the declarant according to the laws of intestate succession or under any will of declarant or codicil thereto or life insurance policy of declarant, or directly financially responsible for declarant's medical care. I am not a health care provider of the declarant or an employee of the health facility in which the declarant is a patient. If the declarant is a resident in a hospital or nursing care facility at the date of execution of this Declaration, at least one (1) of us is an ombudsman designated by the State Ombudsman, Office of the Governor.

Witness Signature _____   Date _____

Printed Name of Witness _____

Witness Signature _____   Date _____

Printed Name of Witness _____

Acceptance of Health Care Agent and Financial Attorney-in-Fact

I accept my appointment as Health Care Agent:

Signature _____   Date _____

I accept my appointment as Attorney-in-Fact for Financial Affairs:

Signature _____   Date _____

South Dakota Advance Health Care Directive

On this date of _____ , I, _____ , do hereby sign, execute, and adopt the following as my Advance Health Care Directive. I direct any and all persons or entities involved with my health care in any manner that these decisions are my wishes and were adopted without duress or force and of my own free will. I have placed my *initials* next to the sections of this Directive that I have adopted:

[   ] Living Will
[   ] Selection of Health Care Agent (Durable Power of Attorney for Health Care)
[   ] Durable Power of Attorney for Financial Affairs
[   ] Designation of Primary Physician
[   ] Organ Donation

Living Will

This is an important legal document. This document directs the medical treatment you are to receive in the event you are unable to participate in your own medical decisions and you are in a terminal condition. This document may state what kind of treatment you want or do not want to receive. This document can control whether you live or die. Prepare this document carefully. If you use this form, read it completely. You may want to seek professional help to make sure the form does what you intend and is completed without mistakes. This document will remain valid and in effect until and unless you revoke it. Review this document periodically to make sure it continues to reflect your wishes. You may amend or revoke this document at any time by notifying your physician and other health care providers. You should give copies of this document to your physician and your family. This form is entirely optional. If you choose to use this form, please note that the form provides signature lines for you, the two (2) witnesses whom you have selected, and a notary public.

I, _____ , willfully and voluntarily make this declaration as a directive to be followed if I am in a terminal condition and become unable to participate in decisions regarding my medical care. With respect to any life-sustaining treatment, I direct the following (*initial only one of the following optional directives if you agree. If you do not agree with any of the following directives, space is provided below for you to write your own directives*):

[   ] NO LIFE-SUSTAINING TREATMENT. I direct that no life-sustaining treatment be provided. If life-sustaining treatment is begun, terminate it.

[   ] TREATMENT FOR RESTORATION. Provide life-sustaining treatment only if and for so long as you believe treatment offers a reasonable possibility of restoring to me the ability to think and act for myself.

[   ] TREAT UNLESS PERMANENTLY UNCONSCIOUS. If you believe that I am permanently unconscious and are satisfied that this condition is irreversible, then do not provide me with life-sustaining treatment, and if life-sustaining treatment is being provided to me, terminate it. If, and so long as you believe that treatment has a reasonable possibility of restoring consciousness to me, then provide life-sustaining treatment.

[   ] MAXIMUM TREATMENT. Preserve my life as long as possible, but do not provide treatment that is not in accordance with accepted medical standards as then in effect.

Artificial nutrition and hydration is food and water provided by means of a nasogastric tube or tubes inserted into the stomach, intestines, or veins (*if you do not wish to receive this form of treatment, you must initial the statement below which reads: "I intend to include this treatment, among the 'life-sustaining treatment' that may be withheld or withdrawn"*):
WITH RESPECT TO ARTIFICIAL NUTRITION AND HYDRATION, I wish to make clear that (*initial only one*):

[   ] I intend TO include this treatment among the "life-sustaining treatment" that may be withheld or withdrawn.

[   ] I do NOT intend to include this treatment among the "life-sustaining treatment" that may be withheld or withdrawn.

(*If you do not agree with any of the printed directives and want to write your own, write directives in addition to the printed provisions, or express some of your other thoughts, you can do so here*):

Selection of Health Care Agent
(Durable Power of Attorney for Health Care)

I, _____ , hereby appoint _____
(name), of _____ (address),
as my attorney-in-fact to consent to, reject, or withdraw consent for medical procedures, treatment, or intervention.

I have discussed my wishes with my attorney-in-fact and my successor attorney-in-fact, and authorize him or her to make all and any health care decisions for me, including decisions to withhold or withdraw any form of life support. I expressly authorize my agent to make decisions for me regarding the withholding or withdrawal of artificial nutrition and hydration in all medical circumstances.

This power of attorney becomes effective when I can no longer make my own medical decisions and is not affected by physical disability or mental incompetence. The determination of whether I can make my own medical decisions is to be made by my attorney-in-fact, or if he or she is unable, unwilling, or unavailable to act, by my successor attorney-in-fact, unless the attending physician determines that I have the capacity to make my own decisions.

Durable Power of Attorney for Financial Affairs

I, _____ , grant a durable power of attorney for financial affairs to _____ (name), of _____
_____ (address), to act as my attorney-in-fact. This power of attorney shall become effective upon my disability, as certified by my primary physician or, if my primary physician is not available, by any other attending physician. This power of attorney grants no power or authority regarding health care decisions to my designated attorney-in-fact.

I give my attorney-in-fact the maximum power under law to perform the following specific acts on my behalf: all acts relating to any and all of my financial and/or business affairs, including all banking and financial institution transactions, all real estate transactions, all insurance and annuity transactions, all claims and litigation, and all business transactions. My attorney-in-fact is granted full power to act on my behalf in the same manner as if I were personally present.

My attorney-in-fact accepts this appointment and agrees to act in my best interest as he or she considers advisable. This power of attorney may be revoked by me at any time and is automatically revoked on my death. This power of attorney shall not be affected by my present or future disability or incapacity. My attorney-in-fact shall not be compensated for his or her services nor shall my attorney-in-fact be liable to me, my estate, heirs, successors, or assigns for acting or refraining from acting under this document, except for willful misconduct or gross negligence. Any third party who receives a signed copy of this document may act under it. Revocation of this document is not effective unless a third party has actual knowledge of such revocation.

Designation of Primary Physician

I designate the following physician as my primary physician: _____
(name), of _____ (address).

Organ Donation

In the event of my death, I have placed my initials next to the following part(s) of my body that I wish donated for the purposes that I have *initialed* below:

[   ] any organs or parts **OR**

[   ] eyes   [   ] bone and connective tissue   [   ] skin

[   ] heart   [   ] kidney(s)   [   ] liver

[   ] lung(s)   [   ] pancreas   [   ] other _____

for the purposes of:

[   ] any purpose authorized by law **OR**

[   ] transplantation   [   ] research   [   ] therapy

[   ] medical education   [   ] other limitations _____

Signature

I sign this Advance Health Care Directive, consisting of the following sections, which I have *initialed* below and have elected to adopt:

[   ]   Living Will

[   ]   Selection of Health Care Agent (Durable Power of Attorney for Health Care)

[   ]   Durable Power of Attorney for Financial Affairs

[   ]   Designation of Primary Physician

[   ]   Organ Donation

BY SIGNING HERE I INDICATE THAT I UNDERSTAND THE PURPOSE AND EFFECT OF THIS DOCUMENT.

Signature _____   Date _____

City, County, and State of Residence _____

Notary Acknowledgment

State of _____

County of _____

On _____ , _____ came before me personally and, under oath, stated that he or she is the person described in the above document and he or she signed the above document in my presence. I declare under penalty of perjury that the person whose name is subscribed to this instrument appears to be of sound mind and under no duress, fraud, or undue influence.

_____

Notary Public

My commission expires _____

Witness Acknowledgment

The declarant is personally known to me and I believe him or her to be of sound mind and under no duress, fraud, or undue influence. I did not sign the declarant's signature above for or at the direction of the declarant and I am not appointed as the health care agent or attorney-in-fact herein. I am at least eighteen (18) years of age and I am not related to the declarant by blood, adoption, or marriage, entitled to any portion of the estate of the declarant according to the laws of intestate succession or under any will of declarant or codicil thereto, or directly financially responsible for declarant's medical care. I am not a health care provider of the declarant or an employee of the health facility in which the declarant is a patient.

Witness Signature _____ Date _____

Printed Name of Witness _____

Witness Signature _____ Date _____

Printed Name of Witness _____

Acceptance of Health Care Agent and Financial Attorney-in-Fact

I accept my appointment as Health Care Agent:

Signature _____ Date _____

I accept my appointment as Attorney-in-Fact for Financial Affairs:

Signature _____ Date _____

Tennessee Advance Health Care Directive

On this date of _____ , I, _____ , do hereby sign, execute, and adopt the following as my Advance Health Care Directive. I direct any and all persons or entities involved with my health care in any manner that these decisions are my wishes and were adopted without duress or force and of my own free will. I have placed my *initials* next to the sections of this Directive that I have adopted:

[　　] Living Will
[　　] Selection of Health Care Agent (Durable Power of Attorney for Health Care)
[　　] Durable Power of Attorney for Financial Affairs
[　　] Designation of Primary Physician
[　　] Organ Donation

Living Will

I, _____ , willfully and voluntarily make known my desire that my dying shall not be artificially prolonged under the circumstances set forth below, and do hereby declare:

If at any time I should have a terminal condition and my attending physician has determined there is no reasonable medical expectation of recovery and which, as a medical probability, will result in my death, regardless of the use or discontinuance of medical treatment implemented for the purpose of sustaining life or the life process, I direct that medical care be withheld or withdrawn, and that I be permitted to die naturally with only the administration of medications or the performance of any medical procedure deemed necessary to provide me with comfortable care or to alleviate pain.

ARTIFICIALLY-PROVIDED NOURISHMENT AND FLUIDS: By *initialing* the appropriate box below, I specifically:

[　　] DO authorize the withholding or withdrawal of artificially-provided food, water, or other nourishment or fluids.

[　　] do NOT authorize the withholding or withdrawal of artificially-provided food, water, or other nourishment or fluids.

In the absence of my ability to give directions regarding my medical care, it is my intention that this declaration shall be honored by my family and physician as the final expression of my legal right to refuse medical care and accept the consequences of such refusal. The definitions of terms used herein shall be as set forth in the Tennessee Right to Natural Death Act, Tennessee Code Annotated, § 32-11-103. I understand the full import of this declaration, and I am emotionally and mentally competent to make this declaration.

Selection of Health Care Agent
(Durable Power of Attorney for Health Care)

This is an important legal document. Before executing this document, you should know these important facts: This document gives the person you designate as your agent (the attorney-in-fact) the power to make health care decisions for you. Your agent must act consistently with your desires as stated in this document. Except as you otherwise specify in this document, this document gives your agent the power to consent to your doctor not giving treatment or stopping treatment necessary to keep you alive. Notwithstanding this document, you have the right to make medical and other health care decisions for yourself so long as you can give informed consent with respect to the particular decision. In addition, no treatment may be given to you over your objection and health care necessary to keep you alive may not be stopped or withheld if you object at the time. This document gives your agent authority to consent, refuse to consent, or withdraw consent to any care, treatment, service, or procedure to maintain, diagnose, or treat a physical or mental condition. This power is subject to any limitations that you include in this document. You may state in this document any types of treatment that you do not desire. In addition, a court can take away the power of your agent to make health care decisions for you if your agent:

(1) authorizes anything that is illegal, OR

(2) acts contrary to your desires as stated in this document.

You have the right to revoke the authority of your agent by notifying your agent or your treating physician, hospital, or other health care provider orally or in writing of the revocation. Your agent has the right to examine your medical records and consent to their disclosure unless you limit this right in this document. Unless you otherwise specify in this document, this document gives your agent the power after you die to:

(1) authorize an autopsy,

(2) donate your body or parts thereof for transplant, therapeutic, educational, or scientific purposes, and

(3) direct the disposition of your remains.

If there is anything in this document that you do not understand, you should ask an attorney to explain it to you.

I, _____ , state and affirm that I have read the foregoing paragraphs concerning the legal consequences of my executing this document, and I do hereby appoint _____ (name), of _____ _____ (address), as my attorney-in-fact to have the authority to express and carry out my specific and general instructions and desires with respect to medical treatment.

I have discussed my wishes with my attorney-in-fact, and authorize him or her to make all and any health care decisions (as defined by Tennessee law) for me, including decisions to withhold or withdraw any form of life support. I expressly authorize my agent to make decisions for me about tube feeding and medication.

This power of attorney becomes effective when I can no longer make my own medical decisions and shall not be affected by my subsequent disability or incompetence. The determination of whether I can make my own medical decisions is to be made by my attorney-in-fact.

Durable Power of Attorney for Financial Affairs

I, _____ , grant a durable power of attorney for financial affairs to _____ (name), of _____
_____ (address), to act as my attorney-in-fact. This power of attorney shall become effective upon my disability, as certified by my primary physician or, if my primary physician is not available, by any other attending physician. This power of attorney grants no power or authority regarding health care decisions to my designated attorney-in-fact.

I give my attorney-in-fact the maximum power under law to perform the following specific acts on my behalf: all acts relating to any and all of my financial and/or business affairs, including all banking and financial institution transactions, all real estate transactions, all insurance and annuity transactions, all claims and litigation, and all business transactions. My attorney-in-fact is granted full power to act on my behalf in the same manner as if I were personally present.

My attorney-in-fact accepts this appointment and agrees to act in my best interest as he or she considers advisable. This power of attorney may be revoked by me at any time and is automatically revoked on my death. This power of attorney shall not be affected by my present or future disability or incapacity. My attorney-in-fact shall not be compensated for his or her services nor shall my attorney-in-fact be liable to me, my estate, heirs, successors, or assigns for acting or refraining from acting under this document, except for willful misconduct or gross negligence. Any third party who receives a signed copy of this document may act under it. Revocation of this document is not effective unless a third party has actual knowledge of such revocation.

Designation of Primary Physician

I designate the following physician as my primary physician: _____
(name), of _____ (address).

Organ Donation

In the event of my death, I have placed my initials next to the following part(s) of my body that I wish donated for the purposes that I have *initialed* below:

[　　] any organs or parts **OR**

[　　] eyes 　　　　　[　　] bone and connective tissue 　　　　[　　] skin

[　　] heart 　　　　　[　　] kidney(s) 　　　　　　　　　　　　　[　　] liver

[　　] lung(s) 　　　　[　　] pancreas 　　　　　　　　　　　　　[　　] other _____

for the purposes of:

[　　] any purpose authorized by law **OR**

[　　] transplantation 　　　　　[　　] research 　　　　　[　　] therapy

[　　] medical education 　　　　[　　] other limitations _____

Signature

I sign this Advance Health Care Directive, consisting of the following sections, which I have *initialed* below and have elected to adopt:

[　　] Living Will

[　　] Selection of Health Care Agent (Durable Power of Attorney for Health Care)

[　　] Durable Power of Attorney for Financial Affairs

[　　] Designation of Primary Physician

[　　] Organ Donation

BY SIGNING HERE I INDICATE THAT I UNDERSTAND THE PURPOSE AND EFFECT OF THIS DOCUMENT.

Signature _____　　　Date _____

City, County, and State of Residence _____

Notary Acknowledgment

State of _____

County of _____

On _____ , _____ came before me personally and, under oath, stated that he or she is the person described in the above document and he or she signed the above document in my presence. I declare under penalty of perjury that the person whose name is subscribed to this instrument appears to be of sound mind and under no duress, fraud, or undue influence.

_____

Notary Public

My commission expires _____

Witness Acknowledgment

The declarant is personally known to me and I believe him or her to be of sound mind and under no duress, fraud, or undue influence. I did not sign the declarant's signature above for or at the direction of the declarant and I am not appointed as the health care agent or attorney-in-fact herein. I am at least eighteen (18) years of age and I am not related to the declarant by blood, adoption, or marriage, entitled to any portion of the estate of the declarant according to the laws of intestate succession or under any will of declarant or codicil thereto, or directly financially responsible for declarant's medical care. I am not a health care provider of the declarant or an employee of the health facility in which the declarant is a patient.

Witness Signature _____ Date _____

Printed Name of Witness _____

Witness Signature _____ Date _____

Printed Name of Witness _____

Acceptance of Health Care Agent and Financial Attorney-in-Fact

I accept my appointment as Health Care Agent:

Signature _____ Date _____

I accept my appointment as Attorney-in-Fact for Financial Affairs:

Signature _____ Date _____

Texas Advance Health Care Directive

On this date of _____ , I, _____ , do hereby sign, execute, and adopt the following as my Advance Health Care Directive. I direct any and all persons or entities involved with my health care in any manner that these decisions are my wishes and were adopted without duress or force and of my own free will. I have placed my *initials* next to the sections of this Directive that I have adopted:

[   ] Living Will (Directive to Physicians and Family or Surrogates)

[   ] Selection of Health Care Agent (Medical Power of Attorney)

[   ] Durable Power of Attorney for Financial Affairs

[   ] Designation of Primary Physician

[   ] Organ Donation

Living Will (Directive to Physicians and Family or Surrogates)

INSTRUCTIONS FOR COMPLETING THIS DOCUMENT: This is an important legal document known as an Advance Directive. It is designed to help you communicate your wishes about medical treatment at some time in the future when you are unable to make your wishes known because of illness or injury. These wishes are usually based on personal values. In particular, you may want to consider what burdens or hardships of treatment you would be willing to accept for a particular amount of benefit obtained if you were seriously ill. You are encouraged to discuss your values and wishes with your family or chosen spokesperson, as well as your physician. Your physician, other health care provider, or medical institution may provide you with various resources to assist you in completing your advance directive. Brief definitions are listed on the following pages and may aid you in your discussions and advance planning. Initial the treatment choices that best reflect your personal preferences. Provide a copy of your directive to your physician, usual hospital, and family or spokesperson. Consider a periodic review of this document. By periodic review, you can best assure that the directive reflects your preferences. In addition to this advance directive, Texas law provides for other types of directives that can be important during a serious illness. These are the Medical Power of Attorney and the Out-of-Hospital Do-Not-Resuscitate Order. You may wish to discuss these with your physician, family, hospital representative, or other advisers. You may also wish to complete a directive related to the donation of organs and tissues and/or a Durable Power of Attorney for Financial Affairs that will allow another person to handle your financial affairs if you are incapacitated.

I, _____ , recognize that the best health care is based upon a partnership of trust and communication with my physician. My physician and I will make health care decisions together as long as I am of sound mind and able to make my wishes known. If there comes a time that I am unable to make medical decisions about myself because of illness or injury, I direct that the following treatment preferences be honored:

If, in the judgment of my physician, I am suffering with a terminal condition from which I am expected to die within six (6) months, even with available life-sustaining treatment provided in accordance with prevailing standards of medical care (*initial one*):

[   ] I request that all treatments other than those needed to keep me comfortable be discontinued or withheld and my physician allow me to die as gently as possible; **OR**

[   ] I request that I be kept alive in this terminal condition using available life-sustaining treatment. (THIS SELECTION DOES NOT APPLY TO HOSPICE CARE.)

If, in the judgment of my physician, I am suffering with an irreversible condition so that I cannot care for myself or make decisions for myself and am expected to die without life-sustaining treatment provided in accordance with prevailing standards of care (*initial one*):

[   ] I request that all treatments other than those needed to keep me comfortable be discontinued or withheld and my physician allow me to die as gently as possible; **OR**

[   ] I request that I be kept alive in this irreversible condition using available life-sustaining treatment. (THIS SELECTION DOES NOT APPLY TO HOSPICE CARE.)

ADDITIONAL REQUESTS: (*After discussion with your physician, you may wish to consider listing particular treatments in this space that you do or do not want in specific circumstances, such as artificial nutrition and fluids, intravenous antibiotics, etc. Be sure to state whether you do or do not want the particular treatment*):

After signing this directive, if my representative or I elect hospice care, I understand and agree that only those treatments needed to keep me comfortable would be provided and I would not be given available life-sustaining treatments. If, in the judgment of my physician, my death is imminent within minutes to hours, even with the use of all available medical treatment provided within the prevailing standard of care, I acknowledge that all treatments may be withheld or removed except those needed to maintain my comfort. I understand that under Texas law this directive has no effect if I have been diagnosed as pregnant. This directive will remain in effect until I revoke it. No other person may do so.

Selection of Health Care Agent (Medical Power of Attorney)

THIS IS AN IMPORTANT LEGAL DOCUMENT. BEFORE SIGNING THIS DOCUMENT, YOU SHOULD KNOW THESE IMPORTANT FACTS: Except to the extent you state otherwise, this document gives the person you name as your agent the authority to make any and all health care decisions for you in accordance with your wishes, including your religious and moral beliefs, when you are no longer capable of making them yourself. Because "health care" means any treatment, service, or procedure to maintain, diagnose, or treat your physical or mental condition, your agent has the power to make a broad range of health care decisions for you. Your agent may consent, refuse to consent, or withdraw consent to medical treatment and may make decisions about withdrawing or withholding life-sustaining treatment. Your agent may not consent to voluntary inpatient mental health services, convulsive treatment, psychosurgery, or abortion. A physician must comply with your agent's instructions or allow you to be transferred to another physician. Your agent's authority begins when your doctor certifies that you lack the competence to make health care decisions. Your agent is obligated to follow your instructions when making decisions on your behalf. Unless you state otherwise, your agent has the same authority to make decisions about your health care as you would have had. It is important that you discuss this document with your physician or other health care provider before you sign it to make sure that you understand the nature and range of decisions that may be made on your behalf. If you do not have a physician, you should talk with someone else who is knowledgeable about these issues and can answer your questions. You do not need a lawyer's assistance to complete this document, but if there is anything in this document that you do not understand, you should ask a lawyer to explain it to you. The person you appoint as agent should be someone you know and trust. The person must be eighteen (18) years of age or older or a person under eighteen (18) years of age who has had the disabilities of minority removed. If you appoint your health or residential care provider (e.g., your physician or an employee of a home health agency, hospital, nursing home, or residential care home, other than a relative), that person has to choose between acting as your agent or as your health or residential care provider; the law does not permit a person to do both at the same time. You should inform the person you appoint that you want the person to be your health care agent. You should discuss this document with your agent and your physician and give each a signed copy. You should indicate on the document itself the people and institutions who have signed copies. Your agent is not liable for health care decisions made in good faith on your behalf. Even after you have signed this document, you have the right to make health care decisions for yourself as long as you are able to do so and treatment cannot be given to you or stopped over your objection. You have the right to revoke the authority granted to your agent by informing your agent or your health or residential care provider orally or in writing, or by your execution of a subsequent medical power of attorney. Unless you state otherwise, your appointment of a spouse dissolves on divorce. This document may not be changed or modified. If you want to make changes in the document, you must make an entirely new one.

THIS POWER OF ATTORNEY IS NOT VALID UNLESS IT IS SIGNED IN THE PRESENCE OF TWO (2) COMPETENT ADULT WITNESSES. THE FOLLOWING PERSONS MAY NOT ACT AS ONE (1) OF THE WITNESSES:

(1) the person you have designated as your agent,

(2) a person related to you by blood or marriage,

(3) a person entitled to any part of your estate after your death under a will or codicil executed by you or by operation of law,

(4) your attending physician,

(5) an employee of your attending physician,

(6) an employee of your health care facility in which you are a patient if the employee is providing direct patient care to you or is an officer, director, partner, or business office employee of the health care facility or of any parent organization of the health care facility, OR

(7) a person who, at the time this power of attorney is executed, has a claim against any part of your estate after your death.

I, _____ , appoint _____ (name), of _____ (address), as my agent to make any and all health care decisions for me, except to the extent I state otherwise in this document. This medical power of attorney takes effect if I become unable to make my own health care decisions and this fact is certified in writing by my physician.

LIMITATIONS ON THE DECISION-MAKING AUTHORITY OF MY AGENT ARE AS FOLLOWS (*insert limitations*):

LOCATION OF COPIES. The original of this document is kept at _____ _____ (address). The following individuals or institutions have signed copies (*list individuals and/or institutions*):

DURATION. I understand that this power of attorney exists indefinitely from the date I execute this document unless I establish a shorter time or revoke the power of attorney. If I am unable to make health care decisions for myself when this power of attorney expires, the authority I have granted my agent continues to exist until the time I become able to make health care decisions for myself.

PRIOR DESIGNATIONS REVOKED. I revoke any prior medical power of attorney.

ACKNOWLEDGMENT OF DISCLOSURE STATEMENT. I have been provided with a disclosure statement explaining the effect of this document. I have read and understood that information contained in the disclosure statement.

Durable Power of Attorney for Financial Affairs

I, _____ , grant a durable power of attorney for financial affairs to _____ (name), of _____
_____ (address), to act as my attorney-in-fact. This power of attorney shall become effective upon my disability, as certified by my primary physician or, if my primary physician is not available, by any other attending physician. This power of attorney grants no power or authority regarding health care decisions to my designated attorney-in-fact.

I give my attorney-in-fact the maximum power under law to perform the following specific acts on my behalf: all acts relating to any and all of my financial and/or business affairs, including all banking and financial institution transactions, all real estate transactions, all insurance and annuity transactions, all claims and litigation, and all business transactions. My attorney-in-fact is granted full power to act on my behalf in the same manner as if I were personally present.

My attorney-in-fact accepts this appointment and agrees to act in my best interest as he or she considers advisable. This power of attorney may be revoked by me at any time and is automatically revoked on my death. This power of attorney shall not be affected by my present or future disability or incapacity. My attorney-in-fact shall not be compensated for his or her services nor shall my attorney-in-fact be liable to me, my estate, heirs, successors, or assigns for acting or refraining from acting under this document, except for willful misconduct or gross negligence. Any third party who receives a signed copy of this document may act under it. Revocation of this document is not effective unless a third party has actual knowledge of such revocation.

Designation of Primary Physician

I designate the following physician as my primary physician: _____
(name), of _____ (address).

Organ Donation

In the event of my death, I have placed my initials next to the following part(s) of my body that I wish donated for the purposes that I have *initialed* below:

[   ] any organs or parts **OR**

[   ] eyes   [   ] bone and connective tissue   [   ] skin

[   ] heart   [   ] kidney(s)   [   ] liver

[   ] lung(s)   [   ] pancreas   [   ] other _____

for the purposes of:

[   ] any purpose authorized by law **OR**

[   ] transplantation   [   ] research   [   ] therapy

[   ] medical education   [   ] other limitations _____

Signature

I sign this Advance Health Care Directive, consisting of the following sections, which I have *initialed* below and have elected to adopt:

[   ]   Living Will (Directive to Physicians and Family or Surrogates)

[   ]   Selection of Health Care Agent (Medical Power of Attorney)

[   ]   Durable Power of Attorney for Financial Affairs

[   ]   Designation of Primary Physician

[   ]   Organ Donation

BY SIGNING HERE I INDICATE THAT I UNDERSTAND THE PURPOSE AND EFFECT OF THIS DOCUMENT.

Signature _____   Date _____

City, County, and State of Residence _____

Notary Acknowledgment

State of _____

County of _____

On _____ , _____ came before me personally and, under oath, stated that he or she is the person described in the above document and he or she signed the above document in my presence. I declare under penalty of perjury that the person whose name is subscribed to this instrument appears to be of sound mind and under no duress, fraud, or undue influence.

_____

Notary Public

My commission expires _____

Witness Acknowledgment

The declarant is personally known to me and I believe him or her to be of sound mind and under no duress, fraud, or undue influence. I did not sign the declarant's signature above for or at the direction of the declarant and I am not appointed as the health care agent or attorney-in-fact herein. I am at least eighteen (18) years of age and I am not related to the declarant by blood, adoption, or marriage, entitled to any portion of the estate of the declarant according to the laws of intestate succession or under any will of declarant or codicil thereto, or directly financially responsible for declarant's medical care. I am not a health care provider of the declarant or an employee of the health facility in which the declarant is a patient.

Witness Signature _____   Date _____

Printed Name of Witness _____

Witness Signature _____   Date _____

Printed Name of Witness _____

Acceptance of Health Care Agent and Financial Attorney-in-Fact

I accept my appointment as Health Care Agent:

Signature _____   Date _____

I accept my appointment as Attorney-in-Fact for Financial Affairs:

Signature _____   Date _____

Utah Advance Health Care Directive

On this date of _____ , I, _____ , do hereby sign, execute, and adopt the following as my Advance Health Care Directive. I direct any and all persons or entities involved with my health care in any manner that these decisions are my wishes and were adopted without duress or force and of my own free will. I have placed my *initials* next to the sections of this Directive that I have adopted:

[   ]   Living Will (Directive to Physicians and Providers of Medical Services)

[   ]   Selection of Health Care Agent (Special Power of Attorney for Health Care)

[   ]   Durable Power of Attorney for Financial Affairs

[   ]   Designation of Primary Physician

[   ]   Organ Donation

Living Will (Directive to Physicians and Providers of Medical Services)

(PURSUANT TO SECTION 75-2-1104, UCA)

I, _____ , being of sound mind, willfully and voluntarily make known my desire that my life not be artificially prolonged by life-sustaining procedures except as I may otherwise provide in this directive.

I declare that if at any time I should have an injury, disease, or illness which is certified in writing to be a terminal condition or persistent vegetative state by two (2) physicians who have personally examined me, and in the opinion of those physicians that the application of life-sustaining procedures would serve only to unnaturally prolong the moment of my death and unnaturally postpone or prolong the dying process, I direct that these procedures be withheld or withdrawn and my death be permitted to occur naturally.

I expressly intend this directive to be a final expression of my legal right to refuse medical or surgical treatment and to accept the consequences from this refusal which shall remain in effect notwithstanding my future inability to give current medical directions to treating physicians and other providers of medical services.

I understand that the term "life-sustaining procedure" includes artificial nutrition and hydration and any other procedures that I specify below to be considered life-sustaining, but does not include the administration of medication or the performance of any medical procedure which is intended to provide comfort care or to alleviate pain.

OTHER INSTRUCTIONS (*optional*):

I reserve the right to give current medical directions to physicians and other providers of medical services so long as I am able, even though these directions may conflict with the above-written directive that life-sustaining procedures be withheld or withdrawn. I understand the full import of this directive and declare that I am emotionally and mentally competent to make this directive.

Selection of Health Care Agent
(Special Power of Attorney for Health Care)

I, _____ , being of sound mind, willfully and voluntarily appoint _____ (name), of _____ _____ (address), as my agent and attorney-in-fact, without substitution, with lawful authority to execute a directive on my behalf under Section 75-2-1105, governing the care and treatment to be administered to or withheld from me at any time after I incur an injury, disease, or illness which renders me unable to give current directions to attending physicians and other providers of medical services. I have carefully selected my above-named agent with confidence in the belief that this person's familiarity with my desires, beliefs, and attitudes will result in directions to attending physicians and providers of medical services which would probably be the same as I would give if able to do so. This power of attorney shall be and remains in effect from the time my attending physician certifies that I have incurred a physical or mental condition rendering me unable to give current directions to attending physicians and other providers of medical services as to my care and treatment.

Durable Power of Attorney for Financial Affairs

I, _____ , grant a durable power of attorney for financial affairs to _____ (name), of _____ _____ (address), to act as my attorney-in-fact. This power of attorney shall become effective upon my disability, as certified by my primary physician or, if my primary physician is not available, by any other attending physician. This power of attorney grants no power or authority regarding health care decisions to my designated attorney-in-fact.

I give my attorney-in-fact the maximum power under law to perform the following specific acts on my behalf: all acts relating to any and all of my financial and/or business affairs, including all banking and financial institution transactions, all real estate transactions, all insurance

and annuity transactions, all claims and litigation, and all business transactions. My attorney-in-fact is granted full power to act on my behalf in the same manner as if I were personally present.

My attorney-in-fact accepts this appointment and agrees to act in my best interest as he or she considers advisable. This power of attorney may be revoked by me at any time and is automatically revoked on my death. This power of attorney shall not be affected by my present or future disability or incapacity. My attorney-in-fact shall not be compensated for his or her services nor shall my attorney-in-fact be liable to me, my estate, heirs, successors, or assigns for acting or refraining from acting under this document, except for willful misconduct or gross negligence. Any third party who receives a signed copy of this document may act under it. Revocation of this document is not effective unless a third party has actual knowledge of such revocation.

Designation of Primary Physician

I designate the following physician as my primary physician: _____
(name), of _____ (address).

Organ Donation

In the event of my death, I have placed my initials next to the following part(s) of my body that I wish donated for the purposes that I have *initialed* below:

[　　] any organs or parts **OR**

[　　] eyes 　　　　　　　[　　] bone and connective tissue 　　　　　[　　] skin

[　　] heart 　　　　　　　[　　] kidney(s) 　　　　　　　　　　　　[　　] liver

[　　] lung(s) 　　　　　　[　　] pancreas 　　　　　　　　　　　　[　　] other _____

for the purposes of:

[　　] any purpose authorized by law **OR**

[　　] transplantation 　　　　　　[　　] research 　　　　　　　[　　] therapy

[　　] medical education 　　　　　[　　] other limitations _____

Signature

I sign this Advance Health Care Directive, consisting of the following sections, which I have *initialed* below and have elected to adopt:

[　　] Living Will (Directive to Physicians and Providers of Medical Services)

[　　] Selection of Health Care Agent (Special Power of Attorney for Health Care)

[　　] Durable Power of Attorney for Financial Affairs

[　　] Designation of Primary Physician

[　　] Organ Donation

BY SIGNING HERE I INDICATE THAT I UNDERSTAND THE PURPOSE AND EFFECT OF THIS DOCUMENT.

Signature _____ 　　Date _____

City, County, and State of Residence _____

Notary Acknowledgment

State of _____

County of _____

On _____ , _____ came before me personally and, under oath, stated that he or she is the person described in the above document and he or she signed the above document in my presence. I declare under penalty of perjury that the person whose name is subscribed to this instrument appears to be of sound mind and under no duress, fraud, or undue influence.

_____
Notary Public
My commission expires _____

Witness Acknowledgment

The declarant is personally known to me and I believe him or her to be of sound mind and under no duress, fraud, or undue influence. I did not sign the declarant's signature above for or at the direction of the declarant and I am not appointed as the health care agent or attorney-in-fact herein. I am at least eighteen (18) years of age and I am not related to the declarant by blood, adoption, or marriage, entitled to any portion of the estate of the declarant according to the laws of intestate succession or under any will of declarant or codicil thereto, or directly financially responsible for declarant's medical care. I am not a health care provider of the declarant or an employee of the health facility in which the declarant is a patient.

Witness Signature _____ Date _____

Printed Name of Witness _____

Witness Signature _____ Date _____

Printed Name of Witness _____

Acceptance of Health Care Agent and Financial Attorney-in-Fact

I accept my appointment as Health Care Agent:

Signature _____ Date _____

I accept my appointment as Attorney-in-Fact for Financial Affairs:

Signature _____ Date _____

Vermont Advance Health Care Directive

On this date of _____ , I, _____ , do hereby sign, execute, and adopt the following as my Advance Health Care Directive. I direct any and all persons or entities involved with my health care in any manner that these decisions are my wishes and were adopted without duress or force and of my own free will. I have placed my *initials* next to the sections of this Directive that I have adopted:

[   ]   Living Will (Terminal Care Document)
[   ]   Selection of Health Care Agent (Durable Power of Attorney for Health Care)
[   ]   Durable Power of Attorney for Financial Affairs
[   ]   Designation of Primary Physician
[   ]   Organ Donation

Living Will (Terminal Care Document)

To my family, my physician, my lawyer, my clergyman. To any medical facility in whose care I happen to be. To any individual who may become responsible for my health, welfare, or affairs.

Death is as much a reality as birth, growth, maturity, and old age—it is the one certainty of life. If the time comes when I, _____ , can no longer take part in decisions of my own future, let this statement stand as an expression of my wishes, while I am still of sound mind.

If the situation should arise in which I am in a terminal state and there is no reasonable expectation of my recovery, I direct that I be allowed to die a natural death and that my life not be prolonged by extraordinary measures. I do, however, ask that medication be mercifully administered to me to alleviate suffering even though this may shorten my remaining life.

This statement is made after careful consideration and is in accordance with my strong convictions and beliefs. I want the wishes and directions here expressed carried out to the extent permitted by law. Insofar as they are not legally enforceable, I hope that those to whom this will is addressed will regard themselves as morally bound by these provisions.

Copies of this request have been given to (*list name[s] and address[es] of person[s] and attach additional sheets if needed*):

_____ (name), of _____
_____ (address)

_____ (name), of _____
_____ (address)

_____ (name), of _____
_____ (address)

Selection of Health Care Agent
(Durable Power of Attorney for Health Care)

THIS IS AN IMPORTANT LEGAL DOCUMENT. BEFORE SIGNING THIS DOCUMENT, YOU SHOULD KNOW THESE IMPORTANT FACTS: Except to the extent you state otherwise, this document gives the person you name as your agent the authority to make any and all health care decisions for you when you are no longer capable of making them yourself. "Health care" means any treatment, service, or procedure to maintain, diagnose, or treat your physical or mental condition. Your agent therefore can have the power to make a broad range of health care decisions for you. Your agent may consent, refuse to consent, or withdraw consent to medical treatment and may make decisions about withdrawing or withholding life-sustaining treatment. You may state in this document any treatment you do not desire or treatment you want to be sure you receive. Your agent's authority will begin when your doctor certifies that you lack the capacity to make health care decisions. You may attach additional pages if you need more space to complete your statement. Your agent will be obligated to follow your instructions when making decisions on your behalf. Unless you state otherwise, your agent will have the same authority to make decisions about your health care as you would have had. It is important that you discuss this document with your physician or other health care providers before you sign it to make sure that you understand the nature and range of decisions which may be made on your behalf. If you do not have a physician, you should talk with someone else who is knowledgeable about these issues and can answer your questions. You do not need a lawyer's assistance to complete this document, but if there is anything in this document that you do not understand, you should ask a lawyer to explain it to you. The person you appoint as agent should be someone you know and trust and must be at least eighteen (18) years old. If you appoint your health or residential care provider (e.g., your physician, or an employee of a home health agency, hospital, nursing home, or residential care home, other than a relative), that person will have to choose between acting as your agent or as your health or residential care provider; the law does not permit a person to do both at the same time. You should inform the person you appoint that you want him or her to be your health care agent. You should discuss this document with your agent and your physician and give each a signed copy. You should indicate on the document itself the people and institutions who will have signed copies. Your agent will not be liable for health care decisions made in good faith on your behalf. Even after you have signed this document, you have the right to make health care decisions for yourself as long as you are able to do so, and treatment cannot be given to you or stopped over your objection. You have the right to revoke the authority granted to your agent by informing him or her or your health care provider orally or in writing. This document may not be changed or modified. If you want to make changes in the document you must make an entirely new one.

THIS POWER OF ATTORNEY WILL NOT BE VALID UNLESS IT IS SIGNED IN THE PRESENCE OF TWO (2) OR MORE QUALIFIED WITNESSES WHO MUST BOTH BE PRESENT WHEN YOU SIGN OR ACKNOWLEDGE YOUR SIGNATURE. THE FOLLOWING PERSONS MAY NOT ACT AS WIT-

NESSES: The person you have designated as your agent, health or residential care provider or one (1) of their employees, spouse, lawful heirs or beneficiaries named in your will or a deed, or creditors or persons who have a claim against you.

I, _____ , hereby appoint _____
(name), of _____ (address), as my agent to make any and all health care decisions for me, except to the extent I state otherwise in this document. This durable power of attorney for health care shall take effect in the event I become unable to make my own health care decisions.

STATEMENT OF DESIRES, SPECIAL PROVISIONS, AND LIMITATIONS REGARDING HEALTH CARE DECISIONS. (*Here you may include any specific desires or limitations you deem appropriate, such as when or what life-sustaining measures should be withheld, directions whether to continue or discontinue artificial nutrition and hydration, or instructions to refuse any specific types of treatment that are inconsistent with your religious beliefs or unacceptable to you for any other reason. Attach additional pages as necessary*):

THE SUBJECT OF LIFE-SUSTAINING TREATMENT IS OF PARTICULAR IMPORTANCE. (*For your convenience in dealing with that subject, some general statements concerning the withholding or removal of life-sustaining treatment are set forth below. If you agree with one of these statements, you may include the statement by initialing the space before the statement*):

[   ] If I suffer a condition from which there is no reasonable prospect of regaining my ability to think and act for myself, I want only care directed to my comfort and dignity and authorize my agent to decline all treatment which is primarily intended to prolong my life, including artificial nutrition and hydration.

[   ] If I suffer a condition from which there is no reasonable prospect of regaining the ability to think and act for myself, I want care directed to my comfort and dignity and also want artificial nutrition and hydration if needed, but authorize my agent to decline all other treatment which is primarily intended to prolong my life.

[   ] I want my life sustained by any reasonable medical measures, regardless of my condition.

I hereby acknowledge that I have been provided with a disclosure statement explaining the effect of this document. I have read and understand the information contained in the disclosure statement. The original of this document will be kept at _____
_____ (address), and the following person(s) and institution(s) will have signed copies (*list name[s] and address[es] of person[s] and attach additional pages if needed*):

_____ (name), of _____
_____ (address)

_____ (name), of _____
_____ (address)

_____ (name), of _____
_____ (address)

Durable Power of Attorney for Financial Affairs

I, _____ , grant a durable power of attorney for financial affairs to _____ (name), of _____
_____ (address), to act as my attorney-in-fact. This power of attorney shall become effective upon my disability, as certified by my primary physician or, if my primary physician is not available, by any other attending physician. This power of attorney grants no power or authority regarding health care decisions to my designated attorney-in-fact.

I give my attorney-in-fact the maximum power under law to perform the following specific acts on my behalf: all acts relating to any and all of my financial and/or business affairs, including all banking and financial institution transactions, all real estate transactions, all insurance and annuity transactions, all claims and litigation, and all business transactions. My attorney-in-fact is granted full power to act on my behalf in the same manner as if I were personally present.

My attorney-in-fact accepts this appointment and agrees to act in my best interest as he or she considers advisable. This power of attorney may be revoked by me at any time and is automatically revoked on my death. This power of attorney shall not be affected by my present or future disability or incapacity. My attorney-in-fact shall not be compensated for his or her services nor shall my attorney-in-fact be liable to me, my estate, heirs, successors, or assigns for acting or refraining from acting under this document, except for willful misconduct or gross negligence. Any third party who receives a signed copy of this document may act under it. Revocation of this document is not effective unless a third party has actual knowledge of such revocation.

Designation of Primary Physician

I designate the following physician as my primary physician: _____
(name), of _____ (address).

Organ Donation

In the event of my death, I have placed my initials next to the following part(s) of my body that I wish donated for the purposes that I have *initialed* below:

[   ] any organs or parts **OR**

[   ] eyes   [   ] bone and connective tissue   [   ] skin

[   ] heart   [   ] kidney(s)   [   ] liver

[   ] lung(s)   [   ] pancreas   [   ] other _____

for the purposes of:

[   ] any purpose authorized by law **OR**

[   ] transplantation   [   ] research   [   ] therapy

[   ] medical education   [   ] other limitations _____

Signature

I sign this Advance Health Care Directive, consisting of the following sections, which I have *initialed* below and have elected to adopt:

[   ] Living Will (Terminal Care Document)

[   ] Selection of Health Care Agent (Durable Power of Attorney for Health Care)

[   ] Durable Power of Attorney for Financial Affairs

[   ] Designation of Primary Physician

[   ] Organ Donation

BY SIGNING HERE I INDICATE THAT I UNDERSTAND THE PURPOSE AND EFFECT OF THIS DOCUMENT.

Signature _____   Date _____

City, County, and State of Residence _____

Notary Acknowledgment

State of _____

County of _____

On _____ , _____ came before me personally and, under oath, stated that he or she is the person described in the above document and he or she signed the above document in my presence. I declare under penalty of perjury that the person whose name is subscribed to this instrument appears to be of sound mind and under no duress, fraud, or undue influence.

_____

Notary Public

My commission expires _____

Witness Acknowledgment

The declarant is personally known to me and I believe him or her to be of sound mind and under no duress, fraud, or undue influence. I did not sign the declarant's signature above for or at the direction of the declarant and I am not appointed as the health care agent or attorney-in-fact herein. I am at least eighteen (18) years of age and I am not related to the declarant by blood, adoption, or marriage, entitled to any portion of the estate of the declarant according to the laws of intestate succession or under any will of declarant or codicil thereto, or directly financially responsible for declarant's medical care. I am not a health care provider of the declarant or an employee of the health facility in which the declarant is a patient.

Witness Signature _____ Date _____

Printed Name of Witness _____

Witness Signature _____ Date _____

Printed Name of Witness _____

Acceptance of Health Care Agent and Financial Attorney-in-Fact

I accept my appointment as Health Care Agent:

Signature _____ Date _____

I accept my appointment as Attorney-in-Fact for Financial Affairs:

Signature _____ Date _____

Statement of Ombudsman, Hospital Representative, or Other Authorized Person

(To be signed only if the principal is in or is being admitted to a hospital, nursing home, or residential-care home.)
I declare that I have personally explained the nature and effect of this durable power of attorney to the principal and that the principal understands the same (*sign below and insert date, printed name, and address*):

Signature _____ Date _____

Printed Name _____

Address _____

Virginia Advance Health Care Directive

On this date of _____ , I, _____ , do hereby sign, execute, and adopt the following as my Advance Health Care Directive. I direct any and all persons or entities involved with my health care in any manner that these decisions are my wishes and were adopted without duress or force and of my own free will. I have placed my *initials* next to the sections of this Directive that I have adopted:

[   ] Living Will
[   ] Selection of Health Care Agent
[   ] Durable Power of Attorney for Financial Affairs
[   ] Designation of Primary Physician
[   ] Organ Donation

Living Will

I, _____ , willfully and voluntarily make known my desire and do hereby declare: If at any time my attending physician should determine that I have a terminal condition where the application of life-prolonging procedures would serve only to artificially prolong the dying process, I direct that such procedures be withheld or withdrawn, and that I be permitted to die naturally with only the administration of medication or the performance of any medical procedure deemed necessary to provide me with comfort care or to alleviate pain.

I specifically direct that the following procedures or treatments be provided to me (*optional*):

In the absence of my ability to give directions regarding the use of such life-prolonging procedures, it is my intention that this advance directive shall be honored by my family and physician as the final expression of my legal right to refuse medical or surgical treatment and accept the consequences of such refusal.

Selection of Health Care Agent

(Cross through if you do not want to appoint an agent to make health care decisions for you.)

I, _____ , hereby appoint _____

(name), of _____ (address),

as my agent to make health care decisions on my behalf as authorized in this document.

I hereby grant to my agent, named above, full power and authority to make health care decisions on my behalf as described below whenever I have been determined to be incapable of making an informed decision about providing, withholding, or withdrawing medical treatment. The phrase "incapable of making an informed decision" means being unable to understand the nature, extent, and probable consequences of a proposed medical decision or unable to make a rational evaluation of the risks and benefits of a proposed medical decision as compared with the risks and benefits of alternatives to that decision, or unable to communicate such understanding in any way. My agent's authority hereunder is effective as long as I am incapable of making an informed decision.

The determination that I am incapable of making an informed decision shall be made by my attending physician and a second physician or licensed clinical psychologist after a personal examination of me and shall be certified in writing. Such certification shall be required before treatment is withheld or withdrawn, and before, or as soon as reasonably practicable after, treatment is provided, and every one-hundred-eighty (180) days thereafter while the treatment continues.

In exercising the power to make health care decisions on my behalf, my agent shall follow my desires and preferences as stated in this document or as otherwise known to my agent. My agent shall be guided by my medical diagnosis and prognosis and any information provided by my physicians as to the intrusiveness, pain, risks, and side effects associated with treatment or nontreatment. My agent shall not authorize a course of treatment which he or she knows, or upon reasonable inquiry ought to know, is contrary to my religious beliefs or my basic values, whether expressed orally or in writing. If my agent cannot determine what treatment choice I would have made on my own behalf, then my agent shall make a choice for me based upon what he or she believes to be in my best interests.

POWERS OF MY AGENT (*optional*):
(Cross through any language you do not want and add any language you do want.)
The powers of my agent shall include the following:
(1) To consent to, refuse, or withdraw consent to any type of medical care, treatment, surgical procedure, diagnostic procedure, medication, and the use of mechanical or other procedures that affect any bodily function, including, but not limited to, artificial respiration, artificially-administered nutrition and hydration, and cardiopulmonary resuscitation. This authorization specifically includes the power to consent to the administration of dosages of pain-relieving medication in excess of recommended dosages in an amount sufficient to relieve pain, even if such medication carries the risk of addiction or inadvertently hastens my death,

(2) To request, receive, and review any information, verbal or written, regarding my physical or mental health, including but not limited to, medical and hospital records, and to consent to the disclosure of this information,

(3) To employ and discharge my health care providers,

(4) To authorize my admission to or discharge (including transfer to another facility) from any hospital, hospice, nursing home, adult home, or other medical care facility for services other than those for treatment of mental illness requiring admission procedures provided in Article 1 (§ 37.1-63 et seq.) of Chapter 2 of Title 37.1, and

(5) To take any lawful actions that may be necessary to carry out these decisions, including the granting of releases of liability to medical providers.

Further, my agent shall not be liable for the costs of treatment pursuant to his or her authorization, based solely on that authorization. This advance directive shall not terminate in the event of my disability.

Durable Power of Attorney for Financial Affairs

I, _____ , grant a durable power of attorney for financial affairs to _____ (name), of _____ _____ (address), to act as my attorney-in-fact. This power of attorney shall become effective upon my disability, as certified by my primary physician or, if my primary physician is not available, by any other attending physician. This power of attorney grants no power or authority regarding health care decisions to my designated attorney-in-fact.

I give my attorney-in-fact the maximum power under law to perform the following specific acts on my behalf: all acts relating to any and all of my financial and/or business affairs, including all banking and financial institution transactions, all real estate transactions, all insurance and annuity transactions, all claims and litigation, and all business transactions. My attorney-in-fact is granted full power to act on my behalf in the same manner as if I were personally present.

My attorney-in-fact accepts this appointment and agrees to act in my best interest as he or she considers advisable. This power of attorney may be revoked by me at any time and is automatically revoked on my death. This power of attorney shall not be affected by my present or future disability or incapacity. My attorney-in-fact shall not be compensated for his or her services nor shall my attorney-in-fact be liable to me, my estate, heirs, successors, or assigns for acting or refraining from acting under this document, except for willful misconduct or gross negligence. Any third party who receives a signed copy of this document may act under it. Revocation of this document is not effective unless a third party has actual knowledge of such revocation.

Designation of Primary Physician

I designate the following physician as my primary physician: _____
(name), of _____ (address).

Organ Donation

In the event of my death, I have placed my initials next to the following part(s) of my body that I wish donated for the purposes that I have *initialed* below:

[   ] any organs or parts **OR**

[   ] eyes   [   ] bone and connective tissue   [   ] skin

[   ] heart   [   ] kidney(s)   [   ] liver

[   ] lung(s)   [   ] pancreas   [   ] other _____

for the purposes of:

[   ] any purpose authorized by law **OR**

[   ] transplantation   [   ] research   [   ] therapy

[   ] medical education   [   ] other limitations _____

Signature

I sign this Advance Health Care Directive, consisting of the following sections, which I have *initialed* below and have elected to adopt:

[   ] Living Will

[   ] Selection of Health Care Agent

[   ] Durable Power of Attorney for Financial Affairs

[   ] Designation of Primary Physician

[   ] Organ Donation

BY SIGNING HERE I INDICATE THAT I UNDERSTAND THE PURPOSE AND EFFECT OF THIS DOCUMENT.

Signature _____   Date _____

City, County, and State of Residence _____

Notary Acknowledgment

State of _____

County of _____

On _____ , _____ came before me per-sonally and, under oath, stated that he or she is the person described in the above document and he or she signed the above document in my presence. I declare under penalty of perjury that the person whose name is subscribed to this instrument appears to be of sound mind and under no duress, fraud, or undue influence.

_____

Notary Public

My commission expires _____

Witness Acknowledgment

The declarant is personally known to me and I believe him or her to be of sound mind and under no duress, fraud, or undue influence. I did not sign the declarant's signature above for or at the direction of the declarant and I am not appointed as the health care agent or attorney-in-fact herein. I am at least eighteen (18) years of age and I am not related to the declarant by blood, adoption, or marriage, entitled to any portion of the estate of the declarant according to the laws of intestate succession or under any will of declarant or codicil thereto, or directly financially responsible for declarant's medical care. I am not a health care provider of the declarant or an employee of the health facility in which the declarant is a patient.

Witness Signature _____ Date _____

Printed Name of Witness _____

Witness Signature _____ Date _____

Printed Name of Witness _____

Acceptance of Health Care Agent and Financial Attorney-in-Fact

I accept my appointment as Health Care Agent:

Signature _____ Date _____

I accept my appointment as Attorney-in-Fact for Financial Affairs:

Signature _____ Date _____

Washington Advance Health Care Directive

On this date of _____ , I, _____ , do hereby sign, execute, and adopt the following as my Advance Health Care Directive. I direct any and all persons or entities involved with my health care in any manner that these decisions are my wishes and were adopted without duress or force and of my own free will. I have placed my *initials* next to the sections of this Directive that I have adopted:

[   ] Living Will
[   ] Selection of Health Care Agent (Durable Power of Attorney for Health Care)
[   ] Durable Power of Attorney for Financial Affairs
[   ] Designation of Primary Physician
[   ] Organ Donation

Living Will

I, _____ , having the capacity to make health care decisions, willfully, and voluntarily make known my desire that my dying shall not be artificially-prolonged under the circumstances set forth below, and do hereby declare that:

If at any time I should be diagnosed in writing to be in a terminal condition by the attending physician, or in a permanent unconscious condition by two physicians, and where the application of life-sustaining treatment would serve only to artificially prolong the process of my dying, I direct that such treatment be withheld or withdrawn, and that I be permitted to die naturally. I understand by using this form that a terminal condition means an incurable and irreversible condition caused by injury, disease, or illness that would within reasonable medical judgment cause death within a reasonable period of time in accordance with accepted medical standards, and where the application of life-sustaining treatment would serve only to prolong the process of dying. I further understand in using this form that a permanent unconscious condition means an incurable and irreversible condition in which I am medically assessed within reasonable medical judgment as having no reasonable probability of recovery from an irreversible coma or a persistent vegetative state.

In the absence of my ability to give directions regarding the use of such life-sustaining treatment, it is my intention that this directive shall be honored by my family and physician(s) as the final expression of my legal right to refuse medical or surgical treatment and I accept the consequences of such refusal. If another person is appointed to make these decisions for me, whether through a durable power of attorney or otherwise, I request that the person be guided by this directive and any other clear expressions of my desires.

If I am diagnosed to be in a terminal condition or in a permanent unconscious condition (*initial one*):

[   ] I DO want to have artificially-provided nutrition and hydration.

[   ] I do NOT want to have artificially-provided nutrition and hydration.

If I have been diagnosed as pregnant and that diagnosis is known to my physician, this directive shall have no force or effect during the course of my pregnancy. I understand the full import of this directive and I am emotionally and mentally capable to make the health care decisions contained in this directive. I understand that before I sign this directive, I can add to, delete from, or otherwise change the wording of this directive and that I may add to or delete from this directive at any time and that any changes shall be consistent with Washington state law or federal constitutional law to be legally valid. It is my wish that every part of this directive be fully implemented. If for any reason any part is held invalid it is my wish that the remainder of my directive be implemented.

Selection of Health Care Agent
(Durable Power of Attorney for Health Care)

I understand that my wishes as expressed in my living will may not cover all possible aspects of my care if I become incapacitated. Consequently, there may be a need for someone to accept or refuse medical intervention on my behalf, in consultation with my physician. Therefore, I, _____ , designate and appoint _____ _____ (name), of _____ _____ (address), as my attorney-in-fact for health care decisions.

This Power of Attorney shall take effect upon my incapacity to make my own health care decisions, as determined by my treating physician and one (1) other physician, and shall continue as long as the incapacity lasts or until I revoke it, whichever happens first.

The powers of my attorney-in-fact under this Power of Attorney are limited to making decisions about my health care on my behalf. These powers shall include the power to order the withholding or withdrawal of life-sustaining treatment if my attorney-in-fact believes, in his or her own judgment, that is what I would want if I could make the decision myself. The existence of this Durable Power of Attorney for Health Care shall have no effect upon the validity of any other Power of Attorney for other purposes that I have executed or may execute in the future.

In the event that a proceeding is initiated to appoint a guardian of my person under RCW 11.88, I nominate the person designated as my attorney-in-fact for health care decisions to serve as my guardian.

I make the following additional instructions regarding my care (*list instructions if desired*):

Durable Power of Attorney for Financial Affairs

I, _____ , grant a durable power of attorney for financial affairs
to _____ (name), of _____
_____ (address), to act as my attorney-in-fact. This power of attorney
shall become effective upon my disability, as certified by my primary physician or, if my primary
physician is not available, by any other attending physician. This power of attorney grants no
power or authority regarding health care decisions to my designated attorney-in-fact.

I give my attorney-in-fact the maximum power under law to perform the following specific
acts on my behalf: all acts relating to any and all of my financial and/or business affairs,
including all banking and financial institution transactions, all real estate transactions, all insurance and annuity transactions, all claims and litigation, and all business transactions. My
attorney-in-fact is granted full power to act on my behalf in the same manner as if I were
personally present.

My attorney-in-fact accepts this appointment and agrees to act in my best interest as he or she
considers advisable. This power of attorney may be revoked by me at any time and is automatically revoked on my death. This power of attorney shall not be affected by my present or
future disability or incapacity. My attorney-in-fact shall not be compensated for his or her
services nor shall my attorney-in-fact be liable to me, my estate, heirs, successors, or assigns
for acting or refraining from acting under this document, except for willful misconduct or
gross negligence. Any third party who receives a signed copy of this document may act under
it. Revocation of this document is not effective unless a third party has actual knowledge of
such revocation.

Designation of Primary Physician

I designate the following physician as my primary physician: _____
(name), of _____ (address).

Organ Donation

In the event of my death, I have placed my initials next to the following part(s) of my body that I wish donated for the purposes that I have *initialed* below:

[　　] any organs or parts **OR**

[　　] eyes　　　　　[　　] bone and connective tissue　　　　[　　] skin

[　　] heart　　　　　[　　] kidney(s)　　　　　　　　　　　　[　　] liver

[　　] lung(s)　　　　[　　] pancreas　　　　　　　　　　　　[　　] other _____

for the purposes of:

[　　] any purpose authorized by law **OR**

[　　] transplantation　　　　　[　　] research　　　　　　[　　] therapy

[　　] medical education　　　　[　　] other limitations _____

Signature

I sign this Advance Health Care Directive, consisting of the following sections, which I have *initialed* below and have elected to adopt:

[　　] Living Will

[　　] Selection of Health Care Agent (Durable Power of Attorney for Health Care)

[　　] Durable Power of Attorney for Financial Affairs

[　　] Designation of Primary Physician

[　　] Organ Donation

BY SIGNING HERE I INDICATE THAT I UNDERSTAND THE PURPOSE AND EFFECT OF THIS DOCUMENT.

ignature _____　　Date _____

City, County, and State of Residence _____

Notary Acknowledgment

State of _____

County of _____

On _____ , _____ came before me personally and, under oath, stated that he or she is the person described in the above document and he or she signed the above document in my presence. I declare under penalty of perjury that the person whose name is subscribed to this instrument appears to be of sound mind and under no duress, fraud, or undue influence.

_____

Notary Public

My commission expires _____

Witness Acknowledgment

The declarant is personally known to me and I believe him or her to be of sound mind and under no duress, fraud, or undue influence. I did not sign the declarant's signature above for or at the direction of the declarant and I am not appointed as the health care agent or attorney-in-fact herein. I am at least eighteen (18) years of age and I am not related to the declarant by blood, adoption, or marriage, entitled to any portion of the estate of the declarant according to the laws of intestate succession or under any will of declarant or codicil thereto, or directly financially responsible for declarant's medical care. I am not a health care provider of the declarant or an employee of the health facility in which the declarant is a patient.

Witness Signature _____ Date _____

Printed Name of Witness _____

Witness Signature _____ Date _____

Printed Name of Witness _____

Acceptance of Health Care Agent and Financial Attorney-in-Fact

I accept my appointment as Health Care Agent:

Signature _____ Date _____

I accept my appointment as Attorney-in-Fact for Financial Affairs:

Signature _____ Date _____

West Virginia Advance Health Care Directive

On this date of _____ , I, _____ , do hereby sign, execute, and adopt the following as my Advance Health Care Directive. I direct any and all persons or entities involved with my health care in any manner that these decisions are my wishes and were adopted without duress or force and of my own free will. I have placed my *initials* next to the sections of this Directive that I have adopted:

[   ]   Living Will
[   ]   Selection of Health Care Agent (Medical Power of Attorney)
[   ]   Durable Power of Attorney for Financial Affairs
[   ]   Designation of Primary Physician
[   ]   Organ Donation

Living Will

THE KIND OF MEDICAL TREATMENT I WANT AND DON'T WANT IF I HAVE A TERMINAL CONDITION OR AM IN A PERSISTENT VEGETATIVE STATE.

I, _____ , being of sound mind, willfully and voluntarily declare that I want my wishes to be respected if I am very sick and not able to communicate my wishes for myself. In the absence of my ability to give directions regarding the use of life-prolonging medical intervention, it is my desire that my dying shall not be prolonged under the following circumstances:

If I am very sick and not able to communicate my wishes for myself and I am certified by one (1) physician who has personally examined me to have a terminal condition or to be in a persistent vegetative state (that is, if I am unconscious and am neither aware of my environment nor able to interact with others), I direct that life-prolonging medical intervention that would serve solely to prolong the dying process or maintain me in a persistent vegetative state be withheld or withdrawn. I want to be allowed to die naturally and only be given medications or other medical procedures necessary to keep me comfortable. I want to receive as much medication as is necessary to alleviate my pain.

I give the following SPECIAL DIRECTIVES OR LIMITATIONS (*comments about tube feedings, breathing machines, cardiopulmonary resuscitation, and dialysis may be placed here. My failure to provide special directives or limitations does not mean that I want or refuse certain treatments*):

It is my intention that this living will be honored as the final expression of my legal right to refuse medical or surgical treatment and to accept the consequences resulting from such refusal. I understand the full import of this living will.

Selection of Health Care Agent (Medical Power of Attorney)

THE PERSON I WANT TO MAKE HEALTH CARE DECISIONS FOR ME WHEN I CAN'T MAKE THEM FOR MYSELF.

I, _____ , hereby appoint _____
(name), of _____ (address), as my representative to act on my behalf to give, withhold, or withdraw informed consent to health care decisions in the event that I am not able to do so myself.

This appointment shall extend to, but not be limited to, health care decisions relating to medical treatment, surgical treatment, nursing care, medication, hospitalization, care and treatment in a nursing home or other facility, and home health care. The representative appointed by this document is specifically authorized to be granted access to my medical records and other health information and to act on my behalf to consent to, refuse, or withdraw any and all medical treatment, diagnostic procedures, or autopsy if my representative determines that I, if able to do so, would consent to, refuse, or withdraw such treatment or procedures. Such authority shall include, but not be limited to, decisions regarding the withholding or withdrawal of life-prolonging interventions.

I appoint this representative because I believe this person understands my wishes and values and will act to carry into effect the health care decisions that I would make if I were able to do so, and because I also believe that this person will act in my best interest when my wishes are unknown. It is my intent that my family, my physician, and all legal authorities be bound by the decisions that are made by the representative appointed by this document, and it is my intent that these decisions should not be the subject of review by any health care provider or administrative or judicial agency.

It is my intent that this document be legally binding and effective and that this document be taken as a formal statement of my desire concerning the method by which any health care decisions should be made on my behalf during any period when I am unable to make such decisions. In exercising the authority under this medical power of attorney, my representative shall act consistently with my special directives or limitations as stated below.

I am giving the following SPECIAL DIRECTIVES OR LIMITATIONS ON THIS POWER (*comments about tube feedings, breathing machines, cardiopulmonary resuscitation, and dialysis may be placed here. My failure to provide special directives or limitations does not mean that I want or refuse certain treatments*):

THIS MEDICAL POWER OF ATTORNEY SHALL BECOME EFFECTIVE ONLY UPON MY INCAPACITY TO GIVE, WITHHOLD, OR WITHDRAW INFORMED CONSENT TO MY OWN MEDICAL CARE.

Durable Power of Attorney for Financial Affairs

I, _____ , grant a durable power of attorney for financial affairs to _____ (name), of _____ _____ (address), to act as my attorney-in-fact. This power of attorney shall become effective upon my disability, as certified by my primary physician or, if my primary physician is not available, by any other attending physician. This power of attorney grants no power or authority regarding health care decisions to my designated attorney-in-fact.

I give my attorney-in-fact the maximum power under law to perform the following specific acts on my behalf: all acts relating to any and all of my financial and/or business affairs, including all banking and financial institution transactions, all real estate transactions, all insurance and annuity transactions, all claims and litigation, and all business transactions. My attorney-in-fact is granted full power to act on my behalf in the same manner as if I were personally present.

My attorney-in-fact accepts this appointment and agrees to act in my best interest as he or she considers advisable. This power of attorney may be revoked by me at any time and is automatically revoked on my death. This power of attorney shall not be affected by my present or future disability or incapacity. My attorney-in-fact shall not be compensated for his or her services nor shall my attorney-in-fact be liable to me, my estate, heirs, successors, or assigns for acting or refraining from acting under this document, except for willful misconduct or gross negligence. Any third party who receives a signed copy of this document may act under it. Revocation of this document is not effective unless a third party has actual knowledge of such revocation.

Designation of Primary Physician

I designate the following physician as my primary physician: _____
(name), of _____ (address).

Organ Donation

In the event of my death, I have placed my initials next to the following part(s) of my body that I wish donated for the purposes that I have *initialed* below:

[   ] any organs or parts **OR**

[   ] eyes   [   ] bone and connective tissue   [   ] skin

[   ] heart   [   ] kidney(s)   [   ] liver

[   ] lung(s)   [   ] pancreas   [   ] other _____

for the purposes of:

[   ] any purpose authorized by law **OR**

[   ] transplantation   [   ] research   [   ] therapy

[   ] medical education   [   ] other limitations _____

Signature

I sign this Advance Health Care Directive, consisting of the following sections, which I have *initialed* below and have elected to adopt:

[   ] Living Will

[   ] Selection of Health Care Agent (Medical Power of Attorney)

[   ] Durable Power of Attorney for Financial Affairs

[   ] Designation of Primary Physician

[   ] Organ Donation

BY SIGNING HERE I INDICATE THAT I UNDERSTAND THE PURPOSE AND EFFECT OF THIS DOCUMENT.

Signature _____   Date _____

City, County, and State of Residence _____

Notary Acknowledgment

State of _____

County of _____

On _____ , _____ came before me personally and, under oath, stated that he or she is the person described in the above document and he or she signed the above document in my presence. I declare under penalty of perjury that the person whose name is subscribed to this instrument appears to be of sound mind and under no duress, fraud, or undue influence.

_____
Notary Public
My commission expires _____

Witness Acknowledgment

The declarant is personally known to me and I believe him or her to be of sound mind and under no duress, fraud, or undue influence. I did not sign the declarant's signature above for or at the direction of the declarant and I am not appointed as the health care agent or attorney-in-fact herein. I am at least eighteen (18) years of age and I am not related to the declarant by blood, adoption, or marriage, entitled to any portion of the estate of the declarant according to the laws of intestate succession or under any will of declarant or codicil thereto, or directly financially responsible for declarant's medical care. I am not a health care provider of the declarant or an employee of the health facility in which the declarant is a patient.

Witness Signature _____ Date _____

Printed Name of Witness _____

Witness Signature _____ Date _____

Printed Name of Witness _____

Acceptance of Health Care Agent and Financial Attorney-in-Fact

I accept my appointment as Health Care Agent:

Signature _____ Date _____

I accept my appointment as Attorney-in-Fact for Financial Affairs:

Signature _____ Date _____

Wisconsin Advance Health Care Directive

On this date of _____ , I, _____ , do hereby sign, execute, and adopt the following as my Advance Health Care Directive. I direct any and all persons or entities involved with my health care in any manner that these decisions are my wishes and were adopted without duress or force and of my own free will. I have placed my *initials* next to the sections of this Directive that I have adopted:

[   ] Living Will (Declaration to Physicians)
[   ] Selection of Health Care Agent (Power of Attorney for Health Care)
[   ] Durable Power of Attorney for Financial Affairs
[   ] Designation of Primary Physician
[   ] Organ Donation

Living Will (Declaration to Physicians)

I, _____ , being of sound mind, voluntarily state my desire that my dying not be prolonged under the circumstances specified in this document. Under those circumstances, I direct that I be permitted to die naturally. If I am unable to give directions regarding the use of life-sustaining procedures or feeding tubes, I intend that my family and physician honor this document as the final expression of my legal right to refuse medical or surgical treatment

If I have a TERMINAL CONDITION, as determined by two (2) physicians who have personally examined me, I do not want my dying to be artificially-prolonged and I do not want life-sustaining procedures to be used. In addition, the following are my directions regarding the use of feeding tubes (*initial one*):

[   ] YES, I DO want feeding tubes used if I have a terminal condition.
[   ] NO, I do NOT want feeding tubes used if I have a terminal condition.
(If you have not initialed either box, feeding tubes will be used.)

If I am in a PERSISTENT VEGETATIVE STATE, as determined by two (2) physicians who have personally examined me, the following are my directions regarding the use of life-sustaining procedures (*initial one*):

[   ] YES, I DO want life-sustaining procedures used if I am in a persistent vegetative state.
[   ] NO, I do NOT want life-sustaining procedures used if I am in a persistent vegetative state.
(If you have not initialed either box, life-sustaining procedures will be used.)

If I am in a PERSISTENT VEGETATIVE STATE, as determined by two (2) physicians who have personally examined me, the following are my directions regarding the use of feeding tubes (*initial one*):

[   ] YES, I DO want feeding tubes used if I am in a persistent vegetative state.

[   ] NO, I do NOT want feeding tubes used if I am in a persistent vegetative state.

(*If you have not initialed either box, feeding tubes will be used.*)

Selection of Health Care Agent (Power of Attorney for Health Care)

NOTICE TO PERSON MAKING THIS DOCUMENT: You have the right to make decisions about your health care. No health care may be given to you over your objection, and necessary health care may not be stopped or withheld if you object. Because your health care providers in some cases may not have had the opportunity to establish a long-term relationship with you, they are often unfamiliar with your beliefs and values and the details of your family relationships. This poses a problem if you become physically or mentally unable to make decisions about your health care. In order to avoid this problem, you may sign this legal document to specify the person whom you want to make health care decisions for you if you are unable to make those decisions personally. That person is known as your health care agent. You should take some time to discuss your thoughts and beliefs about medical treatment with the person whom you have specified. You may state in this document any types of health care that you do or do not desire and you may limit the authority of your health care agent. If your health care agent is unaware of your desires with respect to a particular health care decision, he or she is required to determine what would be in your best interests in making the decision. This is an important legal document. It gives your agent broad powers to make health care decisions for you. It revokes any prior power of attorney for health care that you may have made. If you wish to change your power of attorney for health care, you may revoke this document at any time by destroying it, directing another person to destroy it in your presence, signing a written and dated statement, or stating that it is revoked in the presence of two (2) witnesses. If you revoke, you should notify your agent, your health care providers, and any other person to whom you have given a copy. If your agent is your spouse and your marriage is annulled or you are divorced after signing this document, the document is invalid. You may also use this document to make or refuse to make an anatomical gift upon your death. If you use this document to make or refuse to make an anatomical gift, this document revokes any prior anatomical gift that you may have made. You may revoke or change any anatomical gift that you make by this document by crossing out the anatomical gifts provision in this document. Do not sign this document unless you clearly understand it. It is suggested that you keep the original of this document on file with your physician.

I, _____ , being of sound mind, intend by this document to create a power of attorney for health care. My executing this power of attorney for health care is voluntary. Despite the creation of this power of attorney for health care, I expect to be fully informed about and allowed to participate in any health care decision for me, to the extent that

I am able. For the purposes of this document, "health care decision" means an informed decision to accept, maintain, discontinue, or refuse any care, treatment, service, or procedure to maintain, diagnose, or treat my physical or mental condition. In addition, I may, by this document, specify my wishes with respect to making an anatomical gift upon my death.

If I am no longer able to make health care decisions for myself, due to my incapacity, I hereby designate _____ (name), _____
_____ (address), to be my health care agent for the purpose of making health care decisions on my behalf.
The health care agent named above is not my health care provider, an employee of my health care provider, an employee of a health care facility in which I am a patient, or a spouse of any of those persons, unless he or she is also my relative. For purposes of this document, "incapacity" exists if two (2) physicians or a physician and a psychologist who have personally examined me sign a statement that specifically expresses their opinion that I have a condition that means that I am unable to receive and evaluate information effectively or to communicate decisions to such an extent that I lack the capacity to manage my health care decisions. A copy of that statement must be attached to this document.

Unless I have specified otherwise in this document, if I ever have incapacity I instruct my health care provider to obtain the health care decision of my health care agent, if I need treatment, for all of my health care and treatment. I have discussed my desires thoroughly with my health care agent and believe that he or she understands my philosophy regarding the health care decisions I would make if I were able. I desire that my wishes be carried out through the authority given to my health care agent under this document. If I am unable, due to my incapacity, to make a health care decision, my health care agent is instructed to make the health care decision for me, but my health care agent should try to discuss with me any specific proposed health care if I am able to communicate in any manner, including by blinking my eyes. If this communication cannot be made, my health care agent shall base his or her decision on any health care choices that I have expressed prior to the time of the decision. If I have not expressed a health care choice about the health care in question and communication cannot be made, my health care agent shall base his or her health care decision on what he or she believes to be in my best interest.

My health care agent may not admit or commit me on an inpatient basis to an institution for mental diseases, an intermediate care facility for the mentally retarded, a state treatment facility, or a treatment facility. My health care agent may not consent to experimental mental health research or psychosurgery, electroconvulsive treatment, or other drastic mental health treatment procedures for me.

My health care agent may admit me to a nursing home or community-based residential facility for short-term stays for recuperative care or respite care. If I have initialed "YES" to the following, my health care agent may admit me for a purpose other than recuperative care or respite care, but if I have initialed "NO" to the following, my health care agent may not so admit me (*initial one*):

(1) A nursing home: YES [   ] **OR**   NO [   ]

(2) A community-based residential facility: YES [   ] **OR**   NO [   ]

(*If I have not initialed either "Yes" or "No" immediately above, my health care agent may only admit me for short-term stays for recuperative care or respite care.*)

If I have initialed "YES" to the following, my health care agent may have a feeding tube withheld or withdrawn from me, unless my physician has advised that, in his or her professional judgment, this will cause me pain or will reduce my comfort. If I have initialed "NO" to the following, my health care agent may not have a feeding tube withheld or withdrawn from me. My health care agent may not have orally-ingested nutrition or hydration withheld or withdrawn from me unless provision of the nutrition or hydration is medically contraindicated (*initial one*):

Withhold or withdraw a feeding tube: YES [   ] **OR**   NO [   ]

(*If I have not initialed either "Yes" or "No" immediately above, my health care agent may not have a feeding tube withdrawn from me.*)

If I have initialed "YES" to the following, my health care agent may make health care decisions for me even if my agent knows I am pregnant. If I have initialed "NO" to the following, my health care agent may not make health care decisions for me if my health care agent knows I am pregnant (*initial one*):

Health care decision if I am pregnant: YES [   ] **OR**   NO [   ]

(*If I have not initialed either "Yes" or "No" immediately above, my health care agent may not make health care decisions for me if my health care agent knows I am pregnant.*)

In exercising authority under this document, my health care agent shall act consistently with my following stated desires, if any, and is subject to any special provisions or limitations that I specify. The following are specific desires, provisions, or limitations that I wish to state (*insert desires, provisions, or limitations*):

Subject to any limitations in this document, my health care agent has the authority to do all of the following:

(1) Request, review, and receive any information, oral or written, regarding my physical or mental health, including medical and hospital records,

(2) Execute on my behalf any documents that may be required in order to obtain this information, and

(3) Consent to the disclosure of this information.

Durable Power of Attorney for Financial Affairs

I, _____ , grant a durable power of attorney for financial affairs to _____ (name), of _____ _____ (address), to act as my attorney-in-fact. This power of attorney shall become effective upon my disability, as certified by my primary physician or, if my primary physician is not available, by any other attending physician. This power of attorney grants no power or authority regarding health care decisions to my designated attorney-in-fact.

I give my attorney-in-fact the maximum power under law to perform the following specific acts on my behalf: all acts relating to any and all of my financial and/or business affairs, including all banking and financial institution transactions, all real estate transactions, all insurance and annuity transactions, all claims and litigation, and all business transactions. My attorney-in-fact is granted full power to act on my behalf in the same manner as if I were personally present.

My attorney-in-fact accepts this appointment and agrees to act in my best interest as he or she considers advisable. This power of attorney may be revoked by me at any time and is automatically revoked on my death. This power of attorney shall not be affected by my present or future disability or incapacity. My attorney-in-fact shall not be compensated for his or her services nor shall my attorney-in-fact be liable to me, my estate, heirs, successors, or assigns for acting or refraining from acting under this document, except for willful misconduct or gross negligence. Any third party who receives a signed copy of this document may act under it. Revocation of this document is not effective unless a third party has actual knowledge of such revocation.

Designation of Primary Physician

I designate the following physician as my primary physician: _____ (name), of _____ (address).

Organ Donation

In the event of my death, I have placed my initials next to the following part(s) of my body that I wish donated for the purposes that I have *initialed* below:

[   ] any organs or parts **OR**

[   ] eyes   [   ] bone and connective tissue   [   ] skin

[   ] heart   [   ] kidney(s)   [   ] liver

[   ] lung(s)   [   ] pancreas   [   ] other _____

for the purposes of:

[   ] any purpose authorized by law **OR**

[   ] transplantation   [   ] research   [   ] therapy

[   ] medical education   [   ] other limitations _____

Signature

I sign this Advance Health Care Directive, consisting of the following sections, which I have *initialed* below and have elected to adopt:

[   ]   Living Will (Declaration to Physicians)

[   ]   Selection of Health Care Agent (Power of Attorney for Health Care)

[   ]   Durable Power of Attorney for Financial Affairs

[   ]   Designation of Primary Physician

[   ]   Organ Donation

BY SIGNING HERE I INDICATE THAT I UNDERSTAND THE PURPOSE AND EF-FECT OF THIS DOCUMENT.

Signature _____   Date _____

City, County, and State of Residence _____

Notary Acknowledgment

State of _____

County of _____

On _____ , _____ came before me per-sonally and, under oath, stated that he or she is the person described in the above document and he or she signed the above document in my presence. I declare under penalty of perjury that the person whose name is subscribed to this instrument appears to be of sound mind and under no duress, fraud, or undue influence.

_____

Notary Public

My commission expires _____

Witness Acknowledgment

The declarant is personally known to me and I believe him or her to be of sound mind and under no duress, fraud, or undue influence. I did not sign the declarant's signature above for or at the direction of the declarant and I am not appointed as the health care agent or attorney-in-fact herein. I am at least eighteen (18) years of age and I am not related to the declarant by blood, adoption, or marriage, entitled to any portion of the estate of the declarant according to the laws of intestate succession or under any will of declarant or codicil thereto, or directly financially responsible for declarant's medical care. I am not a health care provider of the declarant or an employee of the health facility in which the declarant is a patient.

Witness Signature _____ Date _____

Printed Name of Witness _____

Witness Signature _____ Date _____

Printed Name of Witness _____

Acceptance of Health Care Agent and Financial Attorney-in-Fact

I accept my appointment as Health Care Agent:

Signature _____ Date _____

I accept my appointment as Attorney-in-Fact for Financial Affairs:

Signature _____ Date _____

Wyoming Advance Health Care Directive

On this date of _____ , I, _____ , do hereby sign, execute, and adopt the following as my Advance Health Care Directive. I direct any and all persons or entities involved with my health care in any manner that these decisions are my wishes and were adopted without duress or force and of my own free will. I have placed my *initials* next to the sections of this Directive that I have adopted:

[   ]   Living Will
[   ]   Selection of Health Care Agent (Durable Power of Attorney for Health Care)
[   ]   Durable Power of Attorney for Financial Affairs
[   ]   Designation of Primary Physician
[   ]   Organ Donation

Living Will

I, _____ , being of sound mind, willfully and voluntarily make known my desire that my dying shall not be artificially prolonged under the circumstances set forth below, do hereby declare:

If at any time I should have an incurable injury, disease, or other illness certified to be a terminal condition by two (2) physicians who have personally examined me, one (1) of whom shall be my attending physician, and the physicians have determined that my death will occur whether or not life-sustaining procedures are utilized and where the application of life-sustaining procedures would serve only to artificially prolong the dying process, I direct that such procedures be withheld or withdrawn, and that I be permitted to die naturally with only the administration of medication or the performance of any medical procedure deemed necessary to provide me with comfort care.

In the absence of my ability to give directions regarding the use of life-sustaining procedures, it is my intention that this declaration shall be honored by my family and physician(s) and agent as the final expression of my legal right to refuse medical or surgical treatment and accept the consequences from this refusal. I understand the full import of this declaration and I am emotionally and mentally competent to make this declaration.

NOTICE: This document has significant medical, legal, and possible ethical implications and effects. Before you sign this document, you should become completely familiar with these implications and effects. The operation, effects, and implications of this document may be discussed with a physician, lawyer, and clergyman of your choice.

Selection of Health Care Agent
(Durable Power of Attorney for Health Care)

I, _____ , hereby appoint _____
(name), of _____ (address), as
my attorney-in-fact to consent to, reject, or withdraw consent for any medical care, treatment,
service, or procedure.

I authorize my attorney-in-fact to make any and all health care decisions for me, including
decisions to withhold or withdraw any form of life-sustaining procedures. This power of
attorney becomes effective when I can no longer make my own medical decisions and is not
affected by my physical disability or incapacity. The determination of whether I can make my
own medical decisions is to be made by my attorney-in-fact, or if he or she is unable, unwilling, or unavailable to act, by my successor attorney-in-fact, unless the attending physician
determines that I have decisional capacity.

Durable Power of Attorney for Financial Affairs

I, _____ , grant a durable power of attorney for financial affairs
to _____ (name), of _____
_____ (address), to act as my attorney-in-fact. This power of attorney
shall become effective upon my disability, as certified by my primary physician or, if my primary
physician is not available, by any other attending physician. This power of attorney grants no
power or authority regarding health care decisions to my designated attorney-in-fact.

I give my attorney-in-fact the maximum power under law to perform the following specific
acts on my behalf: all acts relating to any and all of my financial and/or business affairs,
including all banking and financial institution transactions, all real estate transactions, all insurance and annuity transactions, all claims and litigation, and all business transactions. My
attorney-in-fact is granted full power to act on my behalf in the same manner as if I were
personally present.

My attorney-in-fact accepts this appointment and agrees to act in my best interest as he or she
considers advisable. This power of attorney may be revoked by me at any time and is automatically
revoked on my death. This power of attorney shall not be affected by my present or future
disability or incapacity. My attorney-in-fact shall not be compensated for his or her services
nor shall my attorney-in-fact be liable to me, my estate, heirs, successors, or assigns for acting
or refraining from acting under this document, except for willful misconduct or gross negligence.
Any third party who receives a signed copy of this document may act under it. Revocation of
this document is not effective unless a third party has actual knowledge of such revocation.

Designation of Primary Physician

I designate the following physician as my primary physician: _____
(name), of _____ (address).

Organ Donation

In the event of my death, I have placed my initials next to the following part(s) of my body that I wish donated for the purposes that I have *initialed* below:

[   ] any organs or parts **OR**

[   ] eyes   [   ] bone and connective tissue   [   ] skin

[   ] heart   [   ] kidney(s)   [   ] liver

[   ] lung(s)   [   ] pancreas   [   ] other _____

for the purposes of:

[   ] any purpose authorized by law **OR**

[   ] transplantation   [   ] research   [   ] therapy

[   ] medical education   [   ] other limitations _____

Signature

I sign this Advance Health Care Directive, consisting of the following sections, which I have *initialed* below and have elected to adopt:

[   ] Living Will

[   ] Selection of Health Care Agent (Durable Power of Attorney for Health Care)

[   ] Durable Power of Attorney for Financial Affairs

[   ] Designation of Primary Physician

[   ] Organ Donation

BY SIGNING HERE I INDICATE THAT I UNDERSTAND THE PURPOSE AND EFFECT OF THIS DOCUMENT.

Signature _____   Date _____

City, County, and State of Residence _____

Notary Acknowledgment

State of _____

County of _____

On _____ , _____ came before me personally and, under oath, stated that he or she is the person described in the above document and he or she signed the above document in my presence. I declare under penalty of perjury that the person whose name is subscribed to this instrument appears to be of sound mind and under no duress, fraud, or undue influence.

_____

Notary Public

My commission expires _____

Witness Acknowledgment

The declarant is personally known to me and I believe him or her to be of sound mind and under no duress, fraud, or undue influence. I did not sign the declarant's signature above for or at the direction of the declarant and I am not appointed as the health care agent or attorney-in-fact herein. I am at least eighteen (18) years of age and I am not related to the declarant by blood, adoption, or marriage, entitled to any portion of the estate of the declarant according to the laws of intestate succession or under any will of declarant or codicil thereto, or directly financially responsible for declarant's medical care. I am not a health care provider of the declarant or an employee of the health facility in which the declarant is a patient.

Witness Signature _____   Date _____

Printed Name of Witness _____

Witness Signature _____   Date _____

Printed Name of Witness _____

Acceptance of Health Care Agent and Financial Attorney-in-Fact

I accept my appointment as Health Care Agent:

Signature _____   Date _____

I accept my appointment as Attorney-in-Fact for Financial Affairs:

Signature _____   Date _____

Appendix

This book is part of Nova Publishing Company's *Law Made Simple Series*. This Appendix contains a summary of the laws relating to living wills and advance health care directives for all states and the District of Columbia (Washington D.C.). It has been compiled directly from the most recently-available statutes and has been abridged for clarity and succinctness. Every effort has been made to assure that the information contained in this guide is accurate and complete. However, laws are subject to constant change. Therefore, prior to reliance on any legal points, the current status of the specific law should be checked.

State Law Reference: This listing specifies the correct state statute book(s) which contain living wills or health care directive law.

State Website: This listing provides the internet website address of the location of the state's statutes pertaining to living wills or health care directive laws. The state's website address should be entered at the browser location as one continuous line, with no spaces or breaks in between. These addresses were current at the time of this book's publication, however, like most websites, the page addresses are subject to change. If an expired state webpage is not directed to a new site, laws can be searched at http://www.findlaw.com or on the internet browser's search engine.

Living Will Form: Under this listing, the exact location of a state's official living will form is provided.

Other Directives: The existence and location of additional official state directives relating to advance health care and powers of attorney are indicated in this listing. Examples of such forms are Durable Power of Attorney for Health Care, Durable Power of Attorney for Financial Affairs, Anatomical Gift Act forms (organ donation forms), Designation of Primary Physician, and other related forms.

Living Will Effective: This listing indicates the requirements of state law regarding when a living will becomes effective. Most states require that two physicians must diagnose and document that a patient either has a terminal illness with no hope of recovery or is in a permanent state of unconsciousness, or some similar diagnosis.

Witness Requirements: Under this listing are noted the specific state requirements for witnesses to the signing of a living will and any related advance health care directives. In general, most states require that there are two witnesses, and that the witnesses be over eighteen, not related by blood or marriage to the declarant, not entitled to any part of the declarant's estate, and not financially responsible for the declarant's health care costs.

Alabama

State Law Reference: Code of Alabama

State Website: http://www.legislature.state.al.us/CodeofAlabama/1975/coatoc.htm

Living Will Form: Living Will, Title 22, Chapter 8A, Section 4.

Other Directives: Durable Power of Attorney Act Section 26-1-2. Anatomical Gift Act 22-19-40 through 22-19-47.

Living Will Effective: Two (2) physicians, one being the attending physician, must diagnose and document in the medical records that you either have a terminal illness or injury or are in a permanent state of unconsciousness.

Witness Requirements: Will must be signed in the presence of two (2) or more witnesses at least nineteen (19) years of age. Witnesses cannot be related by blood, adoption, or marriage, entitled to any part of your estate, or be directly financially responsible for your health care.

Alaska

State Law Reference: Alaska Statutes

State Website: http://www.legis.state.ak.us/folhome.htm

Living Will Form: Declaration Relating to Use of Life-Sustaining Procedures serves as Living Will 18-12-010.

Other Directives: Durable Power of Attorney for Health Care 13-26-388 to 13-26-353. Anatomical Gift Act 13-50-010 through 13-50-090. Durable Power of Attorney 13-26-332.

Living Will Effective: Two (2) physicians determine that you are in a terminal condition and your death will result without using life-sustaining procedures. Your physician must then record your diagnosis and the contents of your Declaration in your medical records.

Witness Requirements: Sign your Declaration, or direct another to sign it, in the presence of two (2) adult witnesses or a notary public. Witnesses cannot be related by blood or marriage.

Arizona

State Law Reference: Arizona Revised Statutes

State Website: http://www.azleg.state.az.us/ars/ars.htm

Living Will Form: Living Will Chapter 36, Section 3261 through 36-3262.

Other Directives: Health Care Power of Attorney 36-3224. Anatomical Gift Act 36-841 through 36-850. Durable Power of Attorney 14-5501.

Living Will Effective: A physician must believe that your condition is terminal, irreversible, or incurable.

Witness Requirements: Sign in the presence of two (2) or more witnesses or a notary public. Witnesses cannot be related by blood, adoption, or marriage, entitled to any part of your estate, or be directly financially responsible for your health care.

Arkansas

State Law Reference: Arkansas Code

State Website: http://www.arkleg.state.ar.us/newwebcode/lpext.dll?f=templates&fn=main-h.htm&2.0

Living Will Form: Declaration serves as Living Will Title 20, Chapter 17, Section 202.

Other Directives: Durable Power of Attorney for Health Care 20-13-104. Anatomical Gift Act 20-17-601. Durable Power of Attorney 26-68-402.

Living Will Effective: Declaration applies when two (2) physicians diagnose you to have an incurable or irreversible condition that will cause death in a relatively short time.

Witness Requirements: Sign in the presence of two (2) witnesses. No other restrictions apply.

California

State Law Reference: Health Care Decisions Law

State Website: http://www.leginfo.ca.gov/index.html

Living Will Form: California Advanced Health Care Directive serves as Living Will AB 891-Chapter 658.

Other Directives: California Advanced Health Care Directive contains Power of Attorney for Health Care, Instructions for Health Care, Donation of Organs, and Appointment of Primary Physician AB 891-Chapter 658. Anatomical Gift Act Health and Safety Code 7150 through 7158. Durable Power of Attorney Probate Code 4120 through 4230.

Living Will Effective: This Directive becomes effective in the event that you have an incurable and irreversible condition that will result in death within a relatively short time, become unconscious and, to a reasonable degree of medical certainty, will not regain consciousness, or the likely risks and burdens of treatment would outweigh the expected benefits.

Witness Requirements: Sign in the presence of two (2) adult witnesses. A witness cannot be the person you appointed as your agent, your health care provider or an employee of your health care provider, or the operator or employee of a residential care facility for the elderly. Witnesses cannot be related to you by blood, marriage, or adoption, or be entitled to any part of your estate.

Colorado

State Law Reference: Colorado Statute
State Website: http://64.78.178.125/stat01/index.htm
Living Will Form: Colorado Declaration as to Medical or Surgical Treatment serves as Living Will Title 15, Chapter 18, Section 103.
Other Directives: Durable Power of Attorney for Health Care Section 15-14-506. Anatomical Gift Act 12-34-101. Durable Power of Attorney 15-1-1301 through 15-1-1320, 15-14-501 through 15-14-509 and 15-14-601 through 15-14-611.
Living Will Effective: Two (2) physicians must determine that you are in a terminal condition and your death will result without using life-sustaining procedures. Your physician must then record your diagnosis and the contents of your Declaration in your medical records.
Witness Requirements: Sign in the presence of two (2) adult witnesses. A witness cannot be a person who has claim against your estate upon your death, stands to inherit from your estate, or a physician, an employee of your attending physician or treating health care facility, or a patient of your treating health care facility.

Connecticut

State Law Reference: Connecticut Statute
State Website: http://www.cslib.org/psaindex.htm
Living Will Form: Connecticut Health Care Instructions serves as Living Will Chapter 19A, Section 575A.
Other Directives: Connecticut Health Care Instructions also contains Appointment of Health Care Agent and Appointment of Attorney-In-Fact for Health Care Decisions. Anatomical Gift Act 19a-270. Durable Power of Attorney 45a-802e.
Living Will Effective: When you have an incurable or irreversible medical condition which, without the use of life support, will result in death in a relatively short period of time, or you are in a permanent coma or a persistent vegetative state.
Witness Requirements: Sign in the presence of two (2) adult witnesses. Your appointed agent cannot be a witness. If you reside in a resident facility operated or licensed by the department of mental health or department of mental retardation, additional witness requirements must be met and you should consult an attorney.

Delaware

State Law Reference: Delaware Code Annotated
State Website: http://198.187.128.12/delaware/lpext.dll?f=templates&fn=tools-contents.htm&cp=Infobase&2.0
Living Will Form: Instructions for Health Care serves as Living Will, Title 16, Section 2503.
Other Directives: Delaware Advance Directive contains Power of Attorney for Health Care and Instructions for Health Care. Anatomical Gift Act 16-2710 through 16-2719. Durable Power of Attorney 12-4901 through 12-4905.
Living Will Effective: Two (2) physicians determine in writing that you have a terminal condition and/or are in a permanent state of unconsciousness.
Witness Requirements: Sign in the presence of two (2) adult witnesses. A witness cannot be a person who has claim against your estate upon your death, stands to inherit from your estate, be directly financially responsible for your health care, or be an owner, operator, or employee of a residential long-term health care institution in which you reside.

District of Columbia (Washington D.C.)

State Law Reference: District of Columbia Code
State Website: http://dccode.westgroup.com/home/dccodes/default.wl
Living Will Form: District of Columbia Declaration serves as Living Will, Title 7, Section 7-622.
Other Directives: Power of Attorney for Health Care 21-2207. Anatomical Gift Act 7-1521.04. Durable Power of Attorney 21-2081.
Living Will Effective: Two (2) physicians determine that you are in a terminal condition and your death will result without using life-sustaining procedures. Your physician must then record your diagnosis and the contents of your Declaration in your medical records.
Witness Requirements: Sign in the presence of two (2) adult witnesses. A witness cannot be your appointed attorney-in-fact, health care provider, or an employee of your health care provider. Witnesses also cannot be related by blood, marriage, or adoption, stand to inherit from your estate, or be financially responsible for your health care.

Florida

State Law Reference: Florida Statutes
State Website: http://www.leg.state.fl.us/statutes/index.cfm?Mode=ViewStatutes&Submenu=1
Living Will Form: Living Will, Title XLIV, Chapter 765, Section 303.
Other Directives: Designation of Health Care Surrogate 765-203. Anatomical Gift Act 732.910 through 732.922. Durable Power of Attorney 709.08.
Living Will Effective: Two (2) physicians determine in writing that you have a terminal condition, and/or are in a permanent state of unconsciousness and can no longer make your own health care decisions.
Witness Requirements: Sign in the presence of two (2) adult witnesses. At least one (1) of your witnesses must not be related to you by marriage or blood.

Georgia

State Law Reference: Georgia Code

State Website: http://www.ganet.org/services/ocode/ocgsearch.htm

Living Will Form: Georgia Living Will, Chapter 31, Article 32, Section 3.

Other Directives: Durable Power of Attorney For Health Care 31-36-1. Anatomical Gift Act 44-4-140. Durable Power of Attorney 10-6-140 through 10-6-142.

Living Will Effective: Two (2) physicians determine in writing that you have a terminal condition, and/or are in a permanent state of unconsciousness.

Witness Requirements: Sign in the presence of two (2) adult witnesses. A witness cannot be a person who has claim against your estate upon your death, stands to inherit from your estate, be directly financially responsible for your health care, or be an owner, operator, or employee of a health care institution in which you are a patient. Witnesses also cannot be related by blood or marriage.

Hawaii

State Law Reference: Hawaii Revised Statutes

State Website: http://www.capitol.hawaii.gov/site1/docs/docs.asp?press1=docs

Living Will Form: Instruction for Health Care serves as Living Will Chapter 327E, Section 3.

Other Directives: Hawaii Advanced Health Care Directive has Durable Power of Attorney for Health Care and Instructions for Health Care 327E-3. Anatomical Gift Act 327-1. Durable Power of Attorney 551D-1 through 551D-7.

Living Will Effective: In the event that you have an incurable and irreversible condition that will result in death within a relatively short time, become unconscious and, to a reasonable degree of medical certainty, will not regain consciousness, or the likely risks and burdens of treatment would outweigh the expected benefits.

Witness Requirements: Sign in the presence of two (2) adult witnesses. At least one (1) of your witnesses cannot be related to you by marriage or blood or entitled to any part of your estate. A witness cannot be the person you appoint as your agent, health care provider, or an employee of your health care provider.

Idaho

State Law Reference: Idaho Statutes

State Website: http://www3.state.id.us/idstat/TOC/idstTOC.html

Living Will Form: Idaho Living Will, Title 39, Chapter 45, Section 04.

Other Directives: Durable Power of Attorney for Health Care 39-4505. Anatomical Gift Act 39-34-13. Durable Power of Attorney 15-5-503.

Living Will Effective: Two (2) physicians determine that you are in a terminal condition, your death will result without using life-sustaining procedures, or you are in a persistent vegetative state.

Witness Requirements: Sign in the presence of two (2) adult witnesses. No other restrictions apply.

Illinois

State Law Reference: Illinois Compiled Statutes

State Website: http://www.legis.state.il.us/ilcs/chapterlist.html

Living Will Form: Illinois Declaration serves as Living Will Chapter 755, Section 35/1.

Other Directives: Durable Power of Attorney for Health Care 755-45/1-4. Anatomical Gift Act 755-50. Durable Power of Attorney 755-45.

Living Will Effective: If death would occur without the use of death-delaying procedures. Your physician must personally examine you and certify in writing that you are terminally ill.

Witness Requirements: Sign in the presence of two (2) adult witnesses. Witnesses cannot be entitled to any part of your estate or financially responsible for your medical care.

Indiana

State Law Reference: Indiana Code

State Website: http://www.ai.org/legislative/ic/code/

Living Will Form: Indiana Living Will Declaration Title 16, Article 36, Chapter 4.

Other Directives: Durable Power of Attorney for Health Care Decisions and Appointment of Health Care Representative are contained within the Living Will document. Anatomical Gift Act 29-2-16-1. Durable Power of Attorney 29-3-5.

Living Will Effective: Your physician must certify in writing that you are in a terminal condition and your death would occur within a short period of time without the use of life-sustaining medical care.

Witness Requirements: Sign in the presence of two (2) adult witnesses. Witnesses cannot be entitled to any part of your estate, related to you by blood or marriage, financially responsible for your medical care, or be the person who signed the Declaration on your behalf.

Iowa

State Law Reference: Code of Iowa

State Website: http://www2.legis.state.ia.us/Code.html

Living Will Form: Iowa Declaration serves as Living Will, Title 4, Chapter 144A, Section 3.

Other Directives: Durable Power of Attorney for Health Care 4-144B.2. Anatomical Gift Act 4-142C. Durable Power of Attorney 633.705.

Living Will Effective: Two (2) physicians must certify in writing that you are in a terminal condition and your death would occur within a short period of time without the use of life-sustaining medical care.

Witness Requirements: Sign in the presence of two (2) witnesses eighteen (18) years or older or a notary public. A witness cannot be your health care provider or an employee of your health care provider.

Kansas

State Law Reference: Kansas Statutes

State Website: http://www.accesskansas.org/legislative/statutes/index.cgi

Living Will Form: Kansas Declaration serves as Living Will, Chapter 65, Article 28, Section 103.

Other Directives: Durable Power of Attorney for Health Care 58-629. Anatomical Gift Act 65-3209. Durable Power of Attorney 58-629.

Living Will Effective: Two (2) physicians must certify in writing that you are in a terminal condition and your death would occur within a short period of time without the use of life-sustaining medical care.

Witness Requirements: Sign in the presence of two (2) witnesses eighteen (18) years or older or a notary public. Witnesses cannot be entitled to any part of your estate, be financially responsible for your medical care, be related to you by blood or marriage, or be the person who signed the Declaration on your behalf.

Kentucky

State Law Reference: Kentucky Revised Statutes

State Website: http://www.lrc.state.ky.us/statrev/frontpg.htm

Living Will Form: Living Will Directive, Chapter 311, Section 625.

Other Directives: Anatomical Gift Act 311.165 through 311.235. Durable Power of Attorney 386.093.

Living Will Effective: When you become unable to make your own medical decisions.

Witness Requirements: Sign in the presence of two (2) witnesses eighteen (18) years or older or a notary public. Witnesses cannot be entitled to any part of your estate, financially responsible for your medical care, or related to you by blood or marriage.

Louisiana

State Law Reference: Louisiana Revised Statutes

State Website: http://www.legis.state.la.us/tsrs/search.htm

Living Will Form: Louisiana Declaration serves as Living Will, Title 40, Article 1299, Section 58-3.

Other Directives: Anatomical Gift Act 17:2354.

Living Will Effective: Two (2) physicians must certify in writing that you are in a terminal condition and your death would occur within a short period of time without the use of life-sustaining medical care.

Witness Requirements: Sign in the presence of two (2) adult witnesses. Witnesses cannot be entitled to any part of your estate or related by blood or marriage.

Maine

State Law Reference: Maine Revised Statutes

State Website: http://janus.state.me.us/legis/statutes/

Living Will Form: Instructions for Health Care serves as Living Will, Title 18A, Article 5, Part 8, Section 04.

Other Directives: Durable Power of Attorney for Health Care 18-5-506. Anatomical Gift Act 22-2-710. Durable Power of Attorney 18-5-502.

Living Will Effective: The Living Will becomes effective in the event that you have an incurable and irreversible condition that will result in death within a relatively short time, become unconscious and, to a reasonable degree of medical certainty, will not regain consciousness, or the likely risks and burdens of treatment would outweigh the expected benefits.

Witness Requirements: Sign in the presence of two (2) adult witnesses. No other restrictions apply.

Maryland

State Law Reference: Maryland State Code

State Website: http://mgasearch.state.md.us/verity.asp

Living Will Form: Advance Medical Directive Health Care Instructions serve as Living Will, Article 5, Section 603.

Other Directives: Appointment of Health Care Agent Article 5-603. Anatomical Gift Act 4-501. Durable Power of Attorney 13-601.

Living Will Effective: Two (2) physicians must agree in writing that you are incapable of making an informed health care decision, but you are not unconscious or unable to communicate by any other means.

Witness Requirements: Sign in the presence of two (2) adult witnesses. The person you assign as your agent cannot be a witness. At least one (1) of your witnesses must be a person who is not entitled to any portion of your estate or financial benefit by reason of your death.

Massachusetts

State Law Reference: None.

State Website: http://www.lawlib.state.ma.us/cmr.html

Living Will Form: No state statute governing the use of Living Wills. However, you have a constitutional right to state your wishes about medical care. A form is provided in this book.

Other Directives: Massachusetts Health Care Proxy.
Living Will Effective: In the event that you develop an irreversible condition that prevents you from making your own medical decisions.
Witness Requirements: Because Massachusetts does not have a statute governing the use of Living Wills, there are no specific requirements to make your Living Will legally binding. We suggest that you sign in the presence of two (2) witnesses eighteen (18) years or older or a notary public. A witness should not be your health care provider or an employee of your health care provider. Witnesses should not be entitled to any part of your estate, financially responsible for your medical care, or related to you by blood or marriage.

Michigan
State Law Reference: None
State Website: http://MichiganLegislature.org/law/Default.asp
Living Will Form: No state statute governing the use of Living Wills. However, you have a constitutional right to state your wishes about medical care. A form is provided in this book.
Other Directives: Michigan Designation of Patient Advocate for Health Care.
Living Will Effective: In the event that you develop an irreversible condition that prevents you from making your own medical decisions.
Witness Requirements: Because Michigan does not have a statute governing the use of Living Wills, there are no specific requirements to make your Living Will legally binding. We suggest that you sign in the presence of two (2) witnesses eighteen (18) years or older or a notary public. A witness should not be your health care provider or an employee of your health care provider. Witnesses should not be entitled to any part of your estate, be financially responsible for your medical care, or be related to you by blood or marriage.

Minnesota
State Law Reference: Minnesota Statutes
State Website: http://www.leg.state.mn.us/leg/statutes.htm
Living Will Form: Health Care Living Will, Chapter 145B, Section 04.
Other Directives: Appointment of Health Care Agent is included in Living Will 145B-04. Anatomical Gift Act 145B.04. Durable Power of Attorney 523.01.
Living Will Effective: Living Will becomes effective in the event that you can no longer make your own medical decisions.

Witness Requirements: Sign in the presence of two (2) witnesses eighteen (18) years or older or a notary public. A witness cannot be the person whom you appointed as your agent. At least one (1) witness cannot be your health care provider or an employee of your health care provider.

Mississippi
State Law Reference: Mississippi Code
State Website: http://www.mscode.com/
Living Will Form: Instructions for Health Care serves as Living Will, Title 41, Chapter 41, Section 209.
Other Directives: Mississippi Advance Health Care Directive contains Power of Attorney for Health Care and Instructions for Health Care 41-209. Anatomical Gift Act 41-39-31 through 41-39-51. Durable Power of Attorney 87-3-1.
Living Will Effective: In the event that you have an incurable and irreversible condition that will result in death within a relatively short time, become unconscious and, to a reasonable degree of medical certainty, will not regain consciousness, or the likely risks and burdens of treatment would outweigh the expected benefits.
Witness Requirements: Sign in the presence of two (2) witnesses eighteen (18) years or older or a notary public. A witness cannot be the person whom you appointed as your agent, health care provider, or an employee of your health care provider. At least one (1) witness cannot be related to you by blood or marriage or entitled to your estate upon your death.

Missouri
State Law Reference: Missouri Revised Statutes
State Website: http://www.moga.state.mo.us/home stat.htm
Living Will Form: Missouri Declaration serves as Living Will, Chapter 459, Section 015.
Other Directives: Power of Attorney for Health Care 404-822. Anatomical Gift Act 194.210 through 194.290. Durable Power of Attorney 404.703.
Living Will Effective: The Declaration becomes effective in the event that you have an incurable or irreversible medical condition which, without the use of life support, will result in death in a relative short period of time, or you are in a permanent coma or persistent vegetative state.
Witness Requirements: Sign in the presence of two (2) adult witnesses. If you have someone sign the Declaration on your behalf, that person cannot serve as a witness.

Montana

State Law Reference: Montana Code

State Website: http://data.opi.state.mt.us/bills/mca_toc/index.htm

Living Will Form: Montana Declaration serves as Living Will, Title 50, Chapter 9, Section 103.

Other Directives: Appointment of Health Care Agent is included in Declaration 50-9-103. Anatomical Gift Act 72-17-101. Durable Power of Attorney 72-1-102.

Living Will Effective: Becomes effective when you have an incurable or irreversible medical condition which, without the use of life support, will result in death in a relatively short period of time, or you are in a permanent coma or persistent vegetative state.

Witness Requirements: Sign in the presence of two (2) adult witnesses. No other restrictions apply. Do not use your appointed health care agent as one of your witnesses.

Nebraska

State Law Reference: Nebraska Statutes

State Website: http://www.unicam.state.ne.us/laws/statutes.htm

Living Will Form: Nebraska Declaration serves as Living Will, Chapter 20, Section 404.

Other Directives: Power of Attorney for Health Care 30-3408. Anatomical Gift Act 71-4804. Durable Power of Attorney 30-2665.

Living Will Effective: Declaration becomes effective when your attending physician determines you to have an incurable or irreversible medical condition which, without the use of life support, will result in death in a relatively short period of time, or you are in a permanent coma or persistent vegetative state.

Witness Requirements: Sign in the presence of two (2) adult witnesses. Witnesses cannot be employees of your life or health insurance provider and at least one (1) witness must not be an administrator or employee of your treating health care provider.

Nevada

State Law Reference: Nevada Revised Statutes

State Website: http://www.leg.state.nv.us/law1.htm

Living Will Form: Nevada Declaration serves as Living Will, Chapter 449, Section 610.

Other Directives: Power of Attorney for Health Care 449-800. Anatomical Gift Act 451.500 through 451.590.

Living Will Effective: Declaration becomes effective when your doctor determines that your death would occur without the use of life-sustaining medical care.

Witness Requirements: Sign in the presence of two (2) adult witnesses. No other restrictions apply.

New Hampshire

State Law Reference: New Hampshire Revised Statutes

State Website: http://sudoc.nhsl.lib.nh.us/rsa/

Living Will Form: New Hampshire Declaration serves as Living Will, Title X, Chapter 137H, Section 3.

Other Directives: Power of Attorney for Health Care 137-J:15. Anatomical Gift Act 921-A. Durable Power of Attorney 506:6.

Living Will Effective: Two (2) physicians must certify in writing that you are in a terminal condition and your death would occur within a short period of time without the use of life-sustaining medical care.

Witness Requirements: Sign in the presence of two (2) witnesses eighteen (18) years or older or a notary public. A witness cannot be a person who has a claim against your estate, stands to inherit from your estate, be your spouse, or be your doctor or a person acting under direction or control of your doctor. If you are a resident of a health care facility or a patient in a hospital, one of your witnesses may be your doctor or an employee of your doctor.

New Jersey

State Law Reference: New Jersey Statutes

State Website: http://www.njleg.state.nj.us/html/statutes.htm

Living Will Form: New Jersey Instruction Directive serves as Living Will, Title 26, Chapter 2H, Section 55.

Other Directives: Appointment of a Health Care Representative 26-2H-58. Anatomical Gift Act 26:6-65. Durable Power of Attorney 3B:13a-10.

Living Will Effective: Your doctor or treating health care institution must receive this document. Your attending physician and one (1) other physician must confirm that you are unable to make health care decisions.

Witness Requirements: Sign in the presence of two (2) witnesses eighteen (18) years or older or a notary public. A witness cannot be the person whom you appointed as your agent.

New Mexico

State Law Reference: New Mexico Statutes

State Website: http://198.187.128.12/newmexico/lpext.dll/Infobase2/10e3?fn=document-frame.htm&f=templates&2.0

Living Will Form: Instructions for Health Care serves as Living Will, Chapter, 24, Article 7A, Section 4.

Other Directives: Power of Attorney for Health Care 24-7A-4. Anatomical Gift Act 24-6A-10 through 42-6A-15. Durable Power of Attorney 45-5-501 through 45-5-505.

Living Will Effective: This document becomes effective in the event that you have an incurable and irreversible condition that will result in death within a relatively short time, become unconscious and, to a reasonable degree of medical certainty, will not regain consciousness, or the likely risks and burdens of treatment would outweigh the expected benefits.

Witness Requirements: The law does not require that your advance directive be witnessed. To avoid future concerns, we recommend that you sign in the presence of two (2) witnesses eighteen (18) years or older or a notary public. A witness should not be the person whom you appointed as your agent.

New York

State Law Reference: New York Consolidated Laws

State Website: http://assembly.state.ny.us/leg/?ul=0

Living Will Form: Is authorized by law created by New York courts, not by legislation.

Other Directives: Health Care Proxy Chapter 45, Article 29-C, Section 2980. Anatomical Gift Act 45-43-4300 through 45-43-4309. Durable Power of Attorney 24A-5-1501 through 24A-5-1506.

Living Will Effective: The Living Will becomes effective when you become terminally ill, permanently unconscious, or minimally conscious due to brain damage and will never regain the ability to make decisions.

Witness Requirements: New York Living Will is authorized by law created by New York courts, not by legislation, therefore there are no requirements guiding its use. We recommend that you sign in the presence of two (2) adult witnesses who do not benefit from your estate.

North Carolina

State Law Reference: North Carolina General Statutes

State Website: http://www.ncga.state.nc.us/Statutes/toc-1.html

Living Will Form: Declaration of a Desire for a Natural Death serves as Living Will 90-23-321.

Other Directives: Health Care Power of Attorney 32A- 2- 25. Anatomical Gift Act 130A-402. Durable Power of Attorney 32A-8 through 32A-14.

Living Will Effective: Two (2) physicians must certify in writing that you are in a terminal condition and your death would occur within a short period of time without the use of life-sustaining medical care.

Witness Requirements: Sign in the presence of two (2) adult witnesses and a notary public. A witness cannot be a person who has claim against your estate upon your death, stands to inherit from your estate, be directly financially responsible for your health care, or be an owner, operator, or employee of a health care institution in which you are a patient. Witnesses also cannot be related by blood or marriage.

North Dakota

State Law Reference: North Dakota Century Code

State Website: http://www.state.nd.us/lr/statutes/centurycode.html

Living Will Form: Declaration serves as Living Will, Chapter 23, Section 6.4.

Other Directives: Power of Attorney for Health Care 23-06.5. Anatomical Gift Act 23-06.2-01 through 23-06.2-12. Durable Power of Attorney 30.1-30.

Living Will Effective: Two (2) physicians must certify in writing that you are in a terminal condition and your death would occur within a short period of time without the use of life-sustaining medical care.

Witness Requirements: Sign in the presence of two (2) adult witnesses and a notary public. A witness cannot be a person who has claim against your estate upon your death, stands to inherit from your estate, be directly financially responsible for your health care, or be your doctor. Witnesses also cannot be related by blood or marriage. If you are presently living in a nursing home or other long-term care facility, one (1) of your witnesses must be one (1) of the following: a member of the clergy, a lawyer licensed to practice in North Dakota, or a person designated by the Department of Human Services or the county court for the county in which the facility is located.

Ohio

State Law Reference: Ohio Revised Code

State Website: http://onlinedocs.andersonpublishing.com/revisedcode/

Living Will Form: Living Will Declaration, Title 37, Chapter 2133, Section 01.

Other Directives: Power of Attorney for Health Care 1337-12. Anatomical Gift Act 2108. Durable Power of Attorney 13-1337-01.

Living Will Effective: Two (2) physicians determine that you are in a terminal condition and your death will result without using life-sustaining procedures, including the determination that there is no reasonable possibility that you will regain the ability to make your own health care decisions.

Witness Requirements: Sign in front of two (2) witnesses eighteen (18) years or older or a notary public. Witnesses cannot be related to you by blood, marriage, or adoption, or be your doctor or the administrator of a nursing home in which you are receiving treatment.

Oklahoma

State Law Reference: Oklahoma State Statutes

State Website: http://oklegal.onenet.net/statutes.basic.html

Living Will Form: Is Part 1 of Advance Directive for Health Care, Title 63, Article 3101, Section 4.

Other Directives: Appointment of Health Care Proxy is Part 2 of Advance Directive for Health Care 63-3101.4. Anatomical Gift Act 63-2201 through 63-2209. Durable Power of Attorney 15-1001 through 15-1024.

Living Will Effective: This Directive goes into effect once it is given to your doctor and you are unable to make your own medical decisions. In order to follow your instructions regarding life-sustaining treatment, your doctor must first consult another doctor to determine that you are persistently unconscious or suffering from a terminal condition.

Witness Requirements: Sign in the presence of two (2) adult witnesses. A witness cannot be any person who would inherit from you under any existing will or by operation of law.

Oregon

State Law Reference: Oregon Revised Statutes

State Website: http://www.leg.state.or.us/ors/

Living Will Form: Health Care Instructions serves as Living Will, Chapter 127, Section 531.

Other Directives: Appointment of Health Care Representative 127-531. Anatomical Gift Act 97.950 through 97.964. Durable Power of Attorney 127.005.

Living Will Effective: Two (2) physicians agree that you have an incurable and irreversible condition that will result in death within a relatively short time, will become unconscious and, to a reasonable degree of medical certainty, will not regain consciousness, or the likely risks and burdens of treatment would outweigh the expected benefits.

Witness Requirements: Sign in the presence of two (2) adult witnesses. If you have someone sign the Declaration on your behalf, that person cannot serve as a witness. Your attending physician cannot be a witness. At least one (1) of your witnesses cannot be related to you by blood, marriage, or adoption, entitled to any portion of your estate, or be an owner, operator, or employee of your treating health care facility.

Pennsylvania

State Law Reference: Penn. Consolidated Statutes

State Website: http://members.aol.com/StatutesPA/Index.html

Living Will Form: Declaration serves as Living Will, Title 20, Chapter 54, Section 04.

Other Directives: Anatomical Gift Act Penn. 20-8613.

Living Will Effective: The Declaration becomes effective when your physician receives a copy of it and determines that you are incompetent and in a terminal condition or a state of permanent unconsciousness.

Witness Requirements: Sign in the presence of two (2) adult witnesses. If you have someone sign the Declaration on your behalf, that person cannot serve as a witness.

Rhode Island

State Law Reference: Rhode Island General Laws

State Website: http://www.rilin.state.ri.us/Statutes/Statutes.html

Living Will Form: Declaration serves as Living Will, Chapter 23, Article 4, Section 11-3.

Other Directives: Power of Attorney for Health Care 23-4-10. Anatomical Gift Act 23-18.6. Durable Power of Attorney 18-3-2.

Living Will Effective: Your doctor must determine that your death would occur without use of life-sustaining medical care.

Witness Requirements: Sign in the presence of two (2) adult witnesses. Witnesses cannot be related to you by blood, marriage, or adoption.

South Carolina

State Law Reference: South Carolina Code of Laws

State Website: http://www.lpitr.state.sc.us/code/statmast.htm

Living Will Form: Declaration of a Desire for a Natural Death serves as Living Will, Title 44, Chapter 77, Section 50.

Other Directives: Health Care Power of Attorney 62-5-501. Anatomical Gift Act 44-43-10 through 44-43-50. Durable Power of Attorney 62-5-501.

Living Will Effective: Two (2) physicians must determine you are in a terminal condition and your death will result without using life-sustaining procedures.

Witness Requirements: Sign in the presence of two (2) adult witnesses and a notary public. A witness cannot be a beneficiary of your life insurance policy, your health care provider, or an employee of your health care provider. Witnesses cannot be related to you by blood, marriage, or adoption, entitled to any part of your estate, or directly financially responsible for your health care. In addition, at least one (1) witness must not be an employee of a health facility in which you are a patient. If you are a resident in a hospital or nursing facility, one of the witnesses must also be an ombudsman designated by the State Ombudsman, Office of the Governor.

South Dakota

State Law Reference: South Dakota Codified Laws
State Website: http://legis.state.sd.us/statutes/index.cfm
Living Will Form: Living Will Declaration, Title 34, Chapter 12D, Section 3.
Other Directives: Power of Attorney for Health Care 34-12C-1. Anatomical Gift Act 34-26-20 through 34-26-47. Durable Power of Attorney 51A-11-4.
Living Will Effective: Declaration is effective when your death will result without using life-sustaining procedures, including the determination that there is no reasonable possibility that you will regain the ability to make your own health care decisions.
Witness Requirements: Sign in the presence of two (2) witnesses eighteen (18) years or older or a notary public. Although South Dakota does not have any restrictions on who can be a witness, we suggest that you not use your appointed attorney-in-fact or your health care provider.

Tennessee

State Law Reference: Tennessee Code
State Website: http://www.michie.com/
Living Will Form: Living Will, Title 32, Chapter 11, Section 105.
Other Directives: Power of Attorney for Health Care 34-6-204. Anatomical Gift Act 68-30-105. Durable Power of Attorney 34-6-204.
Living Will Effective: The Living Will becomes effective when your death will result without using life-sustaining procedures.
Witness Requirements: Sign in the presence of two (2) adult witnesses and a notary public. A witness cannot be a person who has claim against your estate upon your death, stands to inherit from your estate, be your doctor or an employee of your doctor, or be an owner, operator, or employee of a health care institution in which you are a patient. Witnesses also cannot be related by blood or marriage.

Texas

State Law Reference: Texas Statutes
State Website: http://www.capitol.state.tx.us/statutes/statutes.html
Living Will Form: Directive to Physicians and Family or Surrogate serves as Living Will, Chapter 166, Section 033.
Other Directives: Medical Power of Attorney 12-481. Anatomical Gift Act Texas Health and Safety Code 692. Durable Power of Attorney Probate Code 482.
Living Will Effective: This Directive becomes effective when your attending physician certifies in writing that you are in a terminal or irreversible condition.
Witness Requirements: At least one (1) witness cannot be related to you by blood, marriage, or adoption, designated to make treatment decisions for you, entitled to any part of your estate, or be your doctor or an employee of your doctor. A witness cannot be an employee of a health care facility in which you are a patient, an officer, director, partner, or a business office employee of the health care facility or any part of any parent organization of the health care facility, or have a claim against your estate after you die.

Utah

State Law Reference: Utah Code
State Website: http://www.le.state.ut.us/~code/code.htm
Living Will Form: Directive to Physicians and Providers of Medical Services serves as Living Will, Title 75, Chapter 2, Section 1104.
Other Directives: Special Power of Attorney for Health Care 75-2-1106. Anatomical Gift Act 26-28-3. Durable Power of Attorney 75-5-501.
Living Will Effective: Two (2) physicians must physically examine you and certify in writing you are in a terminal condition or persistent vegetative state.
Witness Requirements: Sign in the presence of two (2) witnesses eighteen (18) years or older. A witness cannot be entitled to any part of your estate, be financially responsible for your medical care, be related to you by blood or marriage, be the person who signed the Declaration on your behalf, or be an employee of your health care facility.

Vermont

State Law Reference: Vermont Statutes
State Website: http://www.leg.state.vt.us/statutes/statutes2.htm
Living Will Form: Terminal Care Document serves as Living Will, Title 18, Chapter 111, Section 5253.
Other Directives: Power of Attorney for Health Care 14-121-3466. Anatomical Gift Act 18-109. Durable Power of Attorney 14-4-11-3051.
Living Will Effective: Document becomes effective if death would occur regardless of the use of life-sustaining procedures.
Witness Requirements: Sign in the presence of two (2) witnesses eighteen (18) years or older. A witness cannot be entitled to any part of your estate, be your spouse, attending physician or any person acting under the direction or control of your attending physician, or any person who has a claim against your estate.

Virginia

State Law Reference: Code of Virginia
State Website: http://leg1.state.va.us/000/src.htm
Living Will Form: Advance Medical Directive serves as Living Will, Title 54.1, Chapter 29, Section 84.
Other Directives: Anatomical Gift Act 32.1-290. Durable Power of Attorney 37.1-134.8 through 37.1-137.1.
Living Will Effective: This directive becomes effective in the event that you develop a terminal condition or are in a permanent vegetative state and can no longer make your own medical decisions.
Witness Requirements: Sign in the presence of two (2) witnesses eighteen (18) years or older. Witnesses cannot be related by blood or marriage.

Washington

State Law Reference: Revised Code of Washington
State Website: http://www.leg.wa.gov/wsladm/rcw.cfm
Living Will Form: Health Care Directive serves as Living Will, Title 70, Chapter 122, Section 030.
Other Directives: Power of Attorney for Health Care 11-94-010. Anatomical Gift Act 68.50.540. Durable Power of Attorney 11.94.101 through 11.94.900.
Living Will Effective: Declaration applies when two (2) physicians diagnose you to have a incurable or irreversible condition that will cause death in a relatively short time and you can no longer make your own medical decisions.
Witness Requirements: Sign in the presence of two (2) witnesses eighteen (18) years or older. A witness cannot be entitled to any part of your estate, related by blood or marriage, be your attending physician or any person acting under the direction or control of your attending physician, or be any person who has a claim against your estate.

West Virginia

State Law Reference: West Virginia State Code
State Website: http://www.legis.state.wv.us/Code/toc.html
Living Will Form: Living Will, Title 16, Chapter 30, Section 4.
Other Directives: Medical Power of Attorney 16-30-4. Anatomical Gift Act 16-19-2. Durable Power of Attorney 39-4-1 through 39-4-7.
Living Will Effective: Your physician must certify in writing that you are in a terminal condition and your death would occur within a short period of time without the use of life-sustaining medical care.
Witness Requirements: Sign in the presence of two (2) adult witnesses and a notary public. A witness cannot be a person who stands to inherit from your estate, be directly financially responsible for your health care, be your attending physician, or be your health care representative or successor if you have a medical power of attorney. A witness cannot be related by blood or marriage or be the person who signed the document on your behalf.

Wisconsin

State Law Reference: Wisconsin Statutes
State Website: http://www.legis.state.wi.us/rsb/stats.html
Living Will Form: Declaration to Physicians serves as Living Will, Chapter 154, Section 01.
Other Directives: Power of Attorney for Health Care 155-05. Anatomical Gift Act 157.06. Durable Power of Attorney 243.07-1a.
Living Will Effective: This directive becomes effective in the event that your attending physician and one (1) other physician certifies you have developed a terminal condition or are in a permanent vegetative state and can no longer make your own medical decisions.
Witness Requirements: Sign in the presence of two (2) adult witnesses. A witness cannot be a person who stands to inherit from your estate, be directly financially responsible for your health care, be your attending physician, or be an employee of your health care provider or an inpatient health care facility in which you are a patient, unless the employee is a chaplain or social worker. A witness also cannot be related by blood or marriage.

Wyoming

State Law Reference: Wyoming Statutes
State Website: http://legisweb.state.wy.us/titles/statutes.htm
Living Will Form: Living Will Declaration, Title 35, Chapter 22, Article 1.
Other Directives: Power of Attorney for Health Care 3-5-2. Anatomical Gift Act 35-5-102. Durable Power of Attorney 3-5-101.
Living Will Effective: This Declaration becomes effective when two (2) physicians agree that you have a terminal condition from which there can be no recovery and your death is imminent.
Witness Requirements: Sign in the presence of two (2) witnesses eighteen (18) years or older or a notary public. Witnesses cannot be entitled to any part of your estate or financially responsible for your medical care. A witness cannot be related to you by blood or marriage or be the person who signed the Declaration on your behalf.

★ Nova Publishing Company ★
Small Business and Consumer Legal Books and Software

Law Made Simple Series

Living Wills Simplified

ISBN 0-935755-52-7	Book only	$22.95
ISBN 0-935755-50-0	Book w/Forms-on-CD	$28.95

Liwing Trusts Simplified

ISBN 0-935755-53-5	Book only	$22.95
ISBN 0-935755-51-9	Book w/Forms-on-CD	$28.95

Small Business Library Series

Simplified Small Business Accounting (3rd Edition)

ISBN 0-935755-91-8	Book only	$19.95

The Complete Book of Small Business Legal Forms (3rd Edition)

ISBN 0-935755-84-5	Book w/Forms-on-CD	$24.95

Incorporate Your Business: The National Corporation Kit (3rd Edition)

ISBN 0-935755-88-8	Book w/Forms-on-CD	$24.95

The Complete Book of Small Business Management Forms

ISBN 0-935755-56-X	Book w/Forms-on-CD	$24.95

Small Business Start-up Series

C-Corporations: Small Business Start-up Kit

ISBN 0-935755-78-0	Book w/Forms-on-CD	$24.95

S-Corporations: Small Business Start-up Kit

ISBN 0-935755-77-2	Book w/Forms-on-CD	$24.95

Partnerships: Small Business Start-up Kit

ISBN 0-935755-75-6	Book w/Forms-on-CD	$24.95

Limited Liability Company: Small Business Start-up Kit

ISBN 0-935755-76-4	Book w/Forms-on-CD	$24.95

Sole Proprietorship: Small Business Start-up Kit

ISBN 0-935755-79-9	Book w/Forms-on-CD	$24.95

Quick Reference Law Series

Bankruptcy Exemptions: Laws of the United States

ISBN 0-935755-71-3	Book only	$16.95

Corporations: Laws of the United States

ISBN 0-935755-67-5	Book only	$16.95

Divorce: Laws of the United States

ISBN 0-935755-68-3	Book only	$16.95

Limited Liability Companies: Laws of the United States

ISBN 0-935755-80-2	Book only	$16.95

Partnerships: Laws of the United States

ISBN 0-935755-69-1	Book only	$16.95

Wills and Trusts: Laws of the United State

ISBN 0-935755-70-5	Book only	$16.95

Legal Self-Help Series

Debt Free: The National Bankruptcy Kit (2nd Edition)

ISBN 0-935755-62-4	Book only	$19.95

The Complete Book of Personal Legal Forms (3rd Edition)

ISBN 0-935755-92-6	Book w/Forms-on-CD	$24.95

Divorce Yourself: The National No-Fault Divorce Kit (5th Edition)

ISBN 0-935755-93-4	Book only	$24.95
ISBN 0-935755-94-2	Book w/Forms-on-CD	$34.95

Prepare Your Own Will: The National Will Kit (5th Edition)

ISBN 0-935755-72-1	Book only	$17.95
ISBN 0-935755-73-X	Book w/Forms-on-CD	$27.95

★ Ordering Information ★

Distributed by:
National Book Network
4720 Boston Way
Lanham MD 20706

Shipping/handling: $4.50 for first book or disk and $.75 for each additional
Phone orders with Visa/MC: (800) 462-6420
Fax orders with Visa/MC: (800) 338-4550
Internet: www.novapublishing.com